THE PROPHECIES OF JESUS

By the same author

A Study of Bahá'u'lláh's Tablet to the Christians

The first portion of Jesus' Olivet Discourse (The Gospel According to Matthew, ch. 24), as it appears in one of the earliest surviving manuscripts. This manuscript, known as *Codex Sinaiticus*, is believed to date back to the fourth century and was unknown to modern scholars until it was discovered at the monastery of St Catherine adjacent to Mount Sinai in 1844 by the German biblical scholar L.F. Tischendorf. (Reproduced from Helen and Kirsopp Lake's *Codex Sinaiticus Petroplitanus: The New Testament*, 1911, with permission from the British Museum Library. *Folio 213, from additional ms 43725.*)

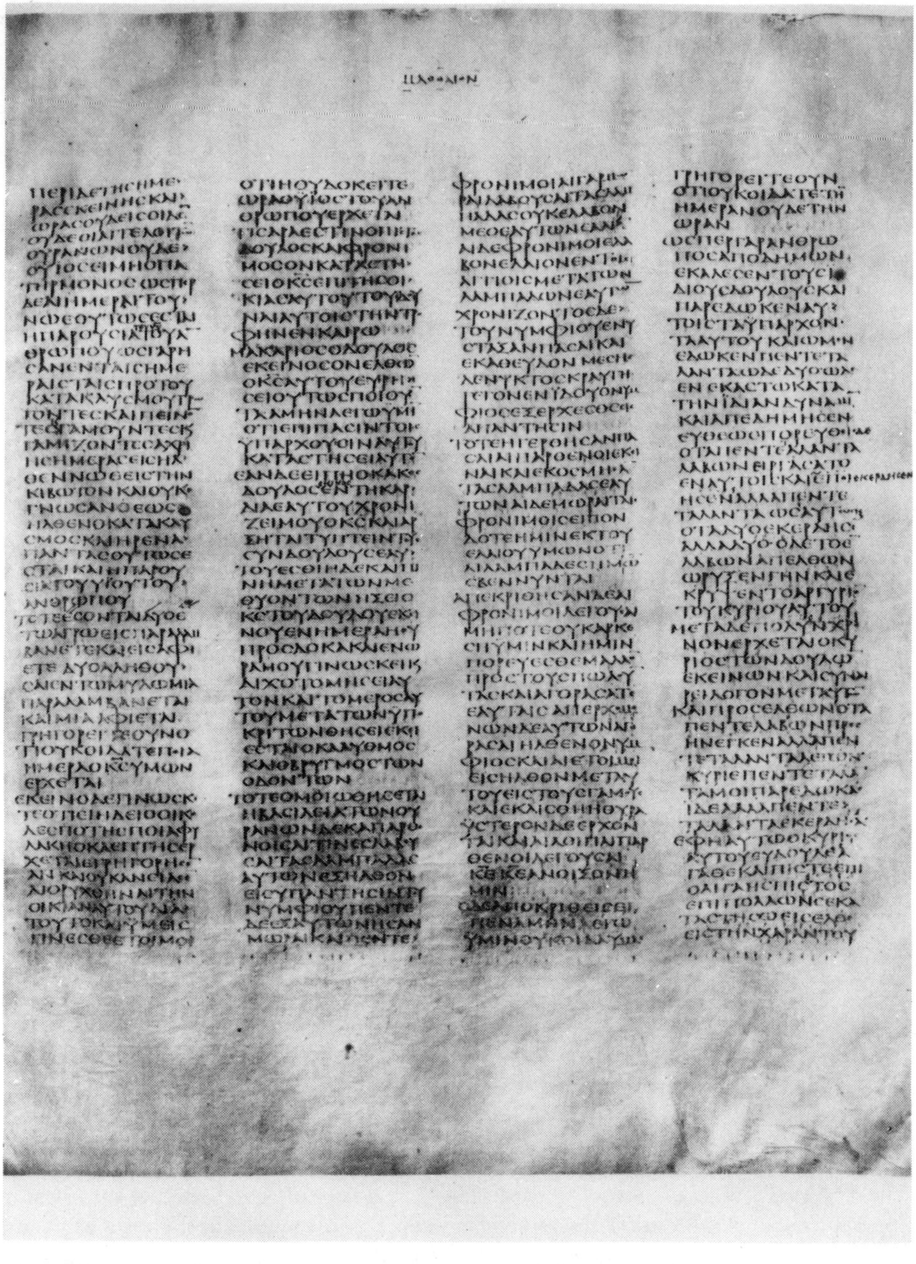

Codex Sinaiticus showing the remaining portion of the Olivet Discourse (The Gospel According to Matthew, ch. 25). (Reproduced from Helen and Kirsopp Lake's *Codex Sinaiticus Petroplitanus: The New Testament*, 1911, with permission from the British Museum Library. *Folio 214, from additional ms 43725.*)

THE PROPHECIES OF JESUS

MICHAEL SOURS

ONEWORLD
OXFORD

The Prophecies of Jesus

Oneworld Publications Ltd
(Sales and Editorial)
185 Banbury Road
Oxford OX2 7AR
England

Oneworld Publications Ltd
(U.S. Sales Office)
County Route 9
P.O. Box 357
Chatham, NY 12037, U.S.A.

© Michael Sours 1991
All rights reserved. Copyright under Berne Convention
Reprinted 1993

A CIP record for this book is available from the British Library

ISBN 1–85168–025–X

Printed and bound in Great Britain

CONTENTS

ILLUSTRATIONS

PREFACE

This book is a commentary on Jesus' great prophetic sermon found in Matthew, chapter 24, commonly known as the Olivet Discourse. This Discourse also corresponds to portions of Mark, chapter 13, and Luke, chapter 21.[1] The purpose of this book is to present and examine Bahá'í claims and Christian interpretations as they relate to Jesus' prophecies. With this objective in mind, an attempt has been made to provide the reader with Bahá'í writings relating to Jesus' Discourse as well as some of the leading Christian views and traditional interpretations. Although differing and sometimes conflicting opinions are presented, in many cases there are Christian interpretations which correspond exactly, or in part, to the Bahá'í teachings. In some instances, the views of Christian expositors are solely relied upon, because there do not appear to be any teachings in the Bahá'í writings which relate to specific aspects of Jesus' Olivet Discourse; nevertheless, these interpretations often provide insights that support the general Bahá'í point of view.

The commentary in this book follows, verse by verse, the text of Matthew, chapter 24, as it appears in the *King James Version* of the Bible. Although many scholars today do not regard this version as the most accurate or reliable translation of the Bible, its style remains widely admired and has come to be regarded as the classic English language translation of the Bible. Moreover, it seems fitting to use this version because it was one of the most widely used translations in the English speaking world at the

1. Matthew's version also includes a number of important parables which appear in chapter 25. These parables are generally accepted as part of the same sermon even though they are not found in the other versions. Every student of prophecy can benefit greatly from the study of these parables. However, they have not been included as part of this commentary, not because of any question concerning their rightful place in Jesus' sermon, but because their meaning is so apparent there is little this commentary can add to what has already been said by the more noteworthy Christian interpreters. See, e.g., *Matthew Henry's Commentary* or *The Expositor's Bible Commentary*, ed. Frank E. Gaebelein.

time Bahá'ís believe the prophecies of Matthew were realized. However, for the purpose of clarity and to benefit from the variety of scholarship available today, various translations of the Bible will be cited and occasionally compared with the *King James Version*. The less archaic *New King James Version* is the version used almost exclusively when explanations are given in the commentaries.

Since many people are unfamiliar with much of the Bible, the Bahá'í Faith, and the technical language of religious scholarship, the commentary has been kept as simple as possible. Some of the more basic, as well as the more technical, information has been deferred to the footnotes and appendices. However, the amount of information contained in this book about the Bahá'í Faith, its history and general teachings is very limited, and those wishing to know more are encouraged to refer to other sources.[2]

This commentary, as with all commentaries, is interpretive, and such interpretation applies not only to the understanding of the prophecies themselves but also to the difficult process of determining what material should be selected for inclusion. The amount of Christian literature available on the subject of prophecy is vast and often very difficult to sort through, particularly the numerous nineteenth-century works, some of which contain much that is obscure to the modern reader. Moreover, some portions of the commentary are the writer's own personal speculations. Consequently, this book is not an 'official' Bahá'í commentary on chapter 24 of Matthew or on Christian millennial beliefs, but an attempt to share the results of the author's own investigation of this complex yet fascinating subject.

For access to much of the literature required for this project I would like to express my gratitude to the Dallas Theological Seminary's Mosher Library, Dallas, Texas; the United States Library of Congress; and the Bodleian Library at the University of Oxford. I would also like to thank the British Museum Library for providing the facsimile reproduction of Matthew, chapter 24, from Kirsopp Lake's *Codex Sinaiticus Petroplitanus*, the Bodleian Library for providing the facsimile reproduction of the title pages from Joseph Mede's *Clavis Apocalyptica* and Sir Isaac Newton's *Dissertation on the Prophecies*, and the Audio-Visual Department of the Bahá'í World Centre for providing photographs of the prison of 'Akká, the Bahá'í Temple of North America and the Seat of the Universal House of Justice.

2. See the bibliography.

INTRODUCTION

Christian Messianic Expectations and Bahá'u'lláh's Claims

In the nineteenth century, there arose among many Christians the strong conviction that they were living in the final days - 'the end time' - prophesied in the Bible. Christians, including lay-persons, preachers, and biblical scholars of virtually every denomination, in both Europe and America, began to assert that the prophecies of the Scriptures were rapidly reaching their culmination and that Jesus' long-awaited Second Advent was drawing near.[3] In connection with Daniel's prophecies concerning the end time, one Christian commentary concluded, 'Without doubt this period is approaching, and not far distant'.[4] Another Christian wrote, 'we may be pretty confident that we shall reach the consummation before the end of this century'.[5] Still another affirmed to an audience at a conference convened for the discussion of prophecy that the terminal periods mentioned in Scripture 'are running out under our own eyes'.[6] Hundreds of others, in statements typical of the time, proclaimed the same hope. Some writers even asserted that, according to well-established methods of biblical interpretation, a chronology of events was evident in the prophecies of Scripture. Many believed this chronology suggested that Christ would return during the mid-nineteenth century.

There were large numbers of Christians who even thought that the year 1844 would be the year of Christ's return. The expectation was so

3. The nineteenth century witnessed what was probably the most dramatic period of Messianic expectation in Christian history. This belief is well documented in Le Roy Edwin Froom's four-volume study *The Prophetic Faith of Our Fathers* (see especially vol. IV).
4. *The Holy Bible Containing the Old and New Testaments with Original Notes*, by Thomas Scott (1815). See vol. III, notes on Daniel, ch. VIII:11-13.
5. Joseph A. Sweiss, *The Last Times and The Great Consummation* 296.
6. Cited from an article by The Revd Dr A.J. Gordon, in *Prophetic Studies of the International Prophetic Conference* (1886) 71.

great and so widespread that historians have called the period immediately following 1844 'the Great Disappointment'.[7] Afterwards, many Christians continued to regard 1844 as a significant year, clearly marked by the prophecies of the Bible, but they acknowledged that the signs which they expected to accompany the appearance of Christ had not occurred. A few attempted to re-evaluate their interpretations to establish a later date for Christ's return, while some began to reassess the methods of interpretation and abandoned the former principles. For others, the failure to see their hopes realized led to disillusionment with the interpretation of prophecy.

The history of these Christians and their expectations has been noted in many subsequent studies. To a large degree their writings are still extant and, in some cases, aspects of their beliefs have endured to this day.[8] What is less well known is that in the Middle East, the lands we commonly know as the lands of the Bible, a similar movement occurred among Muslims at the same time.[9]

In Persia, a Muslim known as Shaykh Ahmad (AD 1753-1834) founded a movement based on the conviction that Islam had become so corrupt that no reform could restore it to its original purpose. Rather, he taught, the 'Judgement Day' prophesied in the Scriptures of Islam was approaching. This judgement would be ushered in by God, who would send the long expected 'Mahdí' (Arabic, meaning 'the Guided One') to renew the Faith of God. After Shaykh Ahmad died, these beliefs were carried on by his successor, Siyyid Kázim, who, as he approached his own death in 1843, directed his followers to wait no longer, but rather to search out the expected Deliverer.

7. See, e.g., *Adventism in America*, ed. Gary Land, 28, and *The Advent Hope in Scripture and History*, ed. V. Norskov Olsen, 170.

8. Most notably, the modern Seventh-Day Adventist Church grew out of the nineteenth-century Advent movement. Also the shift to pre-millennial beliefs can be traced largely to the efforts of early Adventists.

9. In the branch of Islam known as Shí'ah, there were twelve individuals who were regarded as the rightful spiritual successors of Muhammad. The last one, the twelfth Imam, Muhammad al-Mahdí, is said to have disappeared in the year 260 AH. It is believed that this Mahdí would return as a deliverer on the Judgement Day. In the holy Book of Islam, the Qur'án, it is written: 'And they will bid thee to hasten the chastisement. But God cannot fail His threat. And verily, a day with thy Lord is as a thousand years, as ye reckon them!' (40:7). In another verse it is written: 'From the Heaven to the Earth He governeth all things: hereafter shall they come up to him on a day whose length shall be a thousand of such years as ye reckon.' (32:4, trans, Rodwell, cf. 2 Pet. 3:8). From these verses it was understood by some that the return of the Mahdí, the deliverer, would take place on the Judgement Day 1,000 years after his disappearance. Thus, 260 AH plus 1,000 equals 1260 AH. This year, 1260 AH, corresponds exactly to the Christian calendar year 1844.

It was in the following year that one of Siyyid Kázim's students set out for Shíráz, Persia, in his quest to find the Promised One. In that city, in the year 1844, this student and many others met a Person who announced that He was the One they were seeking. He took the title 'the Báb', meaning 'the Gate', and appointed disciples to help spread His teachings.

For a period of six years the Báb preached a new Revelation from God. The Báb claimed to be an independent Prophet whose mission was to renew the eternal Faith of God and to herald a still greater Messenger to come. To a great extent, the Báb's teachings suggested that His mission was similar to that of John the Baptist, who prepared people for the imminent appearance of Christ. The Báb's teachings quickly spread throughout the land, gaining thousands of supporters. But the orthodox Muslim clergy, as well as the civil authorities, clearly saw the Báb as a threat. His teachings were regarded as heretical, and He was arrested.

Only three years after His declaration, the Báb was imprisoned for espousing and preaching His beliefs. He remained a prisoner for the last three years of His ministry. During this time, His followers came under siege from the government and clergy. Thousands died, including many of His disciples, foremost of whom was Quddús.[10] It was also during the time of these conflicts that the Báb was tried and eventually sentenced to death. Amid extraordinary circumstances, He was executed by firing squad in the city of Tabríz in 1850.

It was not long before many came to believe that the Messenger the Báb had spoken of and alluded to so frequently was Bahá'u'lláh, whose name means 'the glory of God'. Bahá'u'lláh openly supported the Cause of His predecessor the Báb, and during the severe persecutions of the years following the Báb's execution He was imprisoned and later exiled. The period of this first imprisonment in Tehran marks the beginning of Bahá'u'lláh's active ministry, but it was only after several years of withdrawal to the mountains of Kurdistan that He formally announced that He was the one whose advent the Báb had anticipated. In the course of His ministry He was exiled repeatedly and was eventually imprisoned in the city of 'Akká,[11] a prison colony of the Ottoman Empire. During the forty years of His ministry, Bahá'u'lláh continued to set forth His teachings and claims in numerous books and Tablets.

10. The Báb gave Quddús the title 'The Last Name of God'. According to the early Bahá'í historian, Nabíl, Quddús suffered a martyr's death at the age of 27 on 16 May, 1849. See *The Dawn-Breakers* 415.
11. A city in present-day Israel.

Today there are people in all the nations of the world who follow Bahá'u'lláh, calling themselves Bahá'ís and accepting Him as the fulfilment of the prophecies of the Bible. Not only have many Christians accepted Bahá'u'lláh; many who were formerly Hindus, Buddhists and Muslims, as well as the followers of other religions, regard Him as the fulfilment of their own sacred Scriptures and traditions.

In this book our purpose will not be to explore these other religious systems and Bahá'u'lláh's relationship to them; instead, we will focus solely on the biblical tradition. The relationship of the Bahá'í Faith to the Bible is, alone, more than can be adequately addressed in any single book. This is especially true since Bahá'u'lláh has not attempted to evade any of the Messianic expectations of Christians by invalidating the legitimacy of the prophecies of the Bible. If Bahá'u'lláh had chosen to disregard large portions of the Bible - for instance, rejecting the prophecies of Daniel, the Gospel versions of Jesus' Olivet Discourse and the Book of Revelation - His claims would not appear so great.

Such an approach cannot be found in Bahá'u'lláh's writings. Instead, He testified to the truth of the Bible, wrote at length in defence of its genuineness, and encouraged both those who choose to follow Him and those who do not to read it.[12] Referring to the Bible, He stated: 'Reflect: the words of the verses themselves eloquently testify to the truth that they are of God' (*Certitude* 84). To Muslims, who objected to the Bible because they mistakenly believed that the Jews and Christians had altered its texts, Bahá'u'lláh pointed out that the Qur'án itself affirmed the truth of the Bible (*Certitude* 20, 84).[13] He argued that textual evidence supports the belief that the Scriptures have not been significantly altered and added that to assert that they have been corrupted is theologically unsound.[14] Bahá'u'lláh so glorified the words of Jesus that on one occasion when He chose to expound

12. The acceptance of the 'divine inspiration of the Gospel' as well as of the 'Sonship and Divinity of Jesus Christ' is central to Bahá'í teachings. In fact, the 'wholehearted and unqualified acceptance' of the divine origin of Christianity and Jesus Christ is among 'the essential prerequisites of admittance into the Bahá'í fold of Jews, Zoroastrians, Hindus, Buddhists, and the followers of other ancient faiths, as well as of agnostics and even atheists'. See Shoghi Effendi, *Promised Day* 114.

13. See Qur'án 5:49-50.

14. Bahá'u'lláh explained that the statements in the Qur'án which indicate that the Jews and Christians had corrupted the Bible have been misunderstood. He states that the meaning is not that the texts have been changed but rather that they have been misinterpreted, and in that sense 'corrupted' (see *Certitude* 86). With regard to textual evidence, He points out that 'the Pentateuch had been spread over the surface of the earth, and was not confined to Mecca and Medina, so that they could privily corrupt and pervert its text' (*Certitude* 86). A theological argument in support of the Gospel can be found in *The Book of Certitude* on pp. 89-90.

at length on a few selected passages of Jesus' great prophetic sermon, the Olivet Discourse, He characterized His explanation as revealing only 'a dewdrop out of the fathomless ocean of the truths treasured' in Jesus' 'holy words' (*Certitude* 28).

It is these teachings, which argue for a strong affirmation of the Bible, that make Bahá'u'lláh's claims especially challenging. From a Christian point of view, none of Bahá'u'lláh's claims are as extraordinary as His claim to have fulfilled the prophecies of the Bible. Bahá'u'lláh wrote:

> He [Bahá'u'lláh], verily, hath again come down from heaven, even as He [Christ] came down from it the first time. Beware lest ye dispute that which He [Bahá'u'lláh] proclaimeth, even as the people [Pharisees] before you disputed His [Christ's] utterances. Thus instructeth you the True One, could ye but perceive it. (*Tablets of Bahá'u'lláh* 11, clarifications added)

This passage alludes to Jesus' statement that He came down from heaven (John 6:38). By claiming to have come from heaven, Jesus symbolically indicated His divine origin. The Jews interpreted Jesus' words literally and disputed with Him for making this claim because, from their point of view, Jesus had simply been physically born of Mary (John 6:41-2). By alluding to the claims of Jesus and how the Jews misunderstood them and failed to perceive Jesus' truth, Bahá'u'lláh is pointing out both His own divine claims and the dangers of failing to comprehend them correctly. In another passage, Bahá'u'lláh states:

> He [Bahá'u'lláh], in truth, hath come unto the world in His most great glory, and all that hath been mentioned in the Gospel hath been fulfilled. (*Epistle* 60, clarification added)

In this passage, Bahá'u'lláh's terminology recalls the prophecy of Matthew 24:30, 'the Son of man coming on the clouds of heaven with power and great glory'. We will examine this prophecy in detail later in the commentary. For now, it is sufficient to observe that Bahá'u'lláh's allusion to Matthew, chapter 24, is followed by words making an open connection between His ministry and the prophecies of the Gospel. There can be little doubt as to the magnitude of the claims Bahá'u'lláh advanced.

For the Christian, the obvious question is: How can Bahá'u'lláh expect anyone to accept that He is the fulfilment of the prophecies of the Bible? Does the Bible not say that there will be a great tribulation, that Christ will appear in the clouds of heaven in great power and glory, that His followers will be caught up in the air to meet Him, that the evil forces of the world will gather together to wage war against Him, that He will defeat them triumphantly, and that finally He will establish the Kingdom of God on earth? How could Bahá'u'lláh, an exile and a prisoner, have fulfilled these prophecies of the Bible?

For Bahá'ís who are acquainted with Bahá'u'lláh's life and teachings, the answers to such questions are not only evident but integral to the Bahá'í experience itself. We have already noted that many Christians expected the Second Advent during the 1800s, in fact in the very year 1844, which marks the beginning of the Bahá'í era. In this book an attempt will be made to provide information which will enable those who accept the authority of the Bible, or those who are interested in the Bahá'í Faith, to understand why many have acknowledged Bahá'u'lláh's biblical claims. Specifically, this book will show how the prophecies, which Christians believed went unfulfilled in the nineteenth century, were, from a Bahá'í point of view, actually fulfilled.

The Significance and Interpretation of Matthew 24

Christians have commonly referred to Chapters 24-5 of Matthew as the Olivet Discourse because these chapters contain a sermon which Jesus delivered on the Mount of Olives, or Olivet.[15] It is also called Jesus' Eschatological[16] Discourse, meaning it is a discourse concerning the time of the end, or the Synoptic Apocalypse. The word 'Apocalypse' is from the Greek word '*apokalupto*' and means 'to reveal'.[17] The Olivet Discourse reveals events that are to unfold in the future. In order to understand the

15. In Jesus' day, this Mount was thickly wooded with olive trees, which is the reason for its name.
16. From the Greek 'eschatos', meaning 'last'. This term is used to refer to those things that are to happen last, i.e., at the end of the age.
17. The last book of the New Testament is frequently entitled the 'Book of Revelation' or the 'Apocalypse'. These titles mean the same thing. 'Revelation' is simply the translation of the Greek word from which 'Apocalypse' is derived. This title appropriately fits the last book of the New Testament because it is a *revelation*, i.e., it contains visions of the future that were *revealed* to John and which *reveal* the future. The word 'Apocalypse' is sometimes used to express catastrophic events, a usage that has evolved due to the nature of some of the images which dominate the contents of the book. The prophecies of the Olivet Discourse are conceptually parallel to the major themes found in the Book of Revelation.

A nineteenth-century etching of olive trees on the slopes of the Mount of Olives. (From Frederic W. Farrar's *The Life of Christ*.)

word 'synoptic' it is important to understand how Jesus' discourse fits into the general composition of the New Testament itself.

In the New Testament there are four versions recounting the Gospel: the Gospel according to Matthew, the Gospel according to Mark, the Gospel according to Luke and the Gospel according to John. The first three versions provide similar brief accounts of the ministry of Jesus Christ and express essentially the same point of view concerning Jesus' life and work. For this reason they are called the 'synoptic' Gospels. Because Jesus' discourse concerning future events is found in all three of these versions, this particular discourse is frequently referred to as the Synoptic Apocalypse. The Olivet Discourse does not appear in John's version of the Gospel.[18]

18. The Gospel according to John differs from the other three versions in the way it recounts Jesus' life by placing a greater emphasis on the divinity and Sonship of Jesus. This accounts for John's version of the Gospel being given the highest esteem among most Christians. The Gospel of John is also the one most frequently alluded to by Bahá'u'lláh and quoted by His son, 'Abdu'l-Bahá. Even though John does not recount an exact parallel to the Olivet Discourse found in Matthew, Mark and Luke, he does, according to Bahá'í interpretation, recount an eschatological message given to the disciples prior to His arrest in Gethsemane. The Comforter (John 14:26, 15:26, 16:5-16) is understood not exclusively as a reference to Pentecost (Acts 2) but as a reference to Christ's second advent. See 'Abdu'l-Bahá, *Some Answered Questions*, ch. 25.

The message is fundamentally the same in Matthew's, Mark's and Luke's accounts of the Gospel. However, the Gospel according to Matthew provides the fullest form of the Olivet Discourse and, at the end, Matthew relates a series of parables and additional teachings concerning the Kingdom of God and the future Judgement. While the accounts themselves are relatively similar, the same cannot be said about the way they have been interpreted since they were first written.

The disagreements over the meaning of the Olivet Discourse and the difficulties involved in its interpretation prompted one Christian commentator to refer to it as 'the biggest problem in the Gospel'.[19] In more recent times, many commentators have avoided even taking it up for discussion, to such an extent that the Christian writer Wilbur M. Smith writes that the Discourse is:

> the most neglected major discourse of our Lord in the literature that has gathered around the Gospel records of His life and teachings. One will come upon a hundred books on the Sermon on the Mount, and sections of this sermon, before he finds an adequate discussion of the Olivet Discourse. (*A Treasury of Books for Bible Study* 235)

The neglect of this Discourse is, however, relative to its importance and the attention that has been given to other passages. Anyone who searches long enough will find that there have been numerous views expressed concerning the meaning of Jesus' prophetic sermon. There is no need to attempt to examine them all here. However, there are two main opposing Christian views which should be noted before introducing a Bahá'í point of view.

The first of these views asserts that the return of Christ will not occur literally in the physical appearance of Jesus, but rather will occur, or has occurred, in a general spiritual unfolding of the Church in the world. Christians who adhere to this view believe that many of the prophecies use symbolic language that should be understood spiritually.[20] The other view holds that the same Jesus of Nazareth will return bodily and literally in the clouds of heaven.[21] Christians who await Jesus to return in this manner usually interpret prophecy literally.

19. A.M. Hunter, *The Gospel According to Saint Mark* 122.
20. See, e.g., *The Second Coming of Christ*, by James M. Campbell, especially pp. 79-116.
21. This belief is based on a literal interpretation of Matthew 24.

The Bahá'í Faith argues that some elements of both these views are correct. Bahá'ís believe Christ will return as a historic and individual Person, but not with the same body or name as that of Jesus of Nazareth.[22] Instead, the return of Christ will be in spirit, that is, the same divine qualities will be made manifest once more in the world by an actual historic Person.

This understanding can be illustrated from the Bible itself by employing the example of Elijah and John the Baptist. According to the Bible, the Prophet Elijah was taken up to heaven without having died (2 Kings. 2:11). Later, the Scripture indicates that the same Elijah will return again (Mal. 4:5). With this in mind, many Jews awaited the literal return of Elijah. When the Jews heard the preaching of John the Baptist they asked him if he claimed to be Elijah. In reply, John denied that he was Elijah (John 1:19-21). However, when the disciples enquired about the matter, Jesus informed them that John the Baptist was, in fact, Elijah (Matt. 17:10-13).[23] This is not a contradiction as some have assumed. John the Baptist was not literally the same Elijah, i.e., the bodily return of Elijah; rather, Elijah had returned 'in the spirit and power' in the person of John the Baptist (Luke 1:17).

John evidently said he was not Elijah because the Jews to whom he was speaking would have understood him to mean he was the literal return of Elijah, which he was not. Jesus, however, told the disciples that John was the return of Elijah because He knew they would understand that John was indeed the fulfilment of Old Testament prophecy. They understood that John the Baptist possessed the same spiritual qualities evident in Elijah.

Similar to Jewish expectations about Elijah, many Christians argue that the same Jesus will return bodily. This expectation rests upon the belief that the Scriptures should be understood literally, meaning that Jesus departed physically and therefore will return in the same manner. However,

22. The belief that Christ will return with a new name and, similarly, bestow a new name on His followers, is accepted by even some conservative Christian expositors of the Bible. This view is based on Revelation 3:12. Some commentators believe the new name referred to is indicated in Revelation 19:13 or 19:16, but other Christian scholars disagree, citing this verse, 'And I will give him a white stone, and on the stone a new name written which no one knows except him who receives it' (Rev. 2:17). See I.T. Beckwith, *The Apocalypse of John*, 468; John Lange, *Commentary on the Holy Scriptures*, vol.12 (see Rev. 19:16); or R.C. Trench, *Commentary on the Epistles to the Seven Churches in Asia*, 198-9. The expectation of a new name is also found in popular Christian literature. Billy Graham writes, 'we have the glorious promise to him that overcometh, "a new name" ' (*Approaching Hoofbeats* 43, 51).

23. See also Matt. 11:13-14.

as the Bible indicates, Elijah was also taken up into heaven without having died. Yet, as we have seen, Elijah returned, not in his former body, but spiritually, in the person of John the Baptist. Moreover, John the Baptist was born on earth and did not literally descend from heaven.

Bahá'ís believe this is also the way Christ's return should be understood: just as Elijah returned not only in the spirit but in the historical person of John the Baptist, Bahá'ís believe the historical Person, Bahá'u'lláh, is the return of Christ in spirit and power. Like Jesus of Nazareth, He is God made manifest in the world - the Word made flesh - that is, God's Word made manifest in the world through a divinely-sent historic Person. Moreover, this appearance of the Word in the Person of Bahá'u'lláh is, from the Bahá'í point of view, in accordance with the overall prophetic teachings of the Bible.

How the Bahá'í Faith is related to biblical prophecies becomes more apparent when we consider the Bahá'í understanding of Scripture. Even though Bahá'u'lláh and His son, 'Abdu'l-Bahá, occasionally interpret the Bible literally, they affirm that to understand Scripture correctly it is also necessary to seek out its deeper spiritual meaning. This meaning is often conveyed through the use of words and phrases which are intended to be interpreted symbolically. In some cases the Scripture may have both inner and outward meanings. Bahá'u'lláh states, 'in the sayings of Him Who is the Spirit (Jesus) unnumbered significances lie concealed' (*Epistle* 148).

Since religion is ultimately concerned with spirituality, salvation, eternal life, and the relationship between ourselves and God, it is important to understand Scripture from a spiritual point of view and to avoid interpreting it in a manner that reduces God's Word to a purely materialistic or worldly meaning. For example, the Scripture teaches that Jesus is Lord. Yet this lordship does not consist of a lordship like that of conventional kings and rulers. Jesus' lordship is over a dominion made up of the hearts of those who believe in Him and willingly accept Him because of the truth of His teachings and the sacrifice He made. This lordship is spiritual and eternal in nature. It is entirely different from the lordship of kings and rulers whose dominions are held together by, and are dependent on, the material force of armies.

Similarly, when Jesus said that He had brought a sword (Matt. 10:34) we know that this was not a literal sword. Jesus used the word 'sword' to symbolize the power of the Word of God to conquer sin (Eph.

6:17). Spiritual lordship, like spiritual power and glory, is altogether different and superior to worldly lordship, material power and material glory. This type of distinction is important to understand when we are interpreting Scripture.

Bahá'u'lláh emphasizes that because people in former ages interpreted prophecies literally, they failed to understand their spiritual meaning. This failure to understand the prophecies is also one of the reasons why people have opposed the Prophets of God. Today there are many conservative Protestant Christians who emphatically reject the explanations of other Christians who interpret some prophecies of the Bible symbolically or allegorically. As one Christian points out, 'Because of the excesses which allegorization has produced in church history, most conservative interpreters today have rejected it.'[24] Consequently, such conservatives are equally opposed to many of the interpretations expounded in the Bahá'í writings.

As the end of the nineteenth century drew near, conservative Christians began increasingly to emphasize literal interpretation in connection with prophecy. This was partly an effort to battle 'modernism' and secular culture. The advent of modern science and Darwinism had shaken people's beliefs in the Bible, especially the traditional, literal interpretation of Scripture. Some Christians accommodated these developments by returning to a more allegorical method of understanding the text. Conservatives resisted this by attempting to refute modern theories and articulating theological arguments that Scripture had to be literal in order to be true. By rejecting symbolic interpretation, they sought to preserve traditional views but, in so doing, they also imposed their own restraints on what God could intend in the Scripture, narrowed their options for understanding its message, and left themselves unprepared in the event they were wrong.

This rejection of allegorical or symbolic interpretation is surprising since Paul himself provides interpretations of the Old Testament which directly support some of the main assumptions of the allegorical method.[25] Moreover, it seems quite hasty to reject an approach largely because Church history indicates that some have carried it to excess, especially since it could be just as easily argued that others have carried the literal approach to excess.

24. See Paul Lee Tan, *The Interpretation of Prophecy* 38.
25. See, e.g., 1 Cor. 10:1-4 and Gal. 4:22-31.

Despite Paul's use of allegory, Jesus' frequent use of symbol and metaphor, and the fact that symbolic imagery is found in the greatest abundance in the prophetic books of the Bible such as Ezekiel, Daniel and Revelation, some Christians insist on denying symbolism whenever possible.[26] There are even some Christians who regard a strict emphasis on the literal approach as essential to the correct acceptance of the Bible itself. In defence of literalism, the Christian evangelical writer Dr Paul L. Tan, for example, argues that symbolism is in concept inconsistent with the nature of God:

> Because of man's finiteness, God does not use an incomprehensible heavenly or 'spiritual' language to write the Scripture. He chooses to convey spiritual truths and principles through the medium of regular, earthly language. Scriptural revelation must therefore be interpreted according to regular rules of earthly grammar and rhetoric. Being divinely intended for human comprehension, the Bible should be interpreted according to the normal mode of communication used among men. (Op. cit., 32-3)

Dr Tan asserts that in order to understand the Bible we must assume that it is using 'words normally and without multiple meaning' (ibid. 30). At the heart of Dr Tan's assumptions, which are widely accepted among conservative Christians, is the conviction that the literal method of interpretation makes it easier for us to understand the meaning of Scripture. Arguing that God intended us to know the meaning of His Word easily, Dr Tan therefore asserts that the literal method is correct.

These assumptions may sound appealing, but in practice they do not stand the test of application, especially in the realm of prophecy. This will become self-evident as we examine some of the differing interpretations of the prophecies found in Matthew, chapter 24. Many Christian commentators have used the literal method of interpretation, and yet it is evident that they differ widely as to what they believe to be the meaning of the text. If the Scriptures were written, as some literalists argue, in a simple and plain language so that they could be easily understood, it is reasonable to assume there would not be so many conflicting interpretations.

26. This approach is very widely applied even to discussions of prophecy. See, e.g., an article by The Revd S.H. Tyng, Jr., rector of the Church of the Holy Trinity, New York, cited in *Premillennial Essays of the Prophetic Conference*, (1879) 26.

A simple example which clearly illustrates this point is verse 29 of Matthew 24. The prophecy states that 'the stars shall fall from heaven'. The Scripture provides no clue as to exactly how this could take place literally. Moreover, the text does not indicate whether meteors or literal stars are meant, nor is it stated whether the stars will fall upon the earth. From a scientific point of view, it is not reasonable to accept the possibility of the stars literally falling on the earth. Hence, contrary to the assumptions of the literalists, a literal interpretation confronts the believer with a meaning which becomes extremely difficult, if not impossible, to understand and accept.

However, if we employ a symbolic approach, this verse (v. 29) can be interpreted to mean that spiritual stars, that is, the leaders of the Church who like stars in the sky guided the believers during the night-time of the religion, will fall from the heaven of spiritual guidance. This view, which we will examine in more detail later, has existed since early Christian times and is also asserted by Bahá'u'lláh in His writings. We may ask, which interpretation is easier to understand and believe: the literal or the symbolic?

This type of symbolism is neither difficult to understand nor unfamiliar to normal 'human' language, since it is obvious that people commonly use such metaphors when speaking. As metaphors and symbols are common to human language, it seems ironic that one would preclude the possibility of their existence when interpreting Scripture, especially prophecies.

The purpose of this commentary is not to enter into an analysis of the methods of interpretation or to resolve such debates. Rather, this issue has been brought up simply to point out that the history of the interpretation of Jesus' Olivet Discourse has shown that from the beginning its interpretation is subject to a variety of complex problems, that its intended meaning is not fully agreed upon by the advocates of any method of interpretation, and that the difficulties Christian commentators and modern scholars have had in ascertaining its meaning preclude any dogmatic determinations. Commenting on the methods of interpretation, Bahá'u'lláh's son, 'Abdu'l-Bahá, states:

> It is difficult to comprehend even the words of a philosopher; how much more difficult it is to understand the Words of God. The divine Words are not to be taken according to their outer

sense. They are symbolical and contain realities of spiritual meaning. For instance, in the book of Solomon's songs you will read about the bride and bridegroom. It is evident that the physical bride and bridegroom are not intended. Obviously, these are symbols conveying a hidden and inner significance. In the same way the Revelations of St John are not to be taken literally, but spiritually. These are the mysteries of God. It is not the reading of the words that profits you; it is the understanding of their meanings. Therefore, pray God that you may be enabled to comprehend the mysteries of the divine Testaments. (*Promulgation* 459)

JESUS' OLIVET DISCOURSE

PART I

THE BEGINNING OF SORROWS

CHRIST FORETELLS
THE DESTRUCTION OF THE TEMPLE

[1] And Jesus went out, and departed from the temple: and his disciples came to him for to shew him the buildings of the temple.
[2] And Jesus said unto them, See ye not all these things? verily I say unto you, There shall not be left here one stone upon another, that shall not be thrown down.

COMMENTARY (24:1-2)

Christ and the Disciples at the Jerusalem Temple

Jesus' turbulent three-and-a-half year ministry is now drawing to a close. As the disciples listen to Jesus they unknowingly stand at the eve of the betrayal, trial and crucifixion of Christ. Verses 1 and 2 provide the initial context of what was to be Jesus' last major discourse. Jesus has come out of the Temple in Jerusalem, accompanied by His leading disciples. We can sense the closeness between them. The text tells us that the disciples sought to show Jesus the buildings of the Temple. This is because they were deeply impressed by the beauty of the structure and its surroundings.[27] However, on this occasion Jesus does not extol the Temple;[28] instead, well aware of what was soon to occur, He prophesies its destruction.

The presentation of this account in the Gospel suggests that Jesus is referring literally to the actual Temple building. This has traditionally been the popular understanding of this prophecy, for shortly after Jesus made this prophecy, the Temple was, in fact, literally destroyed. Moreover, this came to pass in a way very much as Jesus states, 'There shall not be left here one

27. This point is more clearly indicated in Luke 21:5 and Mark 13:1.
28. The Gospel tells us that Jesus had previously cleansed the Temple by driving out those who used its sacred precincts to do business. On that occasion He praised the Temple as 'My Father's house' (John 2:16).

stone upon another'.[29] However, this prophecy can be interpreted both literally and symbolically. That is, the literal destruction of the Temple, roughly forty years later in AD 70, can be regarded as an outward symbol of what was soon to happen in the ministry of Christ: the crucifixion (AD 33).

The implications of this prophecy should not be restricted to a sign of Christ's ability to reveal a glimpse of things to come. Even outward facts of history can often be shadows of greater spiritual events or truths. To understand the significance of this prophecy, it is necessary to know why the Temple in Jerusalem is so important and how Jesus symbolized the Temple in the New Testament.

The Symbolic Relationship Between the Temple and Jesus

The Temple was very important to the religious life of the Jews because (1) it was a sign of God's presence among His people; (2) it was a sign that God had chosen them, the Jews, to be the preservers of His message among the nations; (3) it was the place where sacrifices to God were offered to atone for sins; and (4) it was an outward symbol of the religion that united the Hebrew nation.[30]

During His ministry, Christ correlated His own significance to that of the Temple. In this way He indicated that He now represented that for which the Temple in Jerusalem had formerly stood:

> Jesus answered and said to them, 'Destroy this temple, and in three days I will raise it up.' Then the Jews said, 'It has taken forty-six years to build this temple, and will You raise it up in three days?' But He was speaking of the temple of His body. (John 2:19-22)

Moreover, the Temple sacrifices prescribed in the Old Testament were abrogated by the ministry of Christ, for He now acted as High Priest,[31] offering Himself up as a sacrifice for the redemption of humankind (Heb. 7), and He (His presence and, later, the Church), not the physical Temple in Jerusalem, was the sign of God's presence among humankind and the focal

29. The prophecy fits so well that some sceptics have argued that it must have been written after the fact.
30. The tabernacle is a sign of unity: as God is one, so God's people, gathered in diverse tribes and ranks, are united around the tabernacle (Num. 1-10)' (Walter A. Elwell, *Evangelical Dictionary of Theology* 1068).
31. Once a year the Jewish High Priest entered the Temple and offered a sacrifice to atone for the sins of the people. Jesus, in effect, became both the High Priest and the offering sacrificed for the sins of humankind.

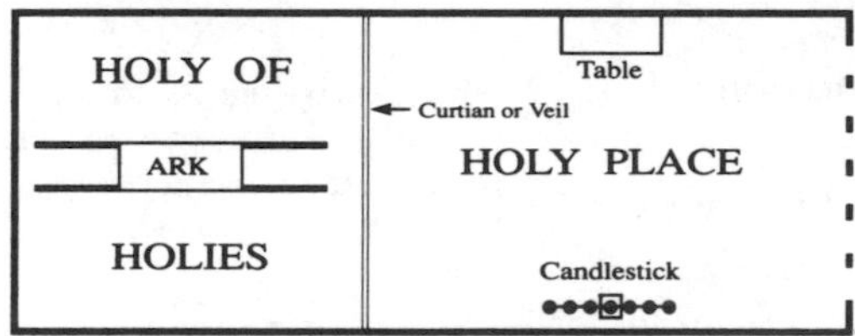

Diagram of the Tabernacle

The Temple had its origin in, and was the successor to, 'the tent of meeting' or Tabernacle, which was built by the Jews in the Sinai wilderness after their exodus from Egyptian captivity. According to Scripture Moses was given detailed instructions by God for the building of the Tabernacle (Exod. 25-31). The Tabernacle was built around a small room called the Holy of Holies. Inside this room was placed the Ark of the Covenant which contained the Law as given at Mount Sinai.

point of unity. After His crucifixion, the establishment of the Church, symbolized by the resurrection, constituted Christ's risen body (Eph. 2:5-6; 5:29-30) and the new Temple (1 Cor. 3:16; 2 Cor. 6:16).[32] It was the Church that was the temple Christ raised up in three days and which became the sign and the source of unity between once divergent peoples (Eph. 2:19-22).[33]

32. 'Abdu'l-Bahá briefly discusses the symbolism of the resurrection in *Some Answered Questions*, ch. 23. For an analysis of 'Abdu'l-Bahá's explanation see Michael Sours, *Understanding Christian Beliefs*, part 4.
33. 'To the second temple [i.e., the reconstructed Temple in Jerusalem], a third court was added, called the court of the gentiles, and designed for the gentile worshippers. This gentile court was accounted holy in no other sense than as a part of the holy city, Jerusalem. In the large covered building of the temple was contained the Holy of Holies; and various sacred emblems. This whole pile of buildings was

Nineteenth-century illustration of the Roman siege of Jesusalem. (Frontispiece from Brown's *Dictionary of the Bible*.)

The Rejection of Jesus and Destruction of the Temple

In the first century BC the Roman Empire took control of the territory where the Jewish nation resided. The Jews had long awaited a Messiah, but now, as they lived and suffered humiliation under Roman domination, the appearance of the promised deliverer seemed especially urgent. The Hebrew Scriptures assured them that the Messiah would lead God's people to victory, that He would establish a Kingdom, and that He would be its ruler (Matt. 2:3-6; John 12:12-13). When Christ appeared He came as a shepherd to gather His flock and lead them into the Kingdom of God. To His followers, Jesus was Lord (i.e., sovereign ruler, Acts 10:36), He did bring a sword (the word of God, Matt. 10:34; Eph. 6:17; 2 Cor. 10:3-5) to defeat the enemy (i.e., sin) and He did establish a kingdom (the Kingdom of God, John 18:36;

called the temple; and it was an emblem of both the human body of Christ; and his visible church on earth' (Ethan Smith, *Key to the Revelation* 154, [1833]). 'Abdu'l-Bahá emphasized unity as the main purpose of temples: 'The real temple is the very Word of God; for to it all humanity must turn, and it is the centre of unity for all mankind' (*Promulgation* 65). 'Temples are the symbols of the divine uniting force so that when the people gather there in the House of God they may recall the fact that the law has been revealed for them and that the law is to unite them' (*Promulgation* 65). 'Bahá'u'lláh hath raised up the tabernacle of the oneness of mankind. Whoso seeketh shelter under this roof will certainly come forth from other dwellings' (*Some Answered Questions* 195).

Despite successive persecutions, only three hundred years had passed since Christ's ministry before the Christians enjoyed state patronage. Extensive church building had already begun in Rome, Constantinople and Palestine in the fourth century. This illustration shows the Church of the Holy Wisdom (or Hagia Sophia, AD 537-47), which still stands as an enduring monument to the early triumph and influence of Christianity. The minarets date from the Turkish conquest in 1453, when the church was converted to a Mosque.

Luke 17:20-1).[34] Thus, Christ did have power and dominion.[35]

But the Jews, having interpreted the prophecies literally, rejected Christ as the Messiah foretold in Scripture.[36] Consequently, Jesus was opposed and eventually brutally crucified. For the Apostles, the arrest of Jesus was an unexpected crisis and they all forsook Him (Matt. 26:56). In this way the Temple of Christ's body (the believers) was destroyed. From this point of view, the crucifixion is central to the symbolic or inner meaning of Jesus' prophecy concerning the destruction of the Temple (Matt. 24:1-2).

34. See Appendix IV, The Kingdom of God.

35. Bahá'u'lláh writes that Christ 'came unto them [the Jews] with manifest dominion' (*Tablets of Bahá'u'lláh* 9).

36. Many Christians believe that the Jews failed to recognize that Christ had fulfilled the prophecies of the Scripture because they were looking to the wrong prophecies. Some Christians believe that Christ fulfilled the prophecies which refer to a suffering servant (e.g., Isa. 53) and that the other prophecies which speak of a ruler are intended for the Second Advent. Bahá'í writings hold that the Jews read the right prophecies but interpreted them incorrectly (Bahá'u'lláh, *Certitude* 18-19; 'Abdu'l-Bahá, *Promulgation* 291-2, 459).

Outwardly, fulfilment of this prophecy can be seen in the eventual destruction of the Jerusalem Temple. These two events are directly related because, rather than follow Jesus and His spiritual teachings, the Jews became impatient with Roman domination and eventually mounted a military revolt against the Romans (AD 66). Rome ordered its army, the supreme military force at that time, to move against the Jews. Jerusalem was destroyed, the Temple was razed to the ground, large numbers of Jews were killed, and the defeated Jews who escaped with their lives were driven out and eventually forbidden to enter the city again.

This event, so closely linked to the rejection of Christ, had a major impact on the future of the Jewish nation, even up to our own time. From the destruction of the Temple onwards the Jews would remain a scattered people living under the rule of other nations. In some regions, where major centres of Jewish population developed, such as in Europe, they would suffer severe persecutions. It was not until the mid-nineteenth century that a significant number of Jews began to return to Jerusalem.[37] This gradual process of emigration back to the Holy Land escalated dramatically following the atrocities they suffered during World War II, and this eventually led to the establishment of the nation of Israel on May 14, 1948.[38] Thus an exile beginning shortly after their rejection of Christ did not end until nearly two thousand years later, during the period that saw the beginnings of the Bahá'í Faith.

The words of the historian Will Durant illustrate how differently history would unfold for Jews and Christians:

> No other people has ever known so long an exile, or so hard a fate. Shut out from their Holy City, the Jews were compelled to surrender it first to paganism, then to Christianity. Scattered into every province and beyond, condemned to poverty and humiliation, unbefriended even by philosophers and saints, they retired from public affairs into private study and worship, passionately preserving the words of their

37. In *Jerusalem, Rebirth of a City*, Martin Gilbert recounts the dramatic changes that occurred in Jerusalem between 1838 and 1898. 'By 1860 Jewish immigration, mostly from Tsarist Russia, had turned the Jews into the largest single group in the city' (xi-xii).

38. 'Abdu'l-Bahá writes, 'Moreover, materially as well (as spiritually), the Israelites will gather in the Holy Land. This is irrefutable prophecy, for the ignominy which Israel has suffered for well-nigh twenty-five hundred years will now be changed into eternal glory, and in the eyes of all, the Jewish people will become glorified to such an extent as to draw the jealousy of its enemies and the envy of its friends' (see Helen Hornby, *Lights of Guidance* 383-4).

> scholars, and preparing to write them down at last in the Talmuds of Babylonia and Palestine. Judaism hid in fear and obscurity while its offspring, Christianity, went out to conquer the world. (*Caesar and Christ* 549)

The dramatically different fate of the Christians reveals the spiritual power that was imparted by Christ to those who accepted His sovereignty. This is reflected in the words of 'Abdu'l-Bahá:

> That mighty Jewish nation toppled and crumbled away, but those few souls who sought shelter beneath the Messianic Tree [Christ] transformed all human life. (*Secret of Divine Civilization* 82-3)

The Christians, who were at first persecuted by the Jews, were also persecuted by the Romans. However, the Word of God carried by the Christians proved not only to be an invincible spiritual stronghold but also an all-conquering spiritual sword. In time Rome felt the effects of Christ's message, and the Kingdom of God that had been established in the hearts of the believers was now established outwardly in the world around the believers as a new civilization - a Christian civilization - emerged. Thus, Christ not only fulfilled prophecy in a spiritual way but, in time, this spiritual fulfilment led to an outward and literal fulfilment in the world. He had become Ruler of an earthly dominion.

This does not mean that the Christian (Byzantine) Empire was a political model of the Kingdom of God or that Constantine,[39] the first ruler to accept Christianity, was a flawless saint. It simply means that the Kingdom of God became manifest in the world to the extent that Jesus' teachings were put into practice or influenced the hearts of those who came to believe in Him. The outward establishment of the Kingdom of God can be seen in the effect the Church had on society: the building of hospitals, the founding of charities and the development of Christian art and culture. The Emperor Constantine was, for example, the first emperor to place a ban

39. Constantine and the whole Byzantine culture have been sharply criticized by western scholars until recent times. Romilly Jenkins attributes some of this criticism to ignorance and some to prejudice arising from the sectarian conflicts between western and eastern Christianity. (See *Byzantium, The Imperial Centuries*, AD 610-1071, 1-14). 'Abdu'l-Bahá emphasizes the change Christianity brought to the empire by pointing out that Constantine established philanthropic institutions for the poor and needy (*Secret of Divine Civilization* 85).

on the human slaughter of the gladiatorial combats. It was the efforts of Christians that led to the eventual elimination of this inhuman practice.[40]

The Jews had rejected Christ and sought deliverance through the use of force, which brought needless destruction upon them and upon Jerusalem, whereas real victory was given to the Christians through Christ's teachings. For the Christian, the destruction of the Temple in Jerusalem appeared to be a sign of God's judgement against those who had turned away from the covenant God had established through Christ.[41] It was a sign that Christ clearly foresaw, a sign that history unfolds according to God's plan, and a sign that real deliverance requires moving with that plan.

Christ was pointing out the inevitable, that which the Jews themselves knew the prophets of former times had warned them about. The Temple served the people only if they remained obedient to God's covenant, otherwise God would cause the destruction of the Temple (Jer. 7:1-15; Ezek. 9; Amos 9:1). When Jesus allowed the Jews to crucify Him,[42] He had, in effect, allowed them to destroy God's Temple, which He then raised up again through the establishment of the Church. The later destruction of the Temple in Jerusalem was an outward shadow in the physical world of what they had brought upon themselves spiritually by rejecting Christ.

Since Jesus had already inaugurated the Christian era, which superseded the Jewish era, there is good reason to believe that His prophecies are not primarily centred upon the fate and destiny of the Jews. Instead, it is logical to assume that His prophecy concerning the destruction of the Temple is essentially involved with His own destiny and the establishment of the Church. Jesus' prophecy came true with the crucifixion, which was the destruction of the Temple (His body) in Jerusalem. The future destruction in AD 70 of the actual building that the Jews continued to regard as the Temple was not in itself necessary for the fulfilment of Jesus' prophecy. Moreover, while the destruction of the Temple - both the crucifixion and the literal destruction in AD 70 -

40. See Sheldon, *History of the Christian Church* 296-9, 399.
41. The Christian historian, Eusebius (AD 263-339) described the tragic destruction of Jerusalem by the Romans and attributed it to God's judgement against the Jews (*The History of the Church* 5:4, pp. 111-12).
42. Jesus allowed Himself to be crucified. It would be incorrect to say that the Jews killed the Messiah against His will. Had Christ wanted to escape He could have done so by recanting His claims. His willingness to die is a great testimony to His truth. This is, according to Bahá'í belief, the meaning of the Qur'ánic verse, 'They [the Jews] declared: "We have put to death the Messiah Jesus the son of Mary, the apostle of Allah." They did not kill him, nor did they crucify him, but they thought they did' (Surah 4:157, *The Koran*, trans. N.J. Dawood).

represented a great loss to the Jews, both events were turned into victory for the Christians. As St Paul said, the crucifixion revealed 'the power of God and the wisdom of God' (1 Cor. 1:24). It proved the invincibility of Jesus' truth, which was essential for the establishment of the Church.[43] The destruction of the Temple in AD 70, as well as further conflicts between the Romans and Jews at Jerusalem (AD 135), compelled the Christians to move out of Israel, spreading the Faith to other areas in the empire, which in turn helped emancipate Christianity from its inhibiting Jewish roots.

It may seem difficult to accept that New Testament symbolism can be applied to this prophecy, because Jesus' words sound very literal. When He refers to the Temple He says, 'There shall not be left here one stone upon another'. However, these words provide an effective use of symbolism to express the initial impact the crucifixion had on the faith of His disciples. When He was first arrested, they all fled (Matt. 26:56), and even Peter, His chief disciple, went on to deny Him (Matt. 26:69-75). The disciples were, in Peter's own words, the stones of the Temple (1 Pet. 2:4-8), every one of which was knocked down and scattered until Jesus' teachings raised the Temple up again through the establishment of the Church.

Naturally, when Christ made this dramatic prophecy the disciples wanted to know more. In the context of their time, the disciples would not have taken such a prophecy lightly.

43. In Bahá'u'lláh's words, 'when the Son of Man [Christ] yielded up His breath to God, the whole creation wept with a great weeping. By sacrificing Himself, however, a fresh capacity was infused into all created things' (*Gleanings* 85).

THE DISCIPLES' QUESTIONS

3 And as he sat upon the mount of Olives, the disciples came unto him privately, saying, Tell us, when shall these things be? and what shall be the sign of thy coming, and of the end of the world?

COMMENTARY (24:3)

The Setting: The Mount of Olives

Perhaps the disciples were too surprised by Jesus' words to ask Him questions while they were still standing near the Temple. Perhaps they did not want to risk being overheard. Matthew doesn't say why, but he does relate that they did enquire about this prophecy later when they were upon the Mount of Olives.

The Mount of Olives is a hill east of the old city walls of Jerusalem. In those days one could walk from the site of the Temple, which is within the city walls, out of the Golden Gate[44] of the Temple courtyard, to the Mount of Olives in a short period of time (less than two hours), and from there gain a view out across the city of Jerusalem. It is here, as the Gospel accounts tell us, that the disciples ask Jesus about the future. It is here that Jesus answers them by giving His last major discourse, the Olivet Discourse, only two days[45] before being tried and crucified.[46] It is also from here that

44. The Golden Gate has been closed since the time of the Crusades. The text does not say, but Jesus and the disciples may have gone through St Stephen's Gate instead.

45. Some scholars argue that Jesus delivered the discourse on Wednesday (April 1), others believe it was delivered on Thursday. The crucifixion took place on the Friday, the Jewish Sabbath, of the same week (John 19:31). According to Jewish reckoning the day begins at sunset.

46. With regard to the belief in a literal resurrection of Jesus, the Mount of Olives is also a traditional site of Jesus' ascension into heaven (Acts 1:9-12). In Christian eschatology it is also commonly believed that upon Christ's return, He will part the Mount in two as He stands on it. This view is based on a literal interpretation of Zechariah 14:4. Understood allegorically, this Old Testament passage could easily refer to Jesus' First Advent, in which case it has already been fulfilled as is suggested by the context of the prophecy in chapters 13 and 14 of Zechariah. One possible interpretation is that the mountain, symbolizing the religion of God, was split into two Faiths, Judaism and Christianity.

The Mount of Olives as viewed from Jerusalem. The enclosed area at the bottom of the slope is the Garden of Gethsemane. (A nineteenth-century etching from Frederic W. Farrar's *The Life of Christ*.)

one can see, on the slopes below, the garden of Gethsemane, where Jesus would soon be betrayed and arrested.

The Three Questions

When the disciples enquired about the future, they asked an essentially threefold question: (1) When will the Temple be destroyed? (2) What will be the sign of Christ's coming?[47] And (3) when will the age end?[48] The fact that these questions are placed together in this way suggests that the disciples believed there was a relationship between these events.

47. The word 'coming' in the Apostles' question is from the Greek word '*parousia*' which signifies not only His appearance but His actual presence. The word literally means 'presence', which some take to mean a consequent future presence of Christ in the world, which suggests a somewhat different meaning from the usual translation 'coming'. See W.E. Vine, *Vine's Expository Dictionary of Biblical Words* 111.

48. The word 'world' is a somewhat inaccurate translation of the original Greek 'aion' which more correctly means 'age'. Thus almost all new versions of the Bible now read 'the end of the age'. See W.E. Vine, *Vine's Expository Dictionary of Biblical Words* 685.

A nineteenth-century rendering of Jerusalem from the Mount of Olives. The most prominent structure is the Shrine (Qubbat al-Sakhra), *the Dome of the Rock*, which is the third most venerated shrine of the Islamic world and stands on the purported site once occupied by the Jerusalem Temple. (From Frederic W. Farrar's *The Life of Christ*.)

THERE WILL BE DECEPTIONS AND FALSE CHRISTS

4 And Jesus answered and said unto them, Take heed that no man
deceive you.
5 For many shall come in my name, saying, I am Christ; and shall
deceive many.

COMMENTARY (24:4-5)

Jesus' Warning Concerning False Christs

As a preface to answering the disciples' questions, Jesus begins with an important warning. They are very eager to know about Christ's Second Advent, perhaps too eager, and therefore Jesus warns them that they must be cautious in order to avoid being deceived by false claimants.

Many Christian commentators point out that, from the earliest Christian times, such individuals did appear. There is, of course, Bar-Jesus mentioned in the Book of Acts 13:6. However, the first truly significant false Christ or Messiah appears to have been Simeon Bar Cochba (AD ?-135), the Jewish rebel leader.[49] The Jews rejected the idea that Jesus of Nazareth - who had not led them in battle against the Romans - was the Messiah, and now they accepted Bar Cochba, who did lead them in rebellion:

> For three years the rebels fought valiantly against the legions; finally they were beaten by lack of food and supplies. The Romans destroyed 985 towns in Palestine, and slew 580,000

49. It seems that the Jews may have regarded Bar Cochba as the Messiah partly for his political ambitions and partly because of his name. The early Church historian, Eusebius (AD 263-339) writes: 'The Jews at that time were under the command of a man called Bar Cochba, which means a star - a bloodthirsty bandit who on the strength of his name [which implies Messiahship: Num. 24:17], as if he had slaves to deal with, paraded himself as a luminary come down from heaven to shine upon their misery.' See Eusebius, *The History of the Church* 157. The word 'Messiah' is Hebrew and has the same meaning as the Greek word 'Christ'.

> men; a still larger number, we are told, perished through starvation, disease, and fire; nearly all Judea was laid waste. Bar Cocheba himself fell in defending Bethar. So many Jews were sold as slaves that their price fell to that of a horse. Thousands hid in underground channels rather than be captured; surrounded by the Romans, they died one by one of hunger, while the living ate the bodies of the dead. (*Caesar and Christ* 548)

Thus there were false Messiahs and many people experienced the bitter consequences of following them.

For many early Christians, Jewish objections to Jesus may have been a test of their faith. An individual like Bar Cochba would have seemed closer to popular Jewish Messianic expectation because of his political character and his promise of deliverance, that is, political deliverance from Rome. This political image fits the literal interpretations of the Scripture common among the Jews at that time. Jesus knew that such political 'messiahs' would arise; therefore, He warned His followers about them. What is particularly important, and perhaps frequently misunderstood, is how this warning relates to the following verses.

THERE WILL BE WARS, FAMINES, PESTILENCES, AND EARTHQUAKES

6 *And ye shall hear of wars and rumours of wars: see that ye be not*
troubled: for all these things must come to pass but the end is not yet.
7 *For nation shall rise against nation, and kingdom against*
kingdom: and there shall be famines, and pestilences, and
earthquakes, in divers places.
8 *All these are the beginning of sorrows.*

COMMENTARY (24:6-8)

Historic Millennial Responses to Catastrophes

Throughout history Christians have looked upon wars, famines, pestilences and earthquakes as the harbingers of the Second Advent. As early as the fourth century, Ambrose (c. 340-97), who was Bishop of Milan, believed that the wars of his time were signs of the approaching end.[50] Similarly, Europe's worst plague, which began in Constantinople in 1347 and spread throughout Europe, appears to have inspired fears that the Judgement Day was at hand.[51] Known as the Black Death, this plague is estimated to have claimed as many as a quarter to three-quarters of the European population. And in the eighteenth century the Lisbon earthquake was

50. See Le Roy Edwin Froom, *The Prophetic Faith of Our Fathers*, vol. 1, 420, trans. from Ambrose, *Exposition in Lukam*, book 10, on Luke 21:9, in Migne, *Patrologia Latina* vol. 15, cols. 1898, 1899.

51. Norman Cohn writes, 'It may well have been the particularly severe epidemic of 1368 which inspired Schmid', an individual who claimed to be the Messiah, 'to announce that the Last Judgement would be held and the Millennium begin in the following year' (*The Pursuit of the Millennium* 145). Cohn also writes, 'People were always on the watch for the "signs" which, according to the prophetic tradition, were to herald and accompany the final "time of troubles"; and since the "signs" included bad rulers, civil discord, war, drought, famine, plague, comets, sudden deaths of prominent persons and an increase in general sinfulness, there was never any difficulty about finding them. Invasion or the threat of invasion by Huns, Magyars, Mongols, Saracens or Turks always stirred memories of those hordes of Antichrist, the peoples of Gog and Magog. Above all, any ruler who could be regarded as a tyrant was apt to take on the features of Antichrist; in which case hostile chroniclers would give him the conventional title of *rex iniquus* [ruler of iniquity]' (ibid. 21).

recognized both in America and Europe as a harbinger of the end times.[52]

However, each catastrophe passed and no visible end was to be discerned. If there is any direct relationship between Jesus' prophecies and these specific recorded tragedies, it remains a mystery. Many have noted that such catastrophes, to a greater or lesser extent, have always existed.[53] Moreover, Christ does not say that these events will occur simultaneously just before He appears. Rather, He tells the disciples 'see that ye be not troubled, for all these things must come to pass, but the end is not yet'. He adds that these things are 'the beginning of sorrows'. These words suggest that Christ is not presenting these events as the signs of the end but, rather, as what must occur during the period of time between His crucifixion (i.e. the destruction of the Temple He speaks of in verse 24:1-2) and His later return at the end of the age (Matt. 24:30).

But if these are not signs of the end, why does Christ mention them? The reason becomes apparent in the closeness between Christ's warning about false prophets and His following explanation that such signs 'are the beginning of sorrows' but are not the end. Difficult times and great hardships provide a strong impetus for people to seek help and turn to God for deliverance. It is at such times that people are easy prey for self-seeking or misguided opportunists. Therefore it is during hardships that people should be especially careful to take heed that no one deceives them.

We can learn two significant points from the fact that Jesus, the true Christ, Himself appeared during such a time of severe hardship: (1) People interpreted the outward struggle with Rome as a sign of the end times when the Messiah should appear, but (2) they rejected Christ because His message did not appear to them to be the remedy for the hardships they were suffering. Later, they would be deceived by Bar Cochba. From these facts we can make the following important observation - the people were

52. See Le Roy Edwin Froom, *The Prophetic Faith of Our Fathers*, vol. 2, 674-6; also D.T. Taylor, *The Great Consummation*. Taylor writes at length about the Lisbon earthquake and argues that it is the fulfilment of Jesus' prophecy (198-209). In recent times the Christian writer Hal Lindsey sold millions of copies of his book *The Late Great Planet Earth*, wherein he argues that Jesus' statements refer to the famines, pestilences, earthquakes and wars of the twentieth century - all part of a 'prophetic scenario' nearing its culmination (pp. 127-199).

53. For example, the Lisbon earthquake is estimated to have claimed 60,000 lives, but the list of known earthquakes is long. Only 18 years before the Lisbon earthquake, Calcutta, India may have lost as many as 300,000 people. Japan in 1730, Italy in 1693, China in 1556 and so on, all suffered major earthquakes. People have interpreted prophecy with themselves in the centre of the divine stage, unaware of similar, if not more significant events taking place elsewhere. The Christian writers Carl Olof Jonsson and Wolfgang Herbst present a detailed challenge to the interpretation that such events were the 'sign' Jesus referred to as a herald of His presence. See *The Sign of the Last Days - When?*

focusing their attention on outward signs and, therefore, they were looking for outward remedies. Naturally, they were deceived by those who also pointed to the outward signs and who offered outward remedies.

The greater crisis was not coming from Rome but from inside themselves. Their subjugation by Rome was merely an outward calamity, perhaps visited upon them because of the inner spiritual crisis that the Jewish nation was suffering. The remedy Christ prescribed was to heal this spiritual ailment. As 'Abdu'l-Bahá writes:

> Jesus . . . founded the sacred Law on a basis of moral character and complete spirituality, and for those who believed in Him He delineated a special way of life which constitutes the highest type of action on earth. And while those emblems of redemption [the Christians] were to outward seeming abandoned to the malevolence and persecution of their tormentors, in reality they had been delivered out of the hopeless darkness which encompassed the Jews and they shone forth in everlasting glory at the dawn of that new day. (*Secret of Divine Civilization* 82, clarification added)

By keeping these points in mind, we can help ourselves avoid making the same mistake. People who have seen outward calamities, such as earthquakes, wars, and famines, as signs of Christ's imminent return have not only been repeatedly disappointed but have entirely overlooked the deeper meaning of the Scriptures. If Jesus was truly saying that primarily outward signs were going to herald His Second Advent, especially such signs as earthquakes and famines, the repeated injunction to watch (Matt. 24:42; 2 Pet. 3:12) would be of little concern. In fact, believers could disregard the warning until the ground began to shake under their feet and the end was then upon them. If the final end did not occur, they could cease watching until the next earthquake sounded the alert. Obviously, true faithfulness could not proceed on such a basis.

Distinguishing Material from Spiritual Catastrophes

There is no doubt that outward earthquakes and other physical calamities have awakened many from their apathy and served as potent reminders of Jesus' words, but it must be admitted that such events are not uncommon. Earthquakes, for example, have unquestionably been a part of human existence as long as people have lived on this planet. Today it is commonly accepted that earthquakes are caused by continental drift, a theory which suggests that earthquakes will forever remain a simple and irrevocable geological occurrence.

Instead of being only literal, Jesus' references to wars and earthquakes are likely to also be symbols for catastrophes of a spiritual nature. In fact, if we assume that these prophecies can also be symbolic, a spiritually relevant picture quickly emerges. Such outward signs can be seen as metaphors representing the decline of the Church. Assuming that Jesus' message is ultimately concerned with the salvation of the human soul, it follows that the wars, famines, pestilences and earthquakes are symbols for upheavals which will occur in humankind's spiritual life. It is such inevitable upheaval and darkness which necessitates the return of Christ and the renewal of God's eternal, changeless Faith.

The first calamities to occur are the 'wars', meaning disputes in the Church. In the first centuries of Christianity there were disagreements over the meaning of Christ's message and over the Church's leadership. These disputes grew and some even led to schisms, persecutions and bloodshed - literal wars. The disputes gradually obscured much of the real message of Christ by embittering Christians towards each other and dividing the Church, and this brought on 'famines'. *Famine* means a famine of the spirit as spoken of by the Old Testament Prophet, Amos:

> Behold, the days are coming, says the Lord God,
> That I will send a famine on the land,
> Not a famine of bread,
> Nor a thirst for water,
> But of hearing the words of the LORD. (Amos 8:11)

Included in these catastrophes are 'pestilences', that is, plagues and diseases. These are not plagues of the body but of the spirit; they are heresies and idolatries. History records a succession of such pestilences since early times: the sectarian battles of Arianism, Gnosticism, and many others.[54]

Finally, with such violent disagreements raging in the Church, the absence of Christian practices and the spread of erroneous beliefs, it is only

54. Arianism was founded by an Alexandria presbyter named Arius (d. AD 336). He denied the pre-existent eternality of Jesus Christ, and his movement proved to be a major divisive force in the fourth century. Gnosticism is a term which has been applied to a variety of movements that flourished in the early Christian centuries. They were elitist movements that stressed that salvation could be attained

inevitable that the institutions of the Church would begin to crack and tumble down. This shaking down of Church leadership and Church institutions can be very effectively represented by 'earthquakes'. Earthquakes could thus be a symbol for any period when the Church is racked by controversies and disagreements. Bahá'u'lláh indicates that the earthquakes mentioned in the Scriptures are symbolic (*Certitude* 44-8) and have come to pass in this day:

> Earthquakes have broken loose, and the tribes have lamented, for fear of God, the Lord of Strength, the All-Compelling. (*Epistle* 132)

In one instance Bahá'u'lláh uses the phrase 'earth of human understanding'(*Gleanings* 88), another time He writes of the 'earth of limitations' (*Certitude* 157), and 'Abdu'l-Bahá uses the phrase 'earthquake of doubts' (*Some Answered Questions* 60-1). What these metaphors suggest is being shaken down, then, is not the physical earth but, rather, people's beliefs and ways of thinking.[55]

Viewed from this perspective, Christ's prophecies about catastrophes are not primarily concerned with natural phenomena but with the spiritual life of the believer. He uses the outward world to symbolize the turmoil that occurs within. Outward, actual earthquakes and disasters serve to remind and awaken people to the spiritual truths they symbolize.

This symbolism - the shaking down and destruction of religious institutions - is closer to the world of the soul than those things that happen within the limits of the physical world. Christ's words, 'see that ye be not troubled', are a counsel to rise above these difficulties and to hold on to one's faith. Many people abandon their faith because they become troubled by the corruption in the Church, the disputes over the interpretation of the text, and the denominational divisions that have progressively worsened in the course of Church history. Such people have fallen short of Jesus' assurance that 'he who endures to the end shall be saved' (Matt. 24:13).

When such dramatic problems arose in the Church they were not the

through certain secret teachings or '*gnosis*' (from the Greek meaning knowledge). Many Gnostics rejected the Old Testament, or parts of it, and some accepted a variety of writings not included in the traditional canon, which they argued to be authoritative. See *The New International Dictionary of the Christian Church* 416-18.

55. This type of interpretation does not preclude outward fulfilment in the physical world. A closer examination of the subject of earthquakes mentioned in the Scriptures suggests that both symbolic and literal earthquakes can sometimes be related to this type of prophecy. See Appendix I.

sign of the end but, as Jesus clearly states, 'the beginning of sorrows'. This view is further supported by the following verses.

THERE WILL BE PERSECUTION AND INIQUITY

9 Then shall they deliver you up to be afflicted, and shall kill you: and ye shall be hated of all nations for my name's sake.
10 And then shall many be offended, and shall betray one another, and shall hate one another.
11 And many false prophets shall rise, and shall deceive many.
12 And because iniquity shall abound, the love of many shall wax cold.
13 But he that shall endure unto the end, the same shall be saved.

COMMENTARY (24:9-13)

The Persecution of the Christians

In verse 9, Christ tells the disciples of the coming opposition and suffering they and the rest of the faithful will suffer. Numerous historical accounts record the persecution, suffering and violent deaths of Christian believers. These records testify to the fulfilment of Christ's prophecy.

When Paul preached in Rome, Christians were already 'spoken against everywhere' (Acts 28:22). Christians would later suffer under sporadic violent persecutions. In AD 64 Christians were made the scapegoats for a severe fire that occurred in Rome. They were, according to Roman historian Tacitus, 'fastened on crosses, and, when daylight failed, were burned to serve as lamps by night'.[56] Later, the early Church historian, Eusebius (AD 263-339), would write that the Roman ruler Diocletian decreed that all Christian churches be

56. Tacitus (c. AD 55-c. 120), *The Annals*, trans. John Jackson, see pp. XV-XLIV.

destroyed, Christian books burned and congregations dissolved:

> Everything indeed has been fulfilled in my time; I saw with my own eyes the places of worship thrown down from top to bottom, the foundations, the inspired holy Scriptures committed to the flames in the middle of the public squares. (*The History of the Church* 329)

Christians were hated as atheists because they did not worship the Roman gods, and they were despised as immoral. Because of misunderstandings about Christian sacraments, Christians were even falsely accused of being practitioners of cannibalism and incest.[57] It was not only at the hands of the Romans that faithful Christians were persecuted and killed. Once the Gospel had spread among the Barbarian tribes of Europe, there, too, the faith of the converts was put to the test. The historian, Gibbon relates an instance of a campaign against Goths who converted to Christianity:

> The faith of the new converts was tried by the persecution which he [Athanaric] excited. A wagon, bearing aloft the shapeless image of Thor, perhaps, or of Woden, was conducted in solemn procession through the streets of the camp, and the rebels who refused to worship the god of their fathers were immediately burnt with their tents and families. (*Decline and Fall* 519, clarification added)

Such episodes suggest that, as Christ had said, the believers would, and did, become the 'hated of all nations' for His name's sake.[58] Referring to

57. These Roman accusations are evident in the surviving writings of the Church Fathers who specifically call attention to them and proceed at length to refute them. See Justin Martyr (c. AD 100-c. 167), The First Apology of Justin; Athenagoras' A Plea For the Christians, *Classical Readings in Christian Apologetics, AD 100-1800*, ed. L. Russ Bush, 7, 37-40, 43-5, 57-9.

58. 'Abdu'l-Bahá called attention to this verse when He referred to the accusations made against the Bahá'í Faith: 'Grieve thou not over what the Pharisees, and the purveyors of false rumours among writers for the press, are saying of Bahá. Call thou to mind the days of Christ, and the afflictions heaped upon Him by the people, and all the torments and tribulations inflicted upon His disciples. Since ye are lovers of the Abhá Beauty, ye also must, for His love's sake, incur the peoples' blame, and all that befell those of a former age must likewise befall you. Then will the faces of the chosen be alight with the splendours of the Kingdom of God, and will shine down the ages, yea, down all the cycles of time, while the deniers shall remain in their manifest loss. It will be even as was said by the Lord Christ: they shall persecute you for My name's sake' (*Selections From the Writings of 'Abdu'l-Bahá* 39-40).

the fortitude of the early Christian believers, 'Abdu'l-Bahá writes:

> After the ascension of Jesus to the Realm of Glory, these few souls [the Apostles] stood up with their spiritual qualities and with deeds that were pure and holy, and they arose by the power of God and the life-giving breaths of the Messiah to save all the peoples of the earth. Then all the idolatrous nations as well as the Jews rose up in their might to kill the Divine fire that had been lit in the lamp of Jerusalem. 'Fain would they put out God's light with their mouths: but God hath willed to perfect His light, albeit the infidels abhor it' (Qur'án 9:33). Under the fiercest tortures, they did every one of these holy souls to death . . . In spite of this agonizing requital, the Christians continued to teach the Cause of God. (*Secret of Divine Civilization* 45, clarification added)

Apostasy and Betrayal Among Christians

Jesus' words, 'And then shall many be offended' refer to the apostasy of many who once professed the faith. That is, seeing the persecution and fearing for themselves, they renounced their faith.[59] Eusebius writes that during the persecution of Diocletian's reign, he saw:

> the pastors of the churches hiding disgracefully in one place or another, while others suffered the indignity of being held up to ridicule by their enemies. (*The History of the Church* 329)

When Jesus prophesied that they will 'betray one another', He may have meant that the deserters will betray those who adhere to their faith. They 'shall hate one another' may mean that, because the people's faith will weaken, hate will enter in among them. The Christian commentator J. P. Lange interprets this verse in the context of Christian sectarian conflict and strife.[60]

59. 'Persecution from without (v. 9) leads to treachery inside the church' (Robert H. Gundry, *Matthew: A Commentary on His Literary and Theological Art* 479). Lange writes, 'This betraying one another includes the idea of delivering up to an unauthorized tribunal, i.e., to the . . . magistrate or to the political power, which has no control over consciences; and the word, therefore, is appropriate to all political persecutions, which not only apostates have inflicted upon true Christians, but Christians upon Christians, Arians upon Catholics, and Catholics upon Arians, etc.' True to his age, Lange then adds, 'See this in all Church history, especially the history of all Protestant persecutions' (*The Gospel According to Matthew* 424).

60. Lange, ibid. He adds, ' "And shall hate one another" - the perfect opposite to the vocation of all Christians, "to love one another" (John 15:17).'

False Prophets Among the Christians

The 'many false prophets' that will arise are commonly seen by Christian commentators[61] as 'false prophets' within the Church who will 'deceive many' (see Acts 20:28-31; 2 Pet. 2:1). If these interpretations are correct, it was not long before the emerging Church saw the fulfilment of Christ's words. In early times, Eusebius recorded that there were many who were regarded as such enemies within the Church.

But it is difficult to distinguish clearly, from the accounts that have come down through history, who might best be described as heretics and who as false prophets. One of the two sides of every dispute inevitably imputed the other side to be heretical, while posterity has been kinder to the records of those who prevailed, either by sound arguments or by resort to force. Nevertheless, among the more extreme claimants, Eusebius preserves the names of Simon the Magus and his successor Menander, who 'actually claimed to be the saviour', and Montanus the Paraclete[62] and his female adherents Priscilla and Maximilla, alleged to have been his prophetesses.'

The records of later periods also leave much that is suspect, but if we can trust them, the Mediaeval and Reformation periods seem to have had an abundance of individuals who arose to claim they were the Messiah. Eudes de l'Etoile, Tanchelm, Konrad Schmid, Bockelson and a number of others all appear to have claimed to be Messiahs or divine heralds of the last days. According to the historian Norman Cohn, many such Messiahs led their followers in ruthless campaigns of plunder and conquest as they sought, in the most contradictory of ways, to establish the Kingdom of God.[63]

Neither was the faith of simple Christians protected from the endless procession of doctrinal disputes. Nearly every century appears to have had an unfortunate share of insincere and self-seeking leaders intent on enthroning their views, right or wrong, at the cost of splitting the Church.

61. See, e.g., Lange, *The Gospel According to Matthew* 424; Patte, *The Gospel According to Matthew* 337.; Gill, 'Out of, from among the churches of Christ; at least under the name of Christians', *An Exposition of The New Testament*, vol. 1, 288.; Gundry, *Matthew: A Commentary on His Literary and Theological Art* 479.
62. The word '*Paraclete*' is from Greek, usually translated as 'the Comforter' (KJV) or 'Helper' (NKJV), and refers to 'He' whom Christ said would come after Him, to 'teach you all things' (John 14:26). See also John 14:16, 15:26, 16:7. Paraclete means advocate, intercessor, consoler, and 'corresponds to the name "Menahem" given by the Hebrews to the Messiah' (*Vine's Expository Dictionary of Biblical Words* 111).
63. *The History of the Church* 135, 217.64. See Norman Cohn, *In Pursuit of the Millennium* 36-9, 142-5, 252-3, 268-9, 294-7.

Jesus states that because 'iniquity shall abound, the love of many shall wax cold'. This may mean that, because some followers apostatize and others are led away by false prophets, many faithful believers are torn away from the spiritual guidance of the Gospel. This causes iniquity to abound, which in turn leads to the loss of love among many. The consequences of this can be seen in the violence that occurred among Christians and between Christian nations.[64]

Despite all this persecution, sectarian strife, deception and hatred, Christ assures us that 'he that shall endure unto the end, the same shall be saved' (Matt. 24:13).[65] This verse can be interpreted in two ways: (1) The believer whose faith endures through the hardships of life until the 'end' of his or her life will be saved; and (2) in a corporate sense, those who are found still to be carrying the torch of faith at the 'end' of the age - they will be saved. Whatever the hardships that were to befall the believers, Christ also assures them that it will not extinguish the light of His teachings - not before the teachings have been preached to all nations. This is the assurance of the next verse.

64. Gibbon, who was himself a professed Christian, felt compelled to point out the severity of the conflicts among Christians. He ended his assessment of the numerous accounts of early Christians who died at the hands of Roman persecutors with these words: 'We shall conclude . . . by a melancholy truth which obtrudes itself on the reluctant mind; that, even admitting, without hesitation or inquiry, all that history has recorded, or devotion has feigned, on the subject of martyrdoms, it must still be acknowledged that the Christians, in the course of their intestine dissensions, have inflicted far greater severities on each other than they had experienced from the zeal of infidels' (*Decline and Fall*, vol. 1, 504).

65. Matthew Henry equates those who endure to the end with a 'remnant according to the election of grace' (Rom. 11:5). See *Matthew Henry's Commentary*, vol. V., 351.

THE GOSPEL WILL BE PREACHED TO ALL NATIONS

14 *And this gospel of the kingdom shall be preached in all the world for a witness unto all nations; and then shall the end come.*

COMMENTARY (24:14)

The Christian Effort to Evangelize the Nations

This particular prophecy has inspired the efforts of many missionaries eager to hasten Christ's Second Advent.[66] But there has been debate concerning what is required for the fulfilment of this prophecy.

The prophecy indicates that the Gospel must be preached to all nations in the world. But questions have been raised concerning what Jesus meant by the phrases (1) 'Gospel of the kingdom', (2) 'all the world', (3) 'all nations', and (4) the word 'preached'.

Defining the Terminology

(1) The definition of the 'gospel of the kingdom' is the least difficult and least disputed of all the terms involved in this prophecy. The word 'gospel'[67] is derived from the Anglo-Saxon term 'God-spell', meaning God-story, and is

66. See Johannes Blauw, *The Missionary Nature of the Church* 106. The view that spreading the Gospel would hasten Christ's return does not appear to have been a major motivating factor during the great missionary period of the nineteenth century. Most interpreters of the Bible, as well as most missionaries, appear to have believed that Matt. 24:14 had already been fulfilled because of other statements made in the New Testament. Nevertheless, it must be acknowledged that some nineteenth-century Christians did view contemporary missionary efforts with the parallel verse, Rev.14:6, in mind. See, e.g., W.A. Spicer, *Our Day In the Light of Prophecy* 307-10.

67. Jesus uses the singular 'Gospel' rather than the plural 'Gospels'. It is important to understand that, while there are four accounts of Jesus' life, there is only one Gospel. The Gospel is not the books themselves but, rather, the message preached in those four accounts. This message is also found in the rest of the New Testament (i.e. the Epistles of the Apostles, Paul's writings, and the Book of Revelation). Thus, while it is correct to use the plural 'Gospels' to refer to the four versions in a literary sense, the message itself concerns the one Gospel, i.e., the good news of Christ's ministry. For this reason, the plural word 'Gospels' would have been an unfamiliar term to the Apostles and early Christians. Hence the New Testament and the Qur'án use only the singular form. For Bahá'í teachings related to this point see, e.g., *Selections from the Writings of 'Abdu'l-Bahá* 9, 12, 60, 168, 223.

used to translate the Greek word 'euanelion', which simply means 'glad-tidings' or 'good news'. This can be understood as the good news of the Christ, i.e. Jesus' teachings and the redemption accomplished through Him.

The wording of Matthew 24:14 is more specific in that Jesus does not simply use the term 'gospel' but, rather, uses the phrase 'gospel of the kingdom'. There is general agreement on the definition of this phrase. Matthew Henry writes:

> It is called the gospel of the kingdom, because it reveals the kingdom of grace, which leads to the kingdom of glory. (*Matthew Henry's Commentary* 1327)

A similar view is expressed by William Hendriksen:

> 'the kingdom', that is, of the reign of God in heart and life, by grace and through faith. (*New Testament Commentary* 855)

(2) The greatest debates have been over how much of the world is intended by 'all the world'. It might seem to be a simple matter to take this verse literally, except that Paul, the greatest missionary of Christ, himself proclaimed that the Gospel 'was preached to every creature under heaven' (Col. 1:23). Paul quoted Psalm 19:4 and asserted that the message had 'gone out to all the earth', in fact, 'to the ends of the world' (Rom. 10:18). Also, the Book of Acts (2:5) records that the Apostles preached the Gospel to Jews from 'every nation under heaven'.

Paul's statements have led some commentators to conclude that Jesus' prophecy may have been fulfilled at an early date; some even argue that 'the end' does not refer to the end when Christ returns but, rather, to the destruction of Jerusalem, meaning that the Gospel had been preached to all nations before AD 70, but this point is greatly debated.[68]

68. 'and before the destruction of Jerusalem, it was preached to all the nations under the heavens; and churches were planted in most places, through the ministry of it: for a witness unto all nations; meaning either for a witness against all such in them, as should reject it; or as a testimony of Christ and salvation, unto all such as should believe in him: and then shall the end come; not the end of the world, as the Ethiopic version reads it, and others understand it; but the end of the Jewish state, the end of the city and temple: so that the universal preaching of the Gospel all over the world, was the last criterion and sign of the destruction of Jerusalem' (John Gill, *Exposition of the New Testament* 289). This view can be found in many older Christian commentaries, e.g. Ellicott's and Matthew Henry's. Others disagreed, such as J. P. Lange, who wrote it 'must not be limited to the Roman Empire'.

The optimistic view that the Gospel had already been preached throughout the world can also be found among the early Church fathers.[69] During the time of Christ and the early Church the whole world meant largely the Roman Empire, and 'all nations' meant simply those nations under the rule of Rome.[70] In part, how one interprets Jesus' prophecy depends on how one views the extent of the world.

With the spread of missionaries throughout the world during the early nineteenth century, some saw the 'world' in a broader sense and began to argue that the fulfilment of Jesus' prophecy was in sight. W.A. Spicer writes:

> In 1804 the British and Foreign Bible Society was organized. Students of the prophetic word felt at the time that these agencies were coming in fulfilment of prophecy. (*Our Day in the Light of Prophecy* 308)

To support this view, Spicer quotes several Christian writers, among whom is G.S. Faber:

> The stupendous endeavours of one gigantic community to convey the Scriptures in every language to every part of the globe may well deserve to be considered as an eminent sign even of these eventful times. Unless I be much mistaken, such endeavours are preparatory to the final grand diffusion of Christianity, which is the theme of so many inspired prophets, and which cannot be very far distant in the present day. (*Dissertation on the Prophecies*, vol. II, 406, written in 1844)

However, it is hard to tell how widespread this view was. As previously mentioned, in nineteenth-century missionary literature, the Matthew 24:14

69. Gibbon assesses early claims in these words: 'The progress of Christianity was not confined to the Roman empire; and, according to the primitive fathers, who interpreted facts by prophecy, the new religion, within a century after the death of its Divine Author, had already visited every part of the globe. "There exists not", says Justin Martyr, "a people, whether Greek or barbarian, or any other race of men, by whatsoever appellation or manners they may be distinguished, however ignorant of the arts or agriculture, whether they dwell under tents, or wander about in covered wagons, among whom prayers are not offered up in the name of a crucified Jesus to the Father and Creator of all things." But this splendid exaggeration, which even at present [1776] it would be extremely difficult to reconcile with the real state of mankind, can be considered only as the rash sally of a devout but careless writer, the measure of whose belief was regulated by that of his wishes' (*Decline and Fall* 186).

70. See Harold Fowler, *The Gospel of Matthew*, vol. 4, 434.

prophecy does not appear to have been a dominant concern; but the existence of this view seems undeniable. Grattan Guinness (1835-1910), who founded the East London Institute for training missionaries, wrote:

> the time for evangelising the nations, and gathering in the church of the first-born is speedily to expire . . . if we be right in believing that scarcely a single prophecy in the whole Bible, relating to events prior to the second advent of Christ, remains unfulfilled. (*The Approaching End of the Age* xvii)

(3) The word 'nations', from the Greek 'ethnos', originally meant 'a multitude'. In this context, its plural form could simply mean 'the multitudes', such as those who live outside the Jewish nation.[71] If defined narrowly, it could be taken to mean whole racial groups having organized nation-like societies, in which case, many of the world's smaller tribal societies could be essentially discounted or overlooked. If applied broadly, tribes and people living in any organized community could be included.

(4) The word 'preached' entails the same difficulty of definition. For example, how significant is a small group of English or Spanish missionaries landing on the shores of a newly discovered land and reading the Bible in English, Spanish or another European language to a group of indigenous inhabitants? It seems unlikely that such efforts could be regarded as sufficient to fulfil Jesus' prophecy. If carried to the other extreme, however, it could be argued that all the peoples of every nation must truly hear the message in such a way as to be able to discern its actual character and thus be equipped to make an informed decision of faith.

The difficulties of defining the language of Jesus' prophecy illustrate that it is probably best to avoid trying to fix its meaning legalistically. Therefore, in the opinion of this writer, it seems fruitless to try to fix a precise time when this prophecy was fulfilled. It can be argued that, from the early Christian point of view, the prophecy had been fulfilled before the time of Muhammad (AD 570-632). After the age of exploration (AD 1420-1620), the world-view was considerably expanded, and in the context of this expanded view, it can be argued that it was fulfilled before or roughly at the time of the early days of the Bahá'í Revelation (1844-63).

71. See *Vine's Expository Dictionary of Biblical Words* 426.

The Testimony of the Gospel

Jesus states that the Gospel will be preached as a 'witness' to all nations. The word 'witness' is from the Greek 'marturion', which is also translated as 'testimony'. The meaning is that the Gospel, or Word of God, testifies to the truth of Christ. That is, the Word is itself the 'proof', testifying to the divinity of Christ. Bahá'u'lláh writes that, after the ascension of Christ, the Gospel, 'His Holy Book', remained as Jesus' 'most great testimony' (*Certitude* 89).

In the teachings of the Bahá'í Faith, miracles and prophecies are regarded as proofs,[72] but not conclusive proofs.[73] As proof, miracles are limited to the time and place they happened; inasmuch, as we are unable to go back in time to verify the occurrence of Jesus' miracles or the miracles claimed in other religions, they all remain inconclusive. Prophecies, as is evident from this commentary, are subject to many interpretations and, therefore, are also somewhat uncertain.

However, the Word of God itself, what it teaches about God and how it guides our actions, can affect our lives personally. Thus, we can practise the teachings, the message of Scripture, and know their truth directly. Christ stated:

> If anyone wants to do His will, he shall know concerning the doctrine,[74] whether it is from God or whether I speak on My own authority. (John 7:17)

In this passage Jesus links direct experience of the Word of God to the verification of its truth. Moreover, it is the Word of God that is the channel through which we are 'born again' (John 3:3, 1 Pet. 1:23) and come into 'everlasting life' (John 5:24).

From this understanding it follows that the words and teachings of a Prophet are the criteria for establishing the truth of that Prophet. Christ's teachings and the record of His life are the testimony of His truth, the proof He entrusted to His followers to carry to all the nations.

The End of the Christian Era

Christ speaks of the preaching of the Gospel to all nations and says, 'then

72. See 'Abdu'l-Bahá, *Selections from the Writings of 'Abdu'l-Bahá* 16.
73. See 'Abdu'l-Bahá, *Some Answered Questions* 37.
74. The Greek word '*didache*', here translated 'doctrine', simply means *instruction* or *that which is taught*, i.e. the actual teachings of Christ. See *Vine's Expository Dictionary of Biblical Words* 180.

shall the end come'. As we have seen, some believe the 'end' refers to the destruction of Jerusalem and not the time of the Second Advent. However, the 'end' mentioned in verses 3, 6, and 13 cannot mean the end of the Jewish era, signified by the destruction of the Temple, because the Jewish era ended even before that event. Christ had already inaugurated the Christian era when He called together His Apostles and preached His teachings (Matt. 10). It therefore seems possible that the 'end' refers to the end of the Christian era. As we will see, this is suggested in the following verse of the Sermon.

PART II

THE CORRUPTING OF ISLAM

DANIEL AND THE COMING DESOLATION

15 When ye therefore shall see the abomination of desolation, spoken of by Daniel the prophet, stand in[75] the holy place, (whoso readeth, let him understand:[76])

COMMENTARY (24:15)

Jesus' Reference to the Book of Daniel

Of all Jesus' prophecies, no verse has received so much attention or sparked such controversy as this one. Christ refers to a time when it will be possible to see what He calls 'the abomination of desolation', standing 'in the holy place'. He also states that this was 'spoken of by Daniel the prophet'. In order to understand what is intended by 'the abomination of desolation', we

75. The KJV renders the Greek as 'stand in', and therefore the text appears to be telling the reader or believer to stand in the holy place. However, this is misleading and, hence, an attempt has been made to render it in a clearer manner in newer translations. Cf., e.g., NIV and RSV, which render the Greek as 'standing in'.

76. The last portion of Matthew 24:15 states, 'whoso readeth, let him understand'. This is assumed by some conservative Christian scholars (Lange, Meyer, Whedon) to be an addition by Matthew. T. Colani puts forward the doubtful argument that this statement is evidence that chapter 24 is an apocalyptic work of a Jewish Christian author and not Jesus. That is, the author is urging the reader to reflect upon the apocalypse, whereas they were really not the words of Jesus, but were later incorporated into the Gospel. For critical assessment see G.R. Beasley-Murray, *Jesus and the Future* 17. Modern conservative commentators reject Colani's thesis, but few would argue that the phrase 'whoso readeth, let him understand' are the words of Jesus. Since Jesus was speaking, it is simply assumed that He would have said 'whoso heareth', not 'readeth'. The argument against this view is that the word 'readeth' applies not to the reading of Matthew 24, but to the reading of the Book of Daniel. 'Abdu'l-Bahá appears to view these words as the words of Jesus and as a reference to the reading of Daniel. See *Some Answered Questions* 51. Some object to the idea that Jesus was referring the disciples to the reading of the Book of Daniel on the grounds that Mark 13:14 says 'let him that readeth understand', but does not include a specific reference to Daniel. Readers of the KJV may find this point surprising. The words 'spoken of by Daniel the prophet' are absent from many early Greek manuscripts and, hence, have been dropped from more recent versions of the Bible (e.g., NIV). The absence of a phrase in some manuscripts is not always, however, a conclusive indication of a later addition since later manuscripts containing the phrase were sometimes based on or influenced by copies of other manuscripts earlier than the ones omitting a phrase or word. For example, a thirteenth-century manuscript may be more accurate than a earlier sixth-century manuscript, because the thirteenth-century one may be a copy of a third-century one while the sixth-

will therefore need to refer to the Book of the Prophet Daniel. By making this brief reference to the prophecies of Daniel, Jesus enormously expands the scope of His message and confronts us with the difficulty of understanding the Book of Daniel - not an easy task, especially for the modern reader who is unfamiliar with the ancient terminology and symbolism which appear in Daniel's visions.

Daniel and the Meaning of the Abomination of Desolation

In the Book of Daniel there are many prophecies concerning an 'abomination of desolation'.[77] There is strong evidence that this abomination of desolation refers to what befell the religion of Islam. However, in order to see how this might be, it is necessary to take a close look at the terminology and the events that later unfolded in the Middle East.

An 'abomination' is something that causes loathing, abhorrence, or disgust - a sacrilege (i.e. a violation or transgression of what is sacred).[78] Thus, the prophecy in Matthew concerns something negative that will cause or bring desolation to the 'holy place'. The 'holy place' is generally understood to mean literally the Temple of Jerusalem, particularly its altar in the 'Holy of Holies'.[79] There are two verses that specifically use this terminology: Daniel 11:31 and 12:11. The first of these verses is as follows:

> And forces shall be mustered by him, and they shall defile the sanctuary fortress; then they shall take away the daily

century one may be a copy of a less reliable fifth-century manuscript. Nevertheless, some scholars believe that this ommission means the texts of both Matthew and Mark are therefore referring us to the reading of Jesus' sermon and that these words were incorporated when Jesus' own words were committed to writing. This view, however, is not persuasive since the language in Mark - the same phrase, the 'abomination of desolation' - clearly originates with Daniel and is set in a prophetic context concerning the Messiah. Therefore, it was not essential for Mark to refer by name to the Book of Daniel since the disciples would have readily recognized the source of the terminology. 'In Mark 13:14 the desolating abomination is referred to as well known, without explanation' (*The New International Dictionary of New Testament Theology*, vol. I, 75). 1 Macc. 1:54 provides another early use of this language, but its context does not concern a future event and therefore, does not relate to the questions of the disciples, as does Daniel's Messianic vision. Thus, the most likely explanation for the wording of Matthew 24:15 is that Jesus is referring His audience to the Book of Daniel and urging them to understand its intention.

77. Also translated as 'desolating sacrilege' (RSV) or 'the abomination that causes desolation' (NIV).

78. 'In Daniel the Hebrew expression . . . appears to signify "the abomination which causes (spiritual) desolation", i.e. it creates either a horror in the mind of the beholders or an objective condition of spiritual devastation' (*The New International Dictionary of New Testament Theology*, vol. I, 74). See also Gerhard Kittel, *Theological Dictionary of the New Testament*, vol. I, 598-600.

79. The 'Holy of Holies' was the innermost portion of the Temple where only the Jewish high priest was allowed to enter. The high priest would enter the Holy of Holies once a year and offer a sacrifice to atone for the people's sins. It was originally the place where the Tablets of the Law were kept.

> sacrifices, and place there the abomination of desolation. (Dan. 11:31)

The common understanding of this passage among many Christian commentators is that the 'forces mustered by him' means an enemy of God; 'and they', that is, the enemy's army or followers, will defile the sanctuary, meaning the Jewish Temple in Jerusalem. They will ban sacrificial offerings to God by the Jews, and they will place an image of a false deity on the Jewish altar. This image is an *abomination* that brings *desolation* to the Temple.

Some scholars maintain that Daniel's prophecies concerning the abomination of desolation actually occurred when Antiochus IV, the king then ruling the Seleucid dynasty, captured Jerusalem and placed a pagan idol (Hellenistic statue) on the altar in the Jerusalem Temple, which desecrated its holy precinct.[80] This actual event is thought to have occurred in the year 167 or 168 BC by order of Antiochus IV. [81] This view is supported by 1 Maccabees, an early Jewish account of events between the years 175 and 134 BC, during which time King Antiochus attempted to make the Jews follow the religious practices of his Hellenistic empire. The following verse from the book of Maccabees uses the terminology 'abomination of desolation' found in Daniel (11:31) and Matthew 24, with reference to the Temple:

> they set up the abomination of desolation upon the altar, and builded idol altars throughout the cities of Juda. (1 Macc. 1:54)[82]

However, as many Christian scholars have noted, this interpretation alone, based as it is on pre-Christian events, does not appear to account for the apparent relationship that Christ indicates (Matt. 24:15) exists between Daniel's prophecies and the Apostles' questions concerning future events (Matt. 24:3).

80. Commenting on Mt. 24:15, Samuel Tobias Lachs writes that the terminology is derived from Daniel and 'refers to the altar to Zeus Olympius which was erected by Antiochus IV on the site of the Temple'. He adds, 'The problem, however, is what does it mean here in its NT context?' (*A Rabbinic Commentary on the New Testament* 382-3).
81. See, e.g., *Bible Dictionary* 857.
82. This book was among a number of books declared canonical by the Roman Catholic Church in 1546 but disputed by Protestants. These books, referred to as Apocrypha, were generally included in Protestant Bibles, including the KJV, up until the early nineteenth century.

It is very possible that the events that occurred in 167/8 BC involving Antiochus IV fit Daniel's prophecies. However, this does not preclude Daniel's prophecies from also referring to the same type of event occurring at a later time, which in fact Jesus clearly indicates to be the case. It may be that Jesus intends that these literal events associated with Antiochus IV foreshadow an even greater spiritual crisis that would occur in the future. Whatever its significance, it is, at least, clear that Jesus saw the things spoken of in Daniel's prophecies as symbols of events that would occur in the future. What then remains is to discover which future events Jesus wants us to understand as the meaning of Daniel's prophecies.

Jerusalem Surrounded by Armies

Some Christian commentators believe that the event Jesus refers to as the 'abomination of desolation' has already occurred. That is, they believe Jesus is alluding to the destruction of the Temple in Jerusalem in AD 70.[83] The most compelling reason to accept this view is largely based on Luke 21:20. In what appears to be a slightly different account of Jesus' Olivet Discourse, Luke does not mention Daniel or use the terminology 'abomination of desolation'. Instead, Luke records the following:

> But when you see Jerusalem surrounded by armies, then know that its desolation is near. (Luke 21:20)

Because Luke mentions that Jerusalem will be surrounded by armies, it is assumed to be a clear prophecy of the Jewish Wars in AD 70 and AD 135, in which Roman armies surrounded Jerusalem. In some respects, this understanding is plausible because what Jesus prophesied did occur, at least in part, during the Jewish Wars. But a strict literal interpretation is problematic since records indicate that, unlike Antiochus IV, the Romans did not attempt to force the Jews to accept the Roman religion or worship an idol. They simply destroyed the Temple. Some Christians have also argued that such an interpretation is difficult to fit into the full context of

83. E.g., 'The Roman army is called the abomination for its ensigns and images which were so to the Jews' (Bishop Newton, *Dissertations on the Prophecies* 344). See also John Gill, Matthew Henry and Lange. Some argue the abomination was the desecration of the Temple caused by the Jewish priests during the revolt against the Romans. See Lange, and also Ellicott's *Commentary* 147. Other Christian commentators disagree and maintain that it refers to the time of the end and involves events associated with the Antichrist. See, e.g., Govett, *The Prophecy on Olivet* 41. Govett's book is largely devoted to refuting the belief that the Romans are the abomination. Instead he, like many others, argues that it is an act against the Temple in the end times, perpetrated by the Antichrist.

Jesus' entire discourse.[84] These arguments provide strong reasons to believe that this interpretation regarding the Jewish Wars is not the probable meaning, or at least, by itself, is not likely to be the entire meaning of the passage, nor even its main significance.

As noted previously, it also seems questionable, with the appearance of Christianity, to continue to associate prophecies about the future primarily with issues of Jewish significance, such as the Jerusalem Temple. Jesus had already identified Himself as the Temple (John 2:19-21). In addition, with the crucifixion of Jesus, the actual Temple in Jerusalem was no longer to have the same significance it had had before the founding of Christianity, since Jesus replaced the Temple sacrifices with His own sacrifice on the Cross (Heb. 9). Jesus' warning is directed to His disciples and followers, not the Jews. It is therefore more likely that this prophecy, if it is to be understood literally, refers to a time when Jerusalem is in Christian hands, a time when it is the Christians who look out and see Jerusalem (the City of Peace) surrounded by armies.[85] Furthermore, the fact that Jesus, in Matt. 24:15, puts the desolation of Jerusalem in the context of Daniel's vision - which is full of symbolic imagery - suggests that the reference to the Temple may also be more symbolic than literal.

What, then, is the meaning of these prophecies? What is the *Temple* that is made desolate? To understand Jesus' prophecy requires us to first go back and follow the advice set forth in the text, that is, to examine more of the details 'spoken of by Daniel the prophet'. As we will see, these details reveal what are, without doubt, some of the most startling discoveries we could ever hope to find concealed in the language of prophecy.

Daniel's Vision of the End

The link between Matthew 24:15 and Daniel's prophecies can be discerned by carefully taking note of certain verses in the last five chapters of the Book of Daniel. In these chapters a 'vision' is revealed and partially explained to Daniel. In this vision there is presented not only a great

84. One of the main arguments against associating the abomination with the Roman army, i.e. their ensigns or any of their idols, is that such a historical interpretation does not fit with the following verse, Matt. 24:16. *The Expositor's Bible Commentary* notes: 'by the time the Romans had actually desecrated the temple in AD 70, it was too late for anyone in the city to flee' (500).

85. The term 'Jerusalem', especially in the sense of the heavenly Jerusalem (Rev. 21:1-22:5), like the term 'the Temple', is often used in the Bible as a symbol for the presence of God's reign, law or the spiritual dwelling-place of the community of true believers. Hence it seems likely that the term 'Jerusalem' in Luke's version may have more than just a literal meaning. The word may be formed from 'yaw-raw' and 'shalom', *founded-peaceful*, meaning *City of Peace*. See *New Bible Dictionary* 566-7.

amount of symbolic imagery, but a series of *prophetic time periods*.[86] It is in the context of these extraordinary time periods that Daniel's vision presents the 'abomination of desolation'. According to the vision, the 'transgression of desolation' will end after a period of time consisting of 'two thousand three hundred days', after which 'the sanctuary shall be cleansed' (Dan. 8:13-14). In other words, the abomination of desolation is set up in the Temple, and this transgression does not end until a period of 2,300 days is concluded. According to the Book of Daniel, the angel Gabriel (8:16) explains to Daniel that this 'vision refers to the time of the end' (8:17). This suggests that the sanctuary will be cleansed at the time of the end, when Christ returns. This 'end' which Daniel speaks of is likely to be the same 'end' which the disciples were asking about, and this is the reason why Christ is referring them to the Book of Daniel. As we examine it more closely, the answer to the disciples' questions about the end becomes even clearer.

In the next chapter of the Book of Daniel (ch. 9), it is recorded that the angel Gabriel sets forth a different set of time periods which specifically concern the coming of the Messiah, that is, Jesus' first appearance.[87] These additional periods of time provide the clearest clues for ascertaining when the longer 2,300-day period first begins and, therefore, when it ends. In fact, many Christians have argued that these time periods reveal both when the first appearance of Christ was to occur and the time when the 2,300 days end. This understanding of Daniel's prophecies was particularly popular during the nineteenth century.[88] Christian interest in these numbers is not surprising in light of the fact that the end of the 2,300 days was considered likely to be the time when Christ would return. To understand how this conclusion was arrived at, we can benefit greatly from first examining how these prophecies reveal the date of Christ's first appearance.

86. See Appendix VII: The Chronological Prophecies.

87. After expressing his admiration for the way Daniel predicts the exact time of Christ's appearance, the Christian scholar George Townsend writes in his 1826 publication, 'Of all the prophets, Daniel is the most distinct in the order of time, and easiest to be understood; and on this account, Sir Isaac Newton observes, in those events which concern the last times, he must be the interpreter of the rest. All his predictions relate to each other, as if they were several parts of one general prophecy. The first is the easiest to be understood, and every succeeding prophecy adds something to the former. Though his style is not so lofty and figurative as that of the other prophets, it is more suitable to his subject, being clear and concise; his narratives and descriptions are simple and natural; and, in short he writes more like a historian than a prophet.' He adds, 'Of the genuineness and authenticity of the book of Daniel we have every possible evidence, both external and internal' (*The Old Testament Arranged in Historical and Chronological Order*, vol. II, 807-8). Such views are no longer readily accepted.

88. See Appendix II: A Brief History of Christian Millennial Views.

Daniel's Prophecies Concerning the First Advent

The Christian scholars who believed that Daniel's prophecies foretold Jesus' appearance often based their calculations on a detailed knowledge of Jewish calendars. We will not explore these details but, rather, will examine the simplified explanation which 'Abdu'l-Bahá Himself provides and which has many similarities to Christian views pre-dating the Bahá'í Faith. We will begin by first reviewing the main verses as they appear in Daniel's vision:

> Seventy weeks are determined
> For your people and for your holy city,
> To finish the transgression,
> To make an end of sins,
> To make reconciliation for iniquity,
> To bring in everlasting righteousness,
> To seal up vision and prophecy,
> And to anoint the Most Holy.
>
> Know therefore and understand,
> That from the going forth of the command
> To restore and build Jerusalem
> Until Messiah the Prince,
> There shall be seven weeks and sixty two weeks;
> The street[89] shall be built again, and the wall,
> Even in troubled times. (Dan. 9:24-5, NKJV)

In a discourse recorded by Laura C. Barney,[90] 'Abdu'l-Bahá offers this brief explanation of Daniel's vision:

> This is a prophecy of the manifestation of Christ. These seventy weeks[91] begin with the restoration and the rebuilding

89. 'Street' (Heb. rechôb)can also be translated as 'open square' or a broad, wide place.

90. This discourse was one of many recorded by Barney during the years 1904-6 while 'Abdu'l-Bahá was 'confined to the city of 'Akká by the Turkish government'. 'Abdu'l-Bahá's explanation was written down in Persian and was approved by 'Abdu'l-Bahá Himself. Later Barney translated it into English.

91. The Christian Bible commentator, Matthew Henry, gave various reasons for the prophetic terminology of 'seventy weeks', among which are, 'These years are thus described by weeks, [1] In conformity to the prophetic style, which is, for the most part, abstruse, and out of the common road of speaking, that the things foretold might not lie too obvious. [2] To put an honour upon the division of time into weeks, which is made purely by the sabbath day, and to signify that that should be perpetual. [3] With reference to the seventy years of the captivity' (*Matthew Henry's Commentary*, vol. IV, 1092 [1712]).

> of Jerusalem, concerning which four edicts were issued by three kings. . . .
>
> But Daniel refers especially to the third edict which was issued in the year 457 BC[92] Seventy weeks make four hundred and ninety days. Each day, according to the text of the Holy Book, is a year. For in the Bible it is said: 'The day of the Lord is one year'.[93] Therefore, four hundred and ninety days are four hundred and ninety years. The third edict of Artaxerxes was issued four hundred and fifty-seven years before the birth of Christ, and Christ when He was martyred and ascended was thirty-three years of age. When you add thirty-three to four hundred and fifty-seven, the result is four hundred and ninety, which is the time announced by Daniel for the manifestation of Christ. (*Some Answered Questions* 40-1)

If we write out 'Abdu'l-Bahá's explanation in a formula, with numbers, it appears as follows:

> 70 weeks are appointed between the rebuilding of Jerusalem and the appearance of the Messiah:
>
> 70 weeks is 70 x 7 days = 490 days
>
> 490 days is a symbol for 490 years

92. It should also be noted that this date is not directly stated in the text of the Bible. Instead, the Bible reads 'in the seventh year of king Artaxerxes', which Bible scholars believe was during 457 BC. During Miller's day this date was commonly printed in the margins of the *King James Version* of the Bible. This particular date is still accepted as accurate by many modern scholars. 'Abdu'l-Bahá states that Daniel 'refers especially to the third edict' but He does not explain how this is evident in the Bible. However, careful examination suggest why this is the case. The first edict, issued by Cyrus in 536 BC (Ezra 1), encountered resistance and opposition. Charges of sedition were made against the people of Israel and the king ordered work on the reconstruction of Jerusalem to cease (Ezra 4:19-24). This work was resumed under a second edict, issued by Darius in 519 BC (Ezra 6), but the work accomplished by both the first and second edicts was too inadequate to constitute a 'restoration' of the Temple, either of the building or its place in the hearts of the people. It was the third edict, issued by Artaxerxes in 457 BC (Ezra 7), which permitted Ezra to return to Jerusalem. This opened the way not just for the restoration of the material Temple but for Ezra to purify the people of Israel (Ezra 9-10) and re-institute the Law and the Temple into their religious life (Neh. 8-10). Ezra is given official sanction by the Persian king Artaxerxes to promulgate the religious law established by Moses, to appoint magistrates in the Jewish homeland, and to offer sacrifices. The fourth edict, issued by Artaxerxes in 444 BC (Neh. 2), simply allowed Nehemiah to further the work and complete the wall around Jerusalem. For a detailed nineteenth-century argument of why the third edict should be considered the commencement point, see Carl August Auberlen's *The Prophecies of Daniel and The Revelations of St John*.
93. Cf. Num. 14:34. See also Ezek. 4:6.

According to the traditional understanding of the Gospel, Christ was crucified and ascended at the age of 33. Artaxerxes' edict to rebuild Jerusalem is issued in 457 BC. If we add the 33 years of Jesus' life to the years that span the time from the issuance of the edict to the time of Jesus' birth, we arrive at a period of time equalling 490 years as prophesied by Daniel:

457 years
+ 33 years
= 490 years

The date for the time of Christ is also given by Daniel in another way. 'Abdu'l-Bahá explains:

> But in the twenty-fifth verse of the ninth chapter of the Book of Daniel this is expressed in another manner, as seven weeks and sixty-two weeks; and apparently this differs from the first saying. Many have remained perplexed at these differences, trying to reconcile these two statements. How can seventy weeks be right in one place, and sixty-two weeks and seven weeks in another? These two sayings do not accord.
>
> But Daniel mentions two dates. One of these dates begins with the command of Artaxerxes to Ezra to rebuild Jerusalem; this is the seventy weeks which came to an end with the ascension of Christ, when by His martyrdom the sacrifice and oblation ceased.
>
> The second period, which is found in the twenty-sixth verse, means that after the termination of the rebuilding of Jerusalem until the ascension of Christ, there will be sixty-two weeks; the seven weeks are the duration of the rebuilding of Jerusalem, which took forty-nine years. When you add these seven weeks to the sixty-two weeks, it makes sixty-nine weeks, and in the last week (69-70) the ascension of Christ took place. These seventy weeks are thus completed, and there is no contradiction. (*Some Answered Questions* 41)

'Abdu'l-Bahá clearly affirms the authority and inspiration of Daniel's vision. He sees no contradictions but, rather, a reliable prophetic chronology accurately revealing the first advent of Christ. Written out mathematically, 'Abdu'l-Bahá's explanation is as follows:

62 weeks = (62 x 7) = 434 years
7 weeks = (7 x 7) = 49 years

69 weeks = (69 x 7) = 483 years

Counting forward 483 years from 457 BC brings us to around AD 26/7 :

483
- 457
= 26

This understanding is essentially composed of two equations:

(1) 7 weeks (7 x 7 = 49 years) to rebuild Jerusalem, which brings us to 408 BC.

and

(2) 62 weeks (434 years) from the completion of Jerusalem to the last week,[94] when Christianity begins (with John the Baptist).[95] This last week ends with the crucifixion and ascension of Christ.

The following time chart illustrates the sequence:

457 BC 408 BC AD 26/7 AD 33/4
<--- 49 years ---> <---- 434 years ----> <--- 7 years --->

94. 'Abdu'l-Bahá is referring to the 'one week', Daniel mentions (9:27) after the sixty-two weeks (9:25-6).
95. Some Christian Adventists believed that this calculation corresponded to John the Baptist's ministry, 'John's ministry began in the latter part of AD 26, and ended with the Autumn of AD 27. Here commenced the week of the confirmation of the covenant, i.e., the establishment of the gospel as a divine system, by the mighty works of Christ' (Samuel S. Snow, *Midnight Cry*, as quoted in *The Prophetic Faith of Our Fathers* 799). It appears that 'Abdu'l-Bahá is expressing the same idea. It should be noted that the exact dates both of Jesus' birth and His crucifixion are highly disputed by scholars, as are most dates associated with that period. However, the date of 457 BC for the issuance of the edict to rebuild Jerusalem is largely agreed upon and is accepted by some to be collaborated by recent archaeological discoveries. Therefore, the 490-year period, if counted from the date of the edict, brings us to a time that witnessed the ministry of Christ. The exact dates may be disputed, but the prophecy does bring us to the general period.

The fact that Jesus' appearance could be calculated with such accuracy led many Bible commentators to feel certain that the method, especially the day/year equation, was correct and that the 457 BC edict was the correct edict from which to base their calculations.[96] It should be emphasized that the basic key to these calculations - the prophetic day being equal to a year - was a common method of calculation among Christian scholars for many centuries. For example, the French reformer and theologian John Calvin (1509-64) states that the early Christian Bible translator and scholar Jerome (c. 345-420) 'reports their [the Jews'] confession, that this passage cannot be understood otherwise than of the advent of Messiah'. Calvin adds, 'they [Jews] agree with us, - in considering the Prophet to reckon the weeks not by days but by years, as in Leviticus (ch. xxv. 8.). There is no difference between us and the Jews in numbering the years; they confess the number of years to be 490, but disagree with us entirely as to the close of the prophecy' (John Calvin, *Commentaries on the Book of the Prophet Daniel* 196 ff).

With regard to Christ's First Advent, the details of Daniel's prophetic chronology were easily discernible using the day/year theory; but what remained a mystery was the culmination of the 2,300-day period. Speculation about this date filled the pages of innumerable Bible commentaries, but it was not until the nineteenth century that these calculations became a major controversy.

When Bible scholars and commentators began to assert that the end of the 2,300 days might correspond to the approaching year of 1844, or some other close approaching date, the idea naturally gained a great deal of attention. Many Christian ministers, both in America and throughout Europe, examined the possibilities of these prophecies. Some concluded, and began to preach, that Christ would return in or around the year 1844. For example, in 1829, The Revd P. Homan writes, 'According to the best commentators, this decree was made in the seventh year of Artaxerxes, AD 457: consequently, the 2,300 days, reckoned from this, terminate in AD 1843'.[97]

96. Calculating the appearance of Jesus in accordance with this prophecy, Matthew Henry writes, 'by this we are confirmed in our belief of the Messiah's being come, and that our Jesus is he, that he came just at the time prefixed, a time worthy to be had in everlasting remembrance' (*Matthew Henry's Commentary*, vol. IV, 1093 [1712]). By the mid-nineteenth century most agreed, as this only slightly exaggerated assessment suggests: 'That the seventy weeks represents 490 solar years, I may take for granted as a thing now agreed on by all Christian commentators; and equally so, that they are to be computed from the commission granted to Ezra in 457 BC, there being 490 years between that date and the death of Christ, AD 33' (Robert Wodrow, *The Past History and Future Destiny of Israel* 136 [1844]).

97. Many Christians believed that these prophetic dates also referred to the restoration of the Jews to

For Bahá'ís, these Christian beliefs and calculations have a special significance because 1844, as noted previously, is the year that marks the beginning of the Bahá'í era. We will now examine how this date appears to be clearly set forth in the Book of Daniel.

Daniel's Prophecies Concerning the Second Advent

In order to understand the prophecies of Daniel's vision, we will again begin by first examining the actual words of the vision and then studying 'Abdu'l-Bahá's explanation. The Book of Daniel states:

> Then I [Daniel] heard a holy one speaking; and another holy one said to that certain one who was speaking, 'How long will the vision be, concerning the daily sacrifices and the transgression of desolation, the giving of both the sanctuary and the host to be trampled under foot?'
>
> And he said to me, 'For two thousand three hundred days; then the sanctuary shall be cleansed'. (Dan. 8:13-14, clarification added)

The Book of Daniel then relates that the angel Gabriel explains that 'the vision refers to the time of the end' (Dan. 8:17). This is one of the reasons many Christian commentators were convinced that the 'two thousand three hundred days' is the duration of time until 'the time of the end'. 'Abdu'l-Bahá states:

> Briefly, the purport of this passage is that he appoints two thousand three hundred years, for in the text of the Bible each

Israel. This is also reflected in The Revd Homan's comments: 'There can be no doubt but that the restoration of Israel will take place in a year of Jubilee, that remarkable festival, so clearly typifying their restoration to their own land. According to the computations of many chronologers, the next year of Jubilee will occur in 1843 or 1844'. See The Revd P. Homan, 'Remarks on the period assigned in Scripture for the restoration of Israel', *The Morning Watch*, vol. I (June 1829). Another Christian, The Revd John Fry, writes, 'It is, indeed, a matter of the most awful inquiry, - on the assumption that this hypothesis which directs our attention to AD 1844, is true - what expectation can be formed from the holy Scriptures respecting the event of that epoch. It is said in Daniel, chapter viii. 14, in connection with the expiration of two thousand three hundred days - "then shall the sanctuary be cleaned".' Shortly thereafter he adds, 'But some may be of opinion, that this "cleansing of the sanctuary", should rather be referred to this last vindication of the holy city from the grasp of the last oppressor, and the actual possession of the mountain of the Lord's house, by the entrance of the divine presence, as described in the prophet Ezekiel. This would, indeed, more coincide with the tradition abroad in the Mahomedan world respecting the return of the Messiah to this earth' (*Observations on the Unfulfilled Prophecies* 372-3, [1835]). See also M. Habershon, *A Dissertation on the Prophetic Scriptures*, 451 (1834).

> day is a year. Then from the date of the issuing of the edict of Artaxerxes to rebuild Jerusalem until the day of the birth of Christ there are 456 years, and from the birth of Christ until the day of the manifestation of the Báb there are 1844 years. When you add 456 years to this number it makes 2,300 years. That is to say, the fulfilment of the vision of Daniel took place in the year AD 1844, and this is the year of the Báb's manifestation according to the actual text of the Book of Daniel. Consider how clearly he determines the year of manifestation; there could be no clearer prophecy for a manifestation than this. (*Some Answered Questions* 42)

'Abdu'l-Bahá's statement concerning the date of Jesus' birth appears to reflect a strict calculation based solely on the Bible without referring to other, outside sources. It also reflects the date popularly accepted among many Christians during 'Abdu'l-Bahá's time.[98]

It seems only logical that periods of time provided in the prophetic vision of the Scripture would and should be based only on the information provided for the believer in the same Scripture. It is this same information, provided by the writers of the Gospel, that suggests that the date of Jesus' crucifixion and ascension correspond to the end of the 490 years mentioned in Daniel's vision.[99]

These dates, however, may not intend the exact dates afforded by the Gregorian calendar. 'Abdu'l-Bahá states that Jesus was crucified and ascended at the age of 33, not in the year 33 of the Gregorian calendar. When 'Abdu'l-Bahá calculates the year 1844, He counts 456 years from 457 BC to the birth of Christ, which leaves 34 years out of 490 years mentioned by Daniel. This means that according to 'Abdu'l-Bahá's interpretation of Daniel, Jesus was crucified and ascended around AD 33-4.

98. Most modern scholars reject the first year AD calculation for Jesus' birth. However, Shoghi Effendi, appointed Guardian of the Bahá'í Faith (1921-57), re-affirmed 'Abdu'l-Bahá's view: 'Regarding the date of the birth of Jesus Christ, 'Abdu'l-Bahá's statement on this subject should be considered by the Bahá'ís as the standard, and as the basis of their calculation' (Helen Hornby, *Lights of Guidance* 368).

99. Luke indicates that Jesus was 'about thirty years of age' when He began His ministry (Luke 3:23). The Gospel of John names three Passovers in which Jesus was involved after He began His ministry (John 2:13, 6:4, 11:55). Based on these references, and others, it is widely accepted that Jesus' ministry lasted a little over three years and that Jesus was, therefore, 33 years of age when He was crucified. Moreover, Jesus' crucifixion took place on the Jewish Passover. According to the Gospel, this occurred on the day called 'preparation' (Matt. 27:62; Mark 15:42; Luke 23:54; and John 19:14, 31, 42) which is well known among Jews as referring to Friday. The day of Passover fell on Friday only twice between Jewish years corresponding to AD 26 and AD 36. Some believe this leaves only AD 30 or AD 33 as possible years for the crucifixion.

Therefore 'Abdu'l-Bahá calculates 457 years to the birth of Christ when determining the period of 490 years to the martyrdom of Christ, but when He determines the 2,300 years to the time of the Bahá'í era, He calculates 456 years to the birth of Christ. There is a one-year difference in the calculations, which clearly indicates that the two approaches are not exactly the same. Why is this?

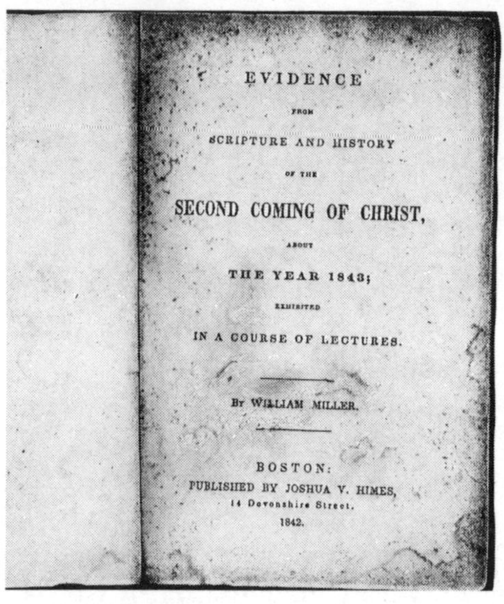

EVIDENCE
FROM
SCRIPTURE AND HISTORY
OF THE
SECOND COMING OF CHRIST,
ABOUT
THE YEAR 1843;
EXHIBITED
IN A COURSE OF LECTURES.

BY WILLIAM MILLER.

BOSTON:
PUBLISHED BY JOSHUA V. HIMES,
14 Devonshire Street.
1842.

A photograph of the title page of *Evidence From Scripture and History of the Second Coming of Christ about the Year 1843* by the Baptist minister William Miller.

'Abdu'l-Bahá does not elaborate on His calculations in His brief explanation, but the reason may be to account for the difference between the Jewish and Gregorian calendars. This difference was understood by nineteenth-century Christians, as can be seen in the writings of such Christian ministers as William Miller and his followers, sometimes called the Millerites. They realized that, according to the Jewish calendar, the 2,300 years might not end in 1843 using the formula 457 - 2,300 = 1843, because the last year fell both in 1843 and 1844. Therefore, the 2,300 years would not be completed until the year 1844. This understanding applies both to the calculation of the crucifixion and ascension of Christ, so that the equation 457 + 33 = 490 should actually be rendered 456 + 34 = 490.

When calculating Daniel's prophecies referring to the time of Christ, 'Abdu'l-Bahá simply adds 457 years to the 33 years which the Gospel implies to be Jesus' age at the time of the crucifixion. Since these calculations were generally accepted, there is no need for 'Abdu'l-Bahá to divert His attention from the main theme to explain the subtleties involved in such calculations and to point out that the prophecy would overlap into AD 34 of the Gregorian calendar.[100] Even without knowledge of the Jewish

100. As already noted, in the nineteenth century it was commonly believed that Christ was 33 years old when He was crucified. It was also accepted that the Gregorian calendar was accurately reckoned from Christ's birth. For this reason it was generally accepted that the crucifixion occurred in AD 33.

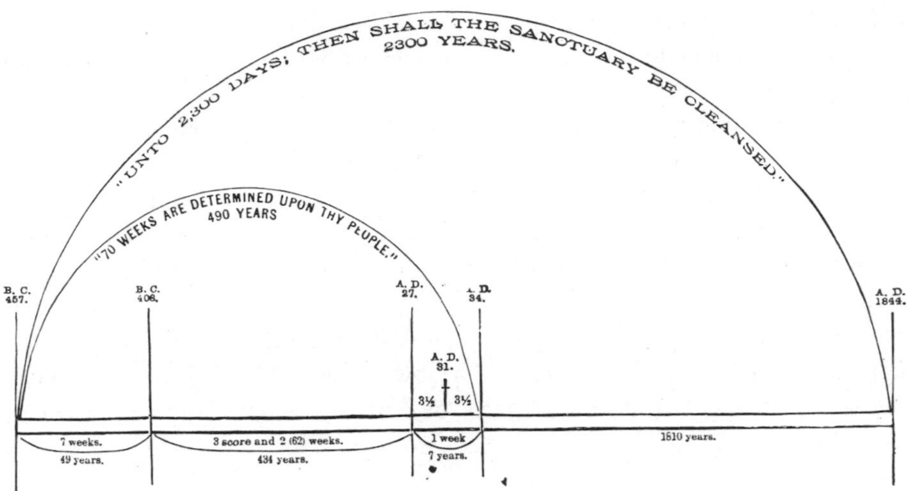

This is one of many Seventh-Day Adventist charts showing the fulfilment of Daniel's prophecies in the year 1844. This chart was made after 1844 and, in the absence of Christ's literal return in the clouds, it was assumed that Daniel's prophecies referred to events that must have taken place in heaven and not on earth. (From *Bible Readings* [1888].)

calendar, this basic formula brings Daniel's prophecy right into the general time of Jesus with great accuracy.

Nevertheless, when this formula is used to calculate the beginning point of the Bahá'í era, the difference needs to be adjusted. This is necessary to avoid the mistaken appearance that the prophecy of 2,300 years and the date 1844 do not agree, since the precise date the Bahá'í Faith began is known to be 1844 and not 1843. Since 'Abdu'l-Bahá does not explain this discrepancy, it can only be assumed that He chose to deduct one year from the 457 years as a concise way of accounting for the difference between the Jewish and Gregorian calendars or the transitional point between BC and AD .[101]

Thus far, there are four important points that now seem clear. (1) Jesus' reference to 'Daniel the prophet' (Matt. 24:15), who speaks of the 2,300 year period, is in response to the disciples' questions which concern Jesus' second coming and the time of the end of the age (Matt. 24:3). This

101. 'a year is gained in our reckoning as we pass directly from 1 BC to AD 1 (without any zero in between)' (*The Expositor's Bible Commentary*, vol. 7, 114).

seems quite obvious since the Apostles' question is concerned with when the time of the end will occur, and the Book of Daniel, which Jesus asks the Apostles to understand, contains prophecies which are also concerned with this. (2) Jesus refers to the 'abomination of desolation', which Daniel's vision indicates will end when the 'sanctuary shall be cleansed' (Daniel 8:14). (3) The sanctuary is cleansed at the end of the 2,300-year period. And (4), we know that the abomination of desolation does not begin before Jesus' first appearance when the 2,300 days begins (that is, in 457 BC), because Jesus speaks of it as something that will occur in the future (Matt. 24:15).

If the sanctuary is cleansed at the end of the 2,300 years, what then remains is to discover when the sanctuary of the Temple was made desolate. In other words, when would Jesus' followers have been able to see what Jesus was foretelling, that is, the beginning of the abomination of desolation?

Prophecies Concerning the Beginning of the Desolation

In the Book of Daniel, several points are mentioned which suggest the nature of the abomination and help us determine when it was to occur. The first point is that the vision states 'both the sanctuary and the host' will be 'trampled under foot' (Dan. 8:13). This indicates that the abomination of desolation is a period of time during which the 'host', that is, the people of God, will suffer. Again, this period ends when the 2,300-year period ends (Dan. 8:13), that is, in 1844.

The inclusion of the believers in this period of time is also indicated in Daniel 12:6-7:

> And one said to the man clothed in linen, who was above the waters of the river, 'How long shall the fulfilment of these wonders be?'
>
> Then I heard the man clothed in linen, who was above the waters of the river, when he held up his right hand and his left hand to heaven, and swore by Him who lives forever, that it shall be for a time, times, and half a time; and *when the power of the holy people* has been completely shattered, all these things shall be finished. (Emphasis added)

The vision states that 'all these things shall be finished' after 'the power of the holy people has been completely shattered'. This again suggests that

Jesus' prophecy concerning 'the abomination of desolation' refers to the beginning of a period of time wherein the believers will suffer; and this period will not end until all is finished, that is, the end of the age.

What is especially interesting is that Daniel's vision provides 'a time, times, and half a time' as the period until the 'fulfilment of these wonders'. How long is 'a time, times, and half a time?' Many Christian commentators argue that it is 1,260 years. It may seem extraordinary that anyone can derive 1,260 years from such a cryptic passage, but once examined in the light of other biblical passages, this appears completely plausible.

For example, in the Book of Revelation it is also prophesied that the holy city will be trodden 'under foot' (Rev. 11:2). It states that this will last 42 months. In the next verse it speaks of 'two witnesses' who will prophesy 1,260 days. Moreover, the Book of Revelation also employs the same terminology found in Daniel's vision, i.e. 'a time, times, and half a time' (Rev. 12:14). Many Christians concluded that a comparison of these time periods revealed that all these passages were written in special prophetic language, and that they all pointed to the same sequential period of time.

The Bible uses the term 'a time' to refer to a year.[102] Thus a 'time, times, and half a time' is equal to a year, plus two years, and half a year, or, in other words, three and a half years, which makes 42 months (3.5 x 12 months = 42 months), which makes 1,260 days (42 x 30 days = 1,260 days). This understanding, like the day/year theory, has existed among Christian scholars for centuries prior to our time.[103] In fact, Christian commentators commonly used such methods of calculations in their books regarding prophecy. One commentator, for example, wrote: 'That these three

102. 'A *time* in the Chaldee language frequently signified a *year*; and is so understood by *Daniel* himself, iv. 25-34; and in the phrase "at the end of *the times*, even of *years*": which is phrased in the English Bible "after certain years", xi. 13, the period therefore denotes *three years and half*, or forty-two months, or (allowing thirty days to the primitive month,) 1,260 days, as this mysterious period is explained in the apocalypse, Rev. xii. 14, xi. 2, 3, xii. 6' (Hales, D.D., Rector of Killesandra, in Ireland; and formerly fellow of Trinity College, and Professor of Oriental Languages in the University of Dublin, *A New Analysis of Chronology and Geography* 521).

103. For example, this point is seen in the writings of The Revd John Cumming (1810-81): 'Every writer upon prophecy is satisfied that a "time" signifies, in prophetic language, a year; "times", two years; and "the dividing of a time", or "half a time", half a prophetic year' (*Lectures on the Book of Daniel* 232). This view is still accepted by some recent conservative Christian scholars such as Paul Tan. Although he does not make any correlations to nineteenth-century Christian Adventist interpretations, he nevertheless writes, 'the "time and times and half a time" (Dan. 7:25, 12:7; Rev. 12:14) must be compared with "forty and two months" (Rev. 11:2, 13:5) and "a thousand two hundred and three score days" (Rev. 12:6), as well as Daniel's prophecy of the 70th week (Dan. 9:26-7)' (Paul Lee Tan, *The Interpretation of Prophecy* 163).

numbers are synchronical, will appear plain to any impartial considerer, that will be at pains to compare them'.[104] He also stated that these numbers 'are not only synchronical, but must be interpreted prophetically, so as years must be understood as days'.[105]

These figures indicate that from the beginning of the abomination of desolation, when the transgression against the sanctuary begins, to the time of the end, when the sanctuary is cleansed, is 1,260 years. Since the 1,260-year period terminates at the time of the end, it also terminates at the time which marks the end of the 2,300 years which, we believe, is 1844. We can now easily calculate when the transgression first occurred by counting back 1,260 years from 1844. If we use the conventional calendar, this subtraction will bring us to the relatively uneventful year of AD 584. However, one of the more startling and indisputable facts about the AD 1844 date is that it corresponds exactly to AH 1260 of the Islamic calendar!

In other words, the calendar that has been used for centuries in the very lands of the Bible, the actual place where Daniel had his vision, corroborates the correctness of the date 1844. In doing so, it provides an amazing correlation that supports the authority of Daniel's vision, affirms the methods of calculation widely used by Christian commentators, and compels a careful consideration of the claims of the Bahá'í Faith.

'Abdu'l-Bahá's own statements affirm the methods of calculation used by Christian commentators, but He differs in that He explains that the prophetic period of time refers to the time span from Muhammad to the Báb, reckoned according to the Islamic calendar and indicating the year AH 1260 (which corresponds exactly to AD 1844):

> Thus three years and a half make forty-two months, and forty-two months are twelve hundred and sixty days. The Báb, the precursor of Bahá'u'lláh, appeared in the year 1260 from the Hejira of Muhammad, by the reckoning of Islam. (*Some Answered Questions* 43)

104. Quoted from Robert Fleming, *The Rise and Fall of Rome Papal*, 1863 reprint of 1701 edn, see p. 37. (This book is also typical of eighteenth- and nineteenth-century Protestant literature with regard to its fierce anti-Roman Catholic polemics.) Another Christian commentator writes, 'All of the different expressions of the period, reckoned (as did the ancients) 360 days to a year, give 1260 years' (Ethan Smith, *Key to the Revelation* 155).
105. Fleming, ibid. 37.

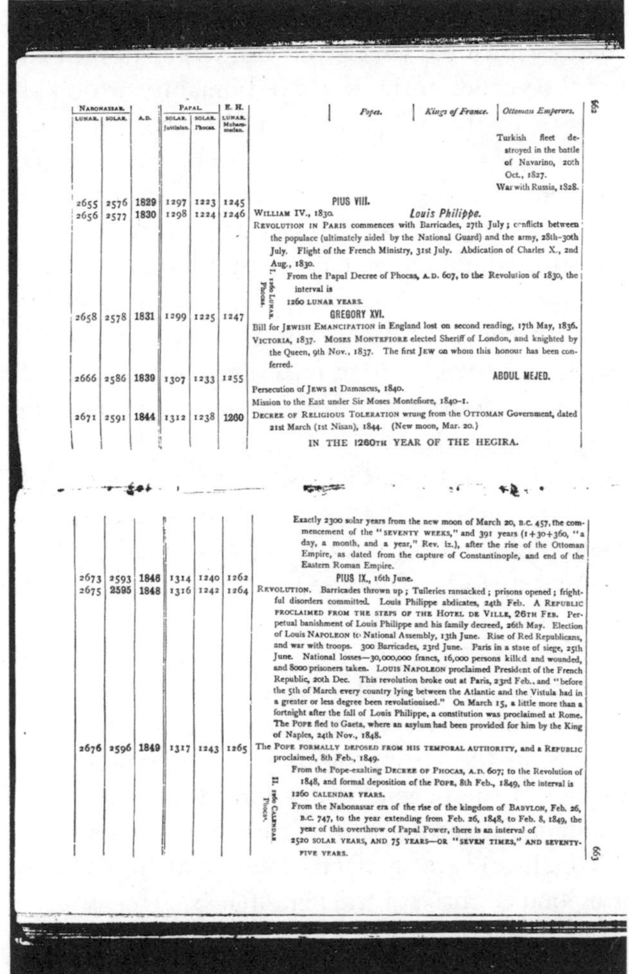

662

NABONASSAR.		A.D.	PAPAL.		E. H.	Popes. | Kings of France. | Ottoman Emperors.
LUNAR.	SOLAR.		SOLAR. Justinian.	SOLAR. Phocas.	LUNAR. Mohammedan.	
						Turkish fleet destroyed in the battle of Navarino, 20th Oct., 1827. War with Russia, 1828.
2655	2576	1829	1297	1223	1245	PIUS VIII.
2656	2577	1830	1298	1224	1246	WILLIAM IV., 1830. *Louis Philippe.* REVOLUTION IN PARIS commences with Barricades, 27th July; conflicts between the populace (ultimately aided by the National Guard) and the army, 28th–30th July. Flight of the French Ministry, 31st July. Abdication of Charles X., 2nd Aug., 1830. [I. 1260 LUNAR. Phocas.] From the Papal Decree of Phocas, A.D. 607, to the Revolution of 1830, the interval is 1260 LUNAR YEARS.
2658	2578	1831	1299	1225	1247	GREGORY XVI. Bill for JEWISH EMANCIPATION in England lost on second reading, 17th May, 1836. VICTORIA, 1837. MOSES MONTEFIORE elected Sheriff of London, and knighted by the Queen, 9th Nov., 1837. The first JEW on whom this honour has been conferred.
2666	2586	1839	1307	1233	1255	ABDUL MEJED. Persecution of JEWS at Damascus, 1840. Mission to the East under Sir Moses Montefiore, 1840–1.
2671	2591	1844	1312	1238	1260	DECREE OF RELIGIOUS TOLERATION wrung from the OTTOMAN Government, dated 21st March (1st Nisan), 1844. (New moon, Mar. 20.) IN THE 1260TH YEAR OF THE HEGIRA.
						Exactly 2300 solar years from the new moon of March 20, B.C. 457, the commencement of the "SEVENTY WEEKS," and 391 years (1+30+360, "a day, a month, and a year," Rev. ix.), after the rise of the Ottoman Empire, as dated from the capture of Constantinople, and end of the Eastern Roman Empire.
2673	2593	1846	1314	1240	1262	PIUS IX., 16th June.
2675	2595	1848	1316	1242	1264	REVOLUTION. Barricades thrown up; Tuileries ransacked; prisons opened; frightful disorders committed. Louis Philippe abdicates, 24th Feb. A REPUBLIC PROCLAIMED FROM THE STEPS OF THE HOTEL DE VILLE, 26TH FEB. Perpetual banishment of Louis Philippe and his family decreed, 26th May. Election of Louis NAPOLEON to National Assembly, 13th June. Rise of Red Republicans, and war with troops. 300 Barricades, 23rd June. Paris in a state of siege, 25th June. National losses—30,000,000 francs, 16,000 persons killed and wounded, and 8000 prisoners taken. LOUIS NAPOLEON proclaimed President of the French Republic, 20th Dec. This revolution broke out at Paris, 23rd Feb., and "before the 5th of March every country lying between the Atlantic and the Vistula had in a greater or less degree been revolutionised." On March 15, a little more than a fortnight after the fall of Louis Philippe, a constitution was proclaimed at Rome. The POPE fled to Gaeta, where an asylum had been provided for him by the King of Naples, 24th Nov., 1848.
2676	2596	1849	1317	1243	1265	The POPE FORMALLY DEPOSED FROM HIS TEMPORAL AUTHORITY, and a REPUBLIC proclaimed, 8th Feb., 1849. [II. 1260 CALENDAR. Phocas.] From the Pope-exalting DECREE OF PHOCAS, A.D. 607; to the Revolution of 1848, and formal deposition of the POPE, 8th Feb., 1849, the interval is 1260 CALENDAR YEARS. From the Nabonassar era of the rise of the kingdom of BABYLON, Feb. 26, B.C. 747, to the year extending from Feb. 26, 1848, to Feb. 8, 1849, the year of this overthrow of Papal Power, there is an interval of 2520 SOLAR YEARS, AND 75 YEARS—OR "SEVEN TIMES," AND SEVENTY-FIVE YEARS.

663

The correlation between the Christian and Islamic calendars did not escape the notice of Christian scholars. H. Gratten Guinness, for example, writes, 'This is the more remarkable also as this [AD 1844] is the 1260th year of the Hegira' (*The Approaching End of the Age* 439). The Islamic calendar is reckoned from the Hijra in the year AD 622. The 'Hejira' (or Hegira) is the latinized version of *Hijra*. Islamic dates are indicated by the European abbreviation AH, which stands for 'Anno Hegirae'. In Islamic history the Hijra signifies the point when Muhammad, owing to severe persecution, broke off relations with the people of the city of Mecca and migrated to Medina. This move marked a dramatic change in the fortunes of Muhammad. This chart from Guinness' *The Approaching End of the Age* [11th edn, 1892] illustates the corresponding dates.

We now know that, according to Bahá'í teachings, there is a relationship between the period of the abomination of desolation and the period of time corresponding to the Islamic era. This means that Jesus' prophecy (Matt. 24:15) concerning the transgression against the sanctuary is related to the Islamic religion.

Islam and the 'Abomination of Desolation'

'Abdu'l-Bahá indicates that the transgression against the sanctuary occurred because, or rather consisted of the fact that, 'the people forfeited all' that

Muhammad and 'Alí[106] - the 'two witnesses' foretold in the Book of Revelation (Rev. 11) - 'had established, which was the foundation of the Law of God, and destroyed the virtues of the world of humanity, which are the divine gifts and the spirit of this religion [Islam]' (*Some Answered Questions* 53).

Jesus' prophecy (Matt. 24:15) is therefore a specific reference to what befell Islam - that is, Islam *is the holy Temple that was desecrated.* But it is very important to realize that Islam was *not* itself the abomination of desolation. Rather, the abomination *is what happened to* Islam over its 1,260-year existence. The transgression against Islam can be seen in a number of ways, most notably: (1) the Christian rejection of Islam, and (2) the destruction of the spirit of Islam from within by those who professed it but did not truly follow its spiritual teachings.

According to the Book of Revelation, God will send 'two witnesses' who, 'clothed in sackcloth' will prophesy 1,260 years. 'Abdu'l-Bahá explains that 'these two witnesses are Muhammad the Messenger of God, and 'Alí, son of Abú Tálib' (*Some Answered Questions*, 48). 'Abdu'l-Bahá further explains:

> It is said they are 'clothed in sackcloth', meaning that they, apparently, were to be clothed in old raiment, not in new raiment; in other words, in the beginning they would possess no splendour in the eyes of the people, nor would their Cause appear new; for Muhammad's spiritual Law corresponds to that of Christ in the Gospel, and most of His laws relating to material things correspond to those of the Pentateuch. This is the meaning of the old raiment. (*Some Answered Questions* 49)

Some Christians had long believed that the transgression against the sanctuary of the Temple was a symbol of the corrupting of the Faith of God.[107] But most Christians applied this understanding of prophecy almost

106. 'Alí (AD 597-661) or 'Alí ibn Abú Tálib (Arabic, lit. son of Abú Tálib) is regarded as the first Muslim, after Muhammad's wife, Khadíjih. He was a pious believer, an ardent promoter of Islam, and the first Imám of Shi'ah Islam. He was also the cousin and son-in-law of Muhammad. When Muhammad entered Mecca and set about destroying the idols that had been set up in the Kaaba, it was 'Alí who accompanied Him.

107. The idea that this period represented a corrupted Church is reflected in the writings of many Christians. E.g., The Revd Cumming writes, 'We are to understand, then, that the saints of God were to be given into the power of the ecclesiastico-political despotism for 1,260 years' (*Lectures on the Book of Daniel* 232).

exclusively to Christianity itself,[108] although some did believe this also referred to Islam.[109] None of these commentators, however, accepted that the religion taught by the Qur'án was true, or that Muhammad was a true Prophet inspired by God.[110]

There were essentially two ways to discover when the 1,260-year period began: (1) ascertain when the Faith of God was corrupted and/or (2) recognize when the two witnesses appeared. Because Christian scholars did not see the significance of the appearance of Muhammad and His chief disciple 'Alí, they commonly calculated the 1,260 years from dates such as 552, 606 and 758, which they believed marked the beginning of the corruption of Christianity. Yet, at none of these dates can we find two witnesses as prophesied in the Book of Revelation. This oversight led many Christians to terminate the 1,260 year period at numerous dates which eventually proved to be insignificant. Because this led to confusion over what the correct dates were, most Christian scholars eventually started to question and reject their own approach to understanding Daniel's prophecies and the Book of Revelation.

What they failed to realize are two rather obvious points: (1) It is when religion is corrupted that God sends Prophets and Messengers. (2) The Book of Revelation states clearly that God will send 'two witnesses' who will prophesy for 1,260 years. This means the two witnesses will appear at the beginning of the 1,260-year period. The Christian scholars

108. Protestants primarily thought of these prophecies in relation to the Papacy: the cleansing of the sanctuary meant the overthrow of the Pope. Others interpreted its meaning more broadly as the cleansing of error from the Church: 'By days we understand years, sanctuary we understand the church, cleansed we may reasonably suppose means that complete redemption from sin' (from a written statement by William Miller made in 1831, quoted in Francis D. Nichol, *The Midnight Cry* 441-2). The Revd Edward Irving wrote that it referred to 'the whole system of doctrine and discipline and customs, actually existing and practically governing Christians in this and every land upon earth. For it is of very small consequence in the sight of God, whether the ambition and pride, and envy and covetousness, and other forms of the natural man be undermined by a Pope and his cardinals, by a Lord Chancellor and his bishops, by a General Assembly and her presbyteries, by dissenting ministers and their congregations. So that they do with a common consent, and with a rival zeal imprison the truth of God under empty forms and lifeless traditions, and constitute a worship in fear and bondage, in order to ingratiate themselves to God' (*The Morning Watch* 269 [Dec. 1832]).

109. See H. Grattan Guinness, *The Approaching End of the Age* 433-8.

110. See Revd J. Cumming, *The Great Preparation* 188. In another work Cumming writes, 'In Palestine and Turkey, and at the sites of the Seven Churches of Asia [Modern Turkey], it is not the Mahometan but the Christian who is sunk deepest in superstition. If I had to choose between the Romanism of the Western Church and the superstition of the Russo-Greek Church, I should be tempted to take Mahometanism in preference; for with all the awful errors of the Mahometans they have never yet worshipped idols. It was the universal idolatry of Christendom that provoked God to raise up the Mahometan scourge. When the Mahometans see men bowing before idols, and pictures, and images, they see something they recoil from with all the instincts of their hearts. A Mahometan mosque is more

were right in realizing that Christianity was being corrupted and that the period of 1,260 years must, therefore, have begun around the time its corruption began. But they did not discern that when that period began, the two witnesses, Muhammad and 'Alí, who arose like Moses and Joshua, had set out to restore the Faith of God and to give light to the people during that period - even as the Bible had prophesied![111]

How was Muhammad a witness? To 'witness' is to give evidence, to testify.[112] In the religious context, this means to give evidence of God and His commands, to testify on behalf of the faithful and against those who have turned against God. It is not well known in the West, but in Muhammad's Book, the Qur'án, the oneness of God is upheld, the fact that Jesus was the Christ is clearly asserted, and the truth of both the Book of Moses and the Gospel are affirmed. Like the Prophets of the Old Testament, Muhammad came to call people back to God at a time when the Faith of God had declined and been corrupted. Christianity in the seventh century was split by severe internal doctrinal conflicts and later by civil war.[113] In fact, the situation had deteriorated to such an extent that, not long after Muhammad appeared, a civil war broke out in the very centre of the Christian world over whether or not it was permissible to make and worship images of Christ. Acceptance of Muhammad's strong

like what a Christian church should be than the Greek cathedrals, and churches, and chapels' (*The Great Tribulation* 56-7). Others concurred with this view: in one Protestant's vehement denunciations of Roman Catholicism, typical of the nineteenth century, he wrote, 'The Arabian . . . was a far more respectable character than any Pope that has ever reigned; and were I to choose between the two superstitions, I would rather be a Moslem than a Papist. It was the glory of Mohammed to destroy idolatry: it is the infamy of the Popes to be the high priests of the "queen of heaven" '(John Thomas, *Elpis Israel* 342). H.M. Balyuzi relates the following tradition: 'Then Muhammad entered the structure of the Ka'bah. Inside were human representations [idols] on the walls. He ordered them to be effaced except for those of the Virgin Mary and the Infant Jesus' (*Muhammad and the Course of Islam* 133). Attitudes are now changing as is evident by the more objective assessments of Islam which have appeared in recent times. See Hans Küng, ed., *Christianity and the World Religions*, esp. 24-8.

111. The failure of the European Christians to understand Islam can be seen in the fact that it was centuries later that the Qur'án was finally translated into a European language. It was not until after the first crusades that Peter the Venerable questioned the policy of killing Muslims and advocated investigating what Muhammad actually taught. See James Kritzeck, *Peter the Venerable and Islam* 20-4. Until that time, most Christians regarded Islam as simply a schism within the Christian Faith, similar, for instance, to Arianism, only worse because it was so successful. This can be seen in Dante's *Inferno*, where Dante imagines Muhammad to be consigned to the lower regions of hell with other schismatics. It should be noted that, despite the almost total lack of credible knowledge about Islam in the West, the important role of 'Alí did not elude Dante. He puts the two witnesses together. See *Inferno*, Canto XXVIII. Peter the Venerable's attempt to increase awareness of Islam (for Christian apologetic reasons) was essentially a failure. Centuries later European writings still recycled the same misconceptions.

112. This title is applied to Muhammad in the Qur'án, see 73:15.

113. In the seventh century, the Christian world was caught up in disputes over the nature of Christ The

affirmation of the oneness of God and of His reiteration of the Old Testament prohibition on the worship of images could have prevented the destructive conflicts experienced by Christians.

We can only speculate what the course of history might have been if all of the Christian world had accepted Islam and *truly* followed the teachings of the Qur'án. Europe and much of Byzantium resisted Islam and sunk into the 'dark ages', while a large portion of Christendom - Syria, all of North Africa and most of what is commonly referred to as the Holy Land - accepted Islam and went on to build a civilization more advanced than any civilization Europe had ever experienced.[114] We can assume that the centuries of violent religious warfare, most notably the crusades, could have been prevented.

But 'Abdu'l-Bahá does not put the responsibility for this transgression chiefly on the shoulders of the Christian world. Rather, He specifically points out that it was the actions of those who followed Islam that caused the most harm. In particular, He focuses attention on a whole despotic dynasty which usurped the leadership of Islam and corrupted its teachings. He equated this dynasty, the Umayyids, with the 'beast' mentioned in the eleventh chapter of Revelation. These individuals, who opposed Muhammad from the very beginning and later converted, were responsible for much internal strife and bloodshed within the Faith of Islam, the effects

larger group, which wielded political influence, was the Chalcedonians. They believed that Christ had two natures, one divine and one human. The other major group was the Monophysites, which believed that Christ had only one nature, that being divine. The Monophysites often viewed the Chalcedonian majority as their oppressors and, consequently, some of them saw the Muslim conquerors as liberators. 'The monophysite Christians welcomed the tolerance shown to their religion and the respect shown to the centres of its worship' (R. Jenkins, *Byzantium, The Imperial Centuries* 9; see also 25, 26, 28, 32). Centuries later, many Protestants also began to envy the tolerance Christians obtained under Islamic rule. The Christian argument that the 'Turk [Muslim] was determined to extirpate the Christian religion was based on prejudice rather than fact; and even in the sixteenth century it was not universally held by the German people. The comparatively large measure of religious toleration practised by the Ottoman government was known to many Germans, and the Turkish policy naturally appealed to such suppressed religious groups as the Lutherans living under Catholic rulers and the Anabaptists who were persecuted by Catholic and Lutheran alike. On the eve of Suleiman's Vienna campaign Luther complained: ". . . I have heard that there are some in Germany who desire the advent of the Turk and wish to come under his regime; they would rather live under the Turk than under the Emperor and princes. With such people it will be hard indeed to fight the Turk!" ' (John W. Bohnstedt, *The Infidel Scourge of God, The Turkish Menace as Seen by German Pamphleteers of the Reformation Era* 20).

114. See R.M. Savory, *Introduction to Islamic Civilization*, chs. 10 and 11. European culture is greatly indebted to Muslim scholars, philosophers and centres of learning, such as Toledo, for the recovery of classical Greek knowledge which inspired the period we call the Renaissance. 'By the time its [Toledo's] importance began to fade, at the close of the thirteenth century, it had furnished scholars with Latin versions of many of the principal works of Greek and Arabic science and philosophy. There was no intellectual centre in Europe that was not touched in some way by, that did not owe some debt to, the school of Toledo' (James Kritzeck, *Peter the Venerable and Islam* 54).

of which have continued to this day. These historical facts correlate to Revelation 11:7, which states that the beast 'made war against' the two witnesses, 'and killed them'. 'Abdu'l-Bahá explains:

> this beast means the Umayyads who attacked them from the pit of error, and who rose against the religion of Muhammad and against the reality of 'Alí - in other words, the love of God.
>
> It is said, 'The beast made war against these two witnesses' - that is to say, a spiritual war; meaning that the beast would act in entire opposition to the teachings, customs and institutions of these two witnesses, to such an extent that the virtues and perfections which were diffused by the power of those two witnesses among the peoples and tribes would be entirely dispelled, and the animal nature and carnal desires would conquer. Therefore, this beast making war against them would gain the victory . . . in other words, that it would destroy the spiritual life which they spread abroad in the midst of the nation, and entirely remove the divine laws and teachings, treading under foot the Religion of God. (*Some Answered Questions* 51)

According to this interpretation, the abomination of desolation refers not to a literal idol being set up in the Temple, but to individuals who, through worldly power, sought to make themselves as idols within the Faith of God. This understanding has not escaped Christians interpreters.[115]

Islam and the Symbolic Meaning of the Temple

The biblical correlation between religion and the Temple suggests that the term 'abomination of desolation' can be applicable to transgressions against any true religion. In all periods of history, there have been those who opposed the religion of God, some who pretended acceptance, and some who failed to live according to its precepts. In this broad sense, the transgression against God's sanctuary, the abomination of desolation, has

115. 'Many exegetes [interpreters], observing that "abomination" is neutral in gender, but the participle "standing where it ought not" is masculine, have concluded that the abomination is the Antichrist, who steps into the place reserved for God (cf. 2 Thess. 2:4). If the term "Antichrist" be extended to mean a power which sets itself against God, it could be employed in this context' (*The New International Dictionary of New Testament Theology*, vol. I, 75). See also Gerhard Kittel, *Theological Dictionary of the New Testament*, vol. I, 600.

occurred in all religions. But it is not surprising that Jesus should specifically use this term (Matt. 24:15) in a prophecy about the tragedy that would befall Islam.[116]

Internal strife quickly rocked the early development of Islam, causing much grief in the Muslim community.[117] Individuals hungry for temporal power and having little regard for spiritual precepts committed murderous acts and offered no worthy leadership to the faithful. As a result of such acts, it became almost impossible for Christians to perceive the truth of the Qur'án.[118]

Moreover, the Christians would themselves take up the sword against the Muslims and show the utmost malevolence towards the Faith Muhammad established. In this way, the house of God was divided and nearly destroyed. In fact, to this day, many individuals point to the violent clashes between Muslims and Christians, such as the Crusades and recent strife in the Middle-East, as a reason for disavowing religion altogether.

In the Bahá'í community, which is now established globally, this antagonism is reconciled. Because of the example and teachings of the Báb and Bahá'u'lláh, the many Bahá'ís in Western countries, such as the Americas and Europe, who come from Christian backgrounds, have

116. 'Abdu'l-Bahá also provides an explanation concerning the holy city being trodden under foot (Rev. 11:2) which is more literal in nature. See Appendix V: The Holy City.

117. The impious and corrupt nature of the Umayyids has been admitted among Muslim historians. Abul Hasan Ali Nadwi writes, 'The then Government was not organized according to the dictates of the Qur'án and the sunnah [example and sayings of Muhammad]; its guiding lights were Arab diplomacy, expediency and interest of the state.' And in another passage, 'The extravagant rulers, surrounded by dissolute parasites who flocked to the capital, demoralized the society and produced an aristocracy resembling the pagan Arab wastrels of the age of Ignorance [i.e., pre-Islamic Arabia] in morals and behaviour' (*Saviours of Islamic Spirit*, vol. 1, 15-16, clarification added). Christianity has also had its share of despotic rulers. But it must be remembered that Muhammad, unlike Christ, specifically provided administrative guidance for the establishment of a just government. The Umayyids wilfully turned their backs on these teachings.

118. The violent propagation of Islam by the use of sword, in a manner which was often inconsistent with the teachings of Muhammad, alienated much of the Christian world from His Faith. 'Abdu'l-Bahá points out that, 'According to the Divine Law of Muhammad, it is not permissible to compel the People of the Book to acknowledge and accept the Faith' (*Secret of Divine Civilization* 43). The 'People of the Book' is an Islamic term referring especially to Christians and Jews. He further states that the injunction to use military force to spread the Faith was directed against 'idolaters of the Days of Ignorance, who in their blindness and bestiality had sunk below the level of human beings' (ibid. 44). These barbarous tribes were characterized by persistent warfare and such cruel practices as burying infants alive. Muhammad's use of force against such people ended such practices and greatly contributed to the civilizing of Arabia. The later use of violence against Christians and Jews, for the purpose of propagation, as well as the violence between Muslims themselves, cannot be regarded as within the intentions of Muhammad's religion. Muhammad's own acceptance of the use of force, e.g., against the Jews, occurred because the Jewish leaders had violated their treaty and were in a state of open hostility towards the Muslim community. It must also be noted that Muhammad sought to establish a theocratic state which governed and protected all its citizens.

accepted the legitimacy and divine inspiration of the Faith of Islam. Moreover, Bahá'u'lláh has taught peoples of the East to abandon their prejudices towards Christians. This is one of the ways in which the Bahá'í Faith has re-established the religion of God and, in doing so, has 'cleansed the sanctuary' and restored the Temple of God.

After verse 15, Christ next tells His followers what they should do when they see the abomination of desolation.

FLEE TO THE MOUNTAINS

> 16 *Then let them which be in Judaea flee into the mountains:*
> 17 *Let him who is on the housetop not come down to take any thing out of his house:*
> 18 *Neither let him which is in the field return back to take his clothes.*

COMMENTARY (24:16-18)

A Physical Crisis as a Metaphor for a Spiritual Crisis

These verses (16-18) are commonly interpreted in a purely literal sense. Many regard them as practical advice for surviving a real, war-like situation. This follows upon the idea that the destruction of the Temple and/or the abomination of desolation refer to the literal destruction of Jerusalem or are a part of a tribulation at the end times. For example, D.A. Carson writes:

> The instructions Jesus gives his disciples about what to do in view of v.15 are so specific that they must be related to the Jewish War. The devastation would stretch far beyond the city; people throughout Judea should flee to the mountains, where the Maccabeans had hidden in caves. Most roofs were flat (cf. Deut. 22:8; Mark 2:4; Acts 10:9) - pleasant places in the cool of the day. Verse 17 implies such haste that fugitives

> will not take time to run downstairs for anything. (*Expositor's Bible Commentary*, vol. 8, 501)

There is probably no need to reject such literalism entirely. However, this type of interpretation alone seems to miss Jesus' persistent concern for saving the soul of the believer and His proportionate lack of emphasis on physical concerns. These instructions are likely to represent the spiritual equivalent of their outward meanings. As already pointed out, it seems improbable that the fall of Jerusalem in AD 70 has any connection with the abomination of desolation. However, it does appear that Jesus is indicating in these verses (16-18) that the abomination is an upheaval of great magnitude requiring His followers to take personal measures necessary to survive its destructive nature.

The measures described are practical steps that might be necessary in any literal conflict of war. This suggests that a war-like condition is probably being used as a metaphor for a broader, spiritual struggle the believer will face. As we have learned, there are many good reasons for believing that Muhammad and 'Alí were the 'two witnesses' and the 'two olive trees' referred to in Revelation (11:3-4), which the Book of Zechariah explains are 'the two anointed ones, who stand beside the Lord of the whole earth' (Zech. 4:14). We know that many Christians accepted Islam and we have also learned that the abomination of desolation represents the corruption of Islam. But when this corruption of Islam occurs, what should the believers do?

The believers are to: (1) flee Judaea, which symbolizes the scene of the abomination of desolation (v. 15-16); (2) set themselves towards the spiritual heights of God's Word, the words of the Old Testament, the Gospel and, at that time, also the Qur'án (v. 16); (3) leave worldly considerations behind, which is to say, be detached from the things of this world (v. 17); and (4) not allow any needs to cause them to turn back, that is, be steadfast (v. 18). The overall thrust of the message is, therefore, very simple but vital - they should respond with urgency, take action, and realize that their souls are in danger if they do not.

Jesus' message can easily apply symbolically to the steps Muslims should take following the corrupting of Islam. The warning is that they should not save their physical lives but, rather, arise to save their spiritual lives. Christ had already taught: 'whoever desires to save his life will lose it, but whoever loses his life for My sake will save it' (Luke 9:24). Therefore Christ is not telling His followers: When you see the religion of God, the Temple, under siege, go and save your physical life from the hardships that will follow. But He says: Take action to follow God's teachings and serve God's cause, because otherwise you will be in danger of losing your spiritual life.

Even though these verses (16-18) are usually interpreted as foretelling the Jewish Wars, it should be kept in mind that the Jewish Wars did not represent a crisis for Christianity. The future would bring many catastrophes of greater destructiveness to Christians - at the hands of Rome, Barbarians and even those who, rather than opposing Christianity, claimed to espouse it.

Taking Refuge in God's Word

Christ tells His followers to flee to the 'mountains': The mountains may symbolize the loftiness and firm stronghold of the Word of God. In the Old Testament the Law comes down from the 'mountain' (Exod. 19), Noah's ark[119] comes to rest upon the mountains (Gen. 8:4), the Book of Isaiah says 'let us go up to the mountain' and prophesied that the Law will go out from the mountain (Isa. 2:2-4), and in the Psalms we read 'His foundation is in the holy mountains' (Ps. 87:1). In the New Testament Jesus 'went up on a mountain' and preached from the mount (Matt. 5:1). Therefore, mountains in Scripture often take on a symbolic character suggesting the source or place from which God's Word and Covenant proceeds - the high ground where the believer finds safety. Christ is enjoining them to turn away from that which brings desolation and to turn instead to the Word of God, the only refuge and hope for spiritual survival.

This instruction is particularly significant with regard to relations between Christianity and Islam. Christians perceived Islam as a threat not because of Muhammad's teachings, of which they knew almost nothing, but because of the imperial and worldly ambitions of those who corrupted His Faith. Had they investigated the Qur'án for themselves and the 'testimony' (Rev. 11:7) of the two witnesses, they could have made it to the safety of 'the mountains' (Matt. 24:16).

The instruction not to attempt to save anything from one's house (v. 17) or go back to retrieve one's clothes (v. 18) may be symbolic of the outer trappings of religion. That is, the 'house' and 'clothes' symbolize the outer forms, the laws adopted from Roman practice, the rituals and the doctrinal

119. Noah's Ark can be understood as a symbol for the Ark of the covenant. The covenant is the agreement between God and humankind mediated and established by the Prophets. By abiding in this covenant, safety is assured from the things that bring on the 'flood'.

controversies that Christianity took upon itself. All of these things must be left behind. Verse 17 further expresses the steadfastness required for following the religious life.

With this interpretation, the relevance of the verses is not restricted to a single set of circumstances at a particular time in history. Their symbolic meanings reflect the infinite and eternal quality of God's Word and the persistent need to follow it. From this point of view, these verses use outward circumstances to convey a spiritual message which is also expressed in Christ's statement, 'No one, having put his hand to the plough, and looking back, is fit for the kingdom of God' (Luke 9:62).

This theme is continued in the following verses.

PERSEVERE

19 *And woe unto them that are with child, and to them that give suck in those days!*
20 *But pray ye that your flight be not in the winter, neither on the sabbath day:*
21 *For then shall be great tribulation, such as was not since the beginning of the world to this time, no, nor ever shall be.*
22 *And except those days should be shortened, there should no flesh be saved: but for the elect's sake those days shall be shortened.*

COMMENTARY (24:19-22)

The Coming Hardships

If understood symbolically, these verses suggest the hardships that must be suffered by the faithful. The believer must remain faithful, even when held back by inescapable responsibilities (v. 19), must struggle at times when it is difficult (v. 21), and even when tradition (the sabbath) and the ruling powers prohibit it (v. 20).

Thus, the well-known requirements and sacrifices of bearing children symbolize the responsibilities and hardships which we must sometimes face in our religious lives. These responsibilities are hard to carry out when we are being persecuted or are suffering discrimination. It is easy to be a follower when there is no opposition or responsibilities to carry.

The hardship of fleeing in winter symbolizes the difficulty of living the religious life during times which are not supportive of such a life, that is, a time when there is little belief and spirituality. Travelling on the sabbath symbolizes having to carry out the religious message or life at a times when tradition opposes it.

A Tribulation Without Parallel

Christ states, 'For then there will be great tribulation, such as has not been since the beginning of the world until this time, no, nor ever shall be'. This verse casts great doubt on the literal interpretations which point solely to the Jewish Wars. Jesus appears to be speaking of a tribulation that is unparalleled in history. The physical suffering during the Jewish Wars was great, but terrifying wars of similar destructiveness, if not worse, such as the modern holocaust in Germany, the oppression under Stalin, or slaughters that took place in Cambodia, as well as many others, have filled the pages of history.

However, interpreting the tribulation in physical terms cannot be entirely ruled out. Such interpretation is, in part, plausible because spiritual tribulation will have an outward influence in the physical life of humankind. But, again, since the spiritual life of humankind is the special concern of Scripture, it seems only appropriate to direct our attention primarily to how this prophecy may be related to our inner lives.

We have already noted that the tribulation is described as an event which has no parallel 'since the beginning of the world until this time, no, nor ever shall be' (v. 21). This verse, if taken literally, suggests a single cataclysmic period which stands alone in history. However, we have seen that terms which appear to be all-embracing often are limited to specific contexts. For example, Paul indicated that the Gospel had been preached 'unto the ends of the world' and 'to every creature which is under heaven' (Rom. 10:18; Col. 1:23). Yet, at that time, Paul had not taken the message beyond the Roman world. These passages demonstrate that the verses of the Bible may be all-inclusive only in their specific contexts. In the case of the tribulation, the context is likely to be the Christian era.

Every religion, from its beginning, undergoes crises and tribulations. But these tribulations must naturally worsen as the religion declines until they reach a degree of severity which threatens to extinguish entirely the spiritual life of all the believers. Hence the words: 'unless those days were shortened, no flesh would be saved' (v. 22).

The word 'flesh' is commonly interpreted literally. Therefore some Christians have, for example, correlated the development of atomic weapons with this prophecy, because these weapons have the potential to destroy all flesh on earth. However, it should be remembered that Paul used such terminology when he spoke of the Church: 'For we are members of His body, and His flesh and of His bones' (Eph. 5:29-30). In the opinion of this writer, Jesus is simply conveying the graveness of the tests that lie ahead and which will nearly extinguish people's faith in God, the true 'flesh' and bones of the Church. The outward form of the religion may remain but its real meaning and practice become increasingly ignored and rejected.

The Meaning of Tribulation

In *The Book of Certitude*, Bahá'u'lláh elaborates on the meaning of chapter 24 of the Gospel of Matthew. The term 'tribulation' is rendered according to its actual Greek meaning 'oppression'. Therefore, in *The Book of Certitude*, the verse reads 'immediately after the oppression of those days'. Bahá'u'lláh indicates that the oppression, or tribulation, is a time when people seek spiritual truth but can find no sure guidance. This, Bahá'u'lláh explains, is chiefly because leaders of humankind, both religious and secular, have become corrupt and self-seeking as well as simply ignorant of the true meaning of Scripture. The appearance of false Christs, false prophets, and of what Paul terms 'deceiving spirits and doctrines of demons' suggests that the latter times, the tribulation, will be a time of great spiritual confusion and destruction. It is this confusion which Bahá'u'lláh suggests is the primary meaning of 'tribulation'. It is a greater calamity for souls to be lost to deception and confusion than for bodies to be lost to destruction. Bahá'u'lláh explains:

> As to the words - 'Immediately after the oppression of those days' - they refer to the time when men shall become oppressed and afflicted, the time when the lingering traces of the Sun of Truth and the fruit of the Tree of knowledge and wisdom will have vanished from the midst of men, when the reins of

> mankind will have fallen into the grasp of the foolish and ignorant, when the portals of divine unity and understanding - the essential and highest purpose in creation - will have been closed, when certain knowledge will have given way to idle fancy, and corruption will have usurped the station of righteousness. Such a condition as this is witnessed in this day when the reins of every community have fallen into the grasp of foolish leaders, who lead after their own whims and desire. On their tongue the mention of God hath become an empty name; in their midst His holy Word a dead letter. (*Certitude* 29)

This interpretation is supported by Paul who said, 'in the last days perilous times will come' (2 Tim. 3:1). Paul describes how immorality will abound and people will be 'always learning and never able to come to the knowledge of the truth' (2 Tim. 3:7). These words suggest that the tribulation is a time when humankind does not know where to turn to 'acquire spiritual knowledge and apprehend the Word of God' (*Certitude* 32).

The cause of this condition, Bahá'u'lláh indicates, is the decline of the influence of religion and the coming to power of corrupt religious leaders 'who lead after their own whims and desire' (ibid. 29). He goes on to state, 'Such is the sway of their desires, that the lamp of conscience and reason hath been quenched in their hearts' (ibid. 29).

Bahá'u'lláh describes such leaders as 'voracious beasts' who have 'gathered and preyed upon the carrion of the souls of men' (ibid. 31). These words of Bahá'u'lláh suggest that Paul's prophecy has been fulfilled:

> For I know this, that after my departure savage wolves will come *in among you*, not sparing the flock. (Acts 20:25, emphasis added)

Moreover, Christ states:

> Not everyone who says to Me, 'Lord, Lord', shall enter the kingdom of heaven, but he who does the will of My Father in heaven. Many will say to me in that day, 'Lord, Lord, have we not prophesied in Your name, cast out demons in Your name,

> and done many wonders in Your name?' And then I will declare to them, 'I never knew you; depart from me you who practise lawlessness!' (Matt. 7:21-3)

The fact that Jesus says these individuals will call Him 'Lord' and 'cast out demons' in His name means they are not persons outside the church but, rather, persons claiming to be Christians.

Christ also states they will prophesy in His name. It does not seem improbable that such false prophets, who prophesy in His name, are among the leaders of the Church today. At present, the Christian Church is divided into thousands of competing sects, and new divisions and disputes emerge every year. If we open a book of doctrine, we are confronted by the Post-tribulational Rapture View, the Partial Rapture View, the Mid-tribulational Rapture View, the Pre-tribulational View and similar confusion over numerous other Bible teachings. Furthermore, we find the Church divided over the moral issues of our time - apartheid, sexism, abortion, divorce and so on. Many Church leaders are afraid to take a moral stand for fear their congregations will desert them. Bahá'u'lláh says:

> Though they recognize in their hearts the Law of God to be one and the same, yet from every direction they issue a new command, and in every season proclaim a fresh decree. No two are found to agree on one and the same law, for they seek no God but their own desire, and tread no path but the path of error. In leadership they have recognized the ultimate object of their endeavour, and account pride and haughtiness as the highest attainments of their heart's desire. (*Certitude* 30)

Moreover, if one is seeking the truth today, which Church can one turn to? In what leader can a Christian place his or her trust? Bahá'u'lláh writes:

> What 'oppression' is more grievous than that a soul seeking the truth, and wishing to attain unto the knowledge of God, should not know where to go for it and from whom to seek it? For opinions have sorely differed, and the ways unto the attainment of God have multiplied. (ibid. 31)

While some Christians are looking outside the Church for the signs of the tribulation, Bahá'u'lláh suggests we should begin instead by looking inside the Church and at the plight of all those who are seeking the truth in today's confused world.

When the Tribulation Occurred

As pointed out before, the tribulation can be understood as the period of spiritual crisis that emerges when a religion declines. In the Christian era this period, according to Bahá'í teachings (*Certitude* 26-33), would correspond to the time before the appearance of Muhammad. Inasmuch as Christians did not embrace Islam, this time of tribulation did not end, but continued. Eventually, this tribulation also occurred in Islam. Today it can be said that the tribulation is a condition embracing the entire world and is the outcome of the decline all previous religions are experiencing. The spread and growth of materialism is no doubt a symptom of this tribulation. The world-wide nature of this tribulation especially suggests a tribulation without any parallel.

According to Bahá'u'lláh, this tribulation, or oppression, is 'the essential feature of every Revelation' (ibid. 31). He writes:

> Unless it cometh to pass, the Sun of Truth will not be made manifest. For the break of the morn of divine guidance must needs follow the darkness of the night of error. For this reason, in all chronicles and traditions reference hath been made unto these things, namely that iniquity shall cover the surface of the earth and darkness shall envelop mankind. (ibid. 31-2)

In this age it appears to many that religion has almost completely lost its moral influence. Some believe it is only a matter of time before religion and belief in God are entirely abandoned. However, Christ assures us this will not happen. He states, 'And unless those days were shortened, no flesh would be saved; but for the elect's sake those days will be shortened' (v. 24:22). That is to say, if things continued as they are, no one would be saved or find eternal life. All would abandon religion, irreligion would prevail, people would be ill-equipped to deal with what would then seem to be the meaningless hardships of life, and destruction would engulf all, inwardly and outwardly. But Christ promised He would re-manifest Himself and the power of the Word of God would be re-established in the world.

From a Bahá'í point of view, verse 22 indicates that the tribulation of the Christian era essentially ended for those who truly took shelter in the teachings of the Qur'án. The present spiritual tribulation ends for those who take shelter in the Faith of Bahá'u'lláh. The tribulation is not, therefore, a single cataclysmic event.

In the next verses Jesus follows His remarks about the tribulation with another warning to His followers.

HIS APPEARANCE WILL NOT BE CONCEALED

23 *Then if any man shall say unto you, Lo, here is Christ, or there; believe it not.*
24 *For there shall arise false Christs, and false prophets, and shall show great signs and wonders; insomuch that, if it were possible, they shall deceive the very elect.*
25 *Behold, I have told you before.*
26 *Wherefore if they shall say unto you, Behold, he is in the desert; go not forth: behold, he is in the secret chambers; believe it not.*
27 *For as lightening cometh out of the east, and shineth even unto the west; so shall also the coming of the Son of man be.*
28 *For wheresoever the carcass is, there will the eagles be gathered together.*

COMMENTARY (24:23-8)

Warnings Concerning Concealed Christs

These warnings concerning false prophets and false Christs are given with regard to those who would claim that He is hidden in a 'secret' place or in a 'desert'. These characteristics indicate that the true appearance of Christ will be openly proclaimed and given to all. It will not be concealed or intended for only a small elite or a limited group of believers. Also, from a Bahá'í point of view, people do not have to seek Him out in one place, hidden or otherwise, because His spiritual presence can be felt, through the effect His teachings have on one's life, by anyone who turns to Him and trusts in Him.

Criteria for Distinguishing True Christs from False

This is the third warning about false Christs in Jesus' Olivet Discourse (24:5,11, 23-4). This emphasis suggests the very real danger such individuals will present. But Christ has not given these warnings without having first provided the believers with clear guidance for distinguishing the true prophets from the false. Previously Christ stated:

> Beware of false prophets, who came to you in sheep's clothing, but inwardly they are ravenous wolves. You will know them by their fruits. Do men gather grapes from thornbushes or figs from thistles? Even so, every good tree bears good fruit, but a bad tree bears bad fruit. A good tree cannot bear bad fruit, nor can a bad tree bear good fruit. Every tree that does not bear good fruit is cut down and thrown into the fire. Therefore by their fruits you will know them. (Matt. 7:15-20)

Christ provides the simple criterion, 'You will know them by their fruits'. That is, we can know false prophets by their qualities or characteristics. Moreover, Christ indicates that they must have the characteristics that are appropriate to their claims: 'Do men gather grapes from thornbushes or figs from thistles?' Grapes are found on the grape vine, figs on fig trees, and thorns on thornbushes. A true prophet will have the qualities of a prophet - divine attributes - and a false prophet will not have such qualities.

Some will be deceived, but Christ's words are clear: if we follow His criterion, we *will* know the good from the bad. He does not say we will be unable to know them even though we examine their qualities. Similarly, Bahá'u'lláh expresses this criterion with these words:

> The proof of the sun is the light thereof, which shineth and envelopeth all things. (*Certitude* 209)

In other words, the light of the sun is the quality by which we are able to recognize the sun's reality. Sunlight is proof of the sun. Likewise, a true prophet is one who raises the spiritually dead to life, who gives sight to the spiritually blind, and who provides spiritual bread to those who hunger for the truth. 'Abdu'l-Bahá likens a true Prophet to a spiritual Teacher:

> The proof of the validity of a Manifestation of God is the penetration and potency of His Word, the cultivation of heavenly attributes in the hearts and lives of His followers and the bestowal of divine education upon the world of humanity. This is absolute proof. The world is a school in which there must be Teachers of the Word of God. The evidence of the ability of these Teachers is efficient education of the graduating classes. (*Promulgation* 341)

To know the truth of Bahá'u'lláh, for example, we need to examine how He has affected the lives of those who follow Him. This evidence is now manifest in the labours of dedicated Bahá'ís. These followers of Bahá'u'lláh, who can now be found throughout the world, are abandoning their age-old prejudices and animosities and are working to build a world that is an outward expression of the Kingdom of God which they have experienced within themselves.

Lightning out of the East

From a Bahá'í point of view, we do not need to seek out so-called prophets in 'deserts' or 'secret chambers'. A prophet's teachings and cause, which are great evidences of His truth, spread quickly and visibly, even as Jesus prophesied, like 'lightning' which 'cometh out of the east, and shineth even unto the west' (v. 27). Bahá'u'lláh indicates the fulfilment of this prophecy with these words:

> Say: In the East the Light of His Revelation hath broken; in the West the signs of His dominion have appeared. (*Tablets of Bahá'u'lláh* 13)

Jesus' prophecy (v. 27) could foretell many things. For example, it could refer to the speed with which the Bahá'í Faith became known to the western world through press accounts or the number of believers who appeared in countries such as England and America during the first years of the twentieth century. In his book, *The Revelation of Bahá'u'lláh*, Adib

Bahá'í House of Worship, Wilmette, Illinois, near the shore of Lake Michigan, north of Chicago. Bahá'u'lláh's son, 'Abdu'l-Bahá, broke the ground for the construction of this temple at a ceremony held in 1912, only forty-nine years after Bahá'u'lláh first proclaimed His mission. (*Photo courtesy of the Bahá'í World Centre, Audio-Visual Department.*)

Taherzadeh suggested that this prophecy may refer to the establishment of the Bahá'í administrative order in Europe and, especially, America.[120] He points out that Persia is regarded as the cradle of the Bahá'í Faith, that is, the place of its birth and early history, and that America is regarded as the cradle of the Bahá'í Administrative Order.

The words 'like lightning' suggest the open visibility of Bahá'u'lláh's proclamation, its startling nature, and the speed of its development. It is a sudden bright light amidst a storm, carrying a forceful message.

120. See Adib Taherzadeh, *The Revelation of Bahá'u'lláh*, vol. IV, 232-3.

The Carrion of the Souls of Men

Jesus follows His reference to lightning with a passage which has perplexed commentators for centuries: 'For wherever the carcass is, there the eagles will be gathered together' (v. 28). Innumerable interpretations have been made regarding the meaning of these words.[121]

The word 'carcass' is from the Greek 'ptoma', meaning dead body, carrion or corpse. The word 'eagles' is from the Greek 'aetos' and is also translated as 'vultures' (NIV). Some Christian scholars believe the vultures gathered around the carcass symbolize the inevitability of God's judgement:

> In Matt. 24:28 and Luke 17:37 the vultures are probably intended. The meaning seems to be that, as these birds of prey gather where the carcass is, so the judgment of God will descend upon the corrupt state of humanity. (*Vine's Expository Dictionary* 189)

Hendriksen writes:

> [The] coming of the Son of man is going to occur when it must occur, because morally and spiritually mankind will have deteriorated to such an extent that it will resemble carrion ready to be devoured by vultures. (*New Testament Commentary* 848)

In Bahá'u'lláh's discourse on Matthew 24:29-30, as mentioned earlier, He speaks of the tribulation as a time when the leaders (of religion, in particular), like 'voracious beasts have gathered and preyed upon the carrion of the souls of men' (*Certitude* 31). This may be a subtle reference to Matthew 24:28. If the vultures are corrupt leaders exploiting the lost souls of humankind, then this is an inevitable condition which, as Scripture indicates, must precede the Second Advent - a subject which the next verse anticipates.

121. See Lange, *Gospel According to Matthew* 426-7. It may reflect an Old Testament proverb, but this is uncertain. (Cf. Job 39:27-30)

PART III

THE SECOND ADVENT

THERE WILL BE SIGNS IN HEAVEN

29 Immediately after the tribulation of those days shall the sun be darkened and the moon shall not give her light, and the stars shall fall from heaven, and the powers of the earth shall be shaken:

COMMENTARY (24:29)

Literal Interpretations of the Signs

These extraordinary references to disturbances in heaven are the final prelude to the Second Advent. However, in the past some Christian commentators argued that the signs spoken of should be taken figuratively, that Jesus was not speaking of His return but of the fall of Jerusalem and the establishment of the Church. Typically, the advocates of this point of view argued that the Second Coming is not related to a second appearance of Christ but to the coming victory of Christ through the efforts of Christians.

Today, most Christian commentators support the view that the passage refers to the Second Coming of Christ. This view finds support in other similar verses in the New Testament, such as 1 Thessalonians, chapter 4. However, there remain different approaches within this second point of view. Commentators appear uncertain as to how literally these passages should be interpreted. For example, William Hendriksen understands these signs using a literal approach, but he cautions,

> In connection with this apocalyptic picture strict literalness must be avoided. Until this prophetic panorama becomes history we shall probably not know how much of this description must be taken literally and how much figuratively. (*New Testament Commentary* 863)

In relatively recent history, a number of outstanding natural phenomena have been interpreted as the signs foretold by Christ. Most notably, on 19 May, 1780 there was a great eclipse of the sun that caused many people to believe that Christ's return was growing close. On the night of that same date many reported that the light of the moon was also obscured, some even said it had the appearance of blood. Such accounts were repeated later by Christian commentators who accepted the signs as heralds of the end. These particular events were regarded as so extraordinary that memory of them endured into the twentieth century.[122]

Other examples include the Lisbon earthquake of 1755, the Dark Day of 1780, and the star-falls of 1833 and 1866. All were interpreted by at least some Christians as literal signs heralding Christ's return. Moreover, such signs seemed to be added confirmations to the Millerites and Adventists of the nineteenth century who expected Christ to return in the year 1844.

These interpretations were expressed in many books and, although the Adventists either revised their views or renounced them following their disappointment in 1844, some Bahá'ís eventually adopted their interpretations of these events.[123] Even though Bahá'u'lláh states that such signs should be understood symbolically, this, of course, does not preclude some physical or natural event acting as an appropriate metaphor signifying the fulfilment of a prophecy, such as, for instance, the meteor shower of 1833. In fact, Bahá'u'lláh later wrote:

> Vain imaginings have withheld them from Him Who is the Self-Subsisting. They speak as prompted by their own caprices, and understand not. Among them are those who have said . . . 'Have the stars fallen?' Say: 'Yea, when He Who is the Self-Subsisting dwelt in the Land of Mystery (Adrianople)'. (*Epistle* 131-2)

The 'Land of Mystery' refers to the city of Adrianople, now Edirne, situated in Turkey on the border with Bulgaria, an area which, at the time of

122. See *The Bible Reader*. Also, D.T. Taylor's *The Great Consummation* which is perhaps one of the most interesting and enthusiastically written books utilizing this type of interpretation of the 'celebrated Dark Day', the darkening of the moon and other such events.

123. Most notably, the Bahá'í author William Sears popularized these interpretations in his book *Thief in the Night*. Sears mentions all three of these signs. Quoting and relying on earlier Christian interpretations, he argues that these events did herald the Second Advent. However, Sears neglects to note that Bahá'u'lláh refers to the signs of Matthew 24:29 in *The Book of Certitude* and explains that Jesus' words are primarily symbols of spiritual occurrences.

A nineteenth-century depiction of the star-fall of 1833. An unusually intense meteor shower believed by many Christians to be a fulfilment of Jesus' prophecy 'the stars shall fall from heaven' (Matt. 24:29) and a confirmation of Christian millennial interpretations. (From *Bible Readings* [1888].)

Bahá'u'lláh, was located in the Ottoman Empire. In 1863 Bahá'u'lláh was exiled to Adrianople, and it was in 1866, during His sojourn there, that a meteor shower took place. It would therefore appear that the 1833 meteor shower cannot be the one referred to in Matthew 24:29 - unless the 1833 meteor shower heralded the Báb and the 1866 meteor shower is understood as a herald of Bahá'u'lláh.

Even as late as 1891, the Christian commentator D.T. Taylor cited numerous accounts of the 1833 and 1866 meteor showers and interpreted them as fulfilments of prophecy. He prefaced these accounts with the statement:

> [This] array of evidence, gathered from authentic sources in every quarter of our world, sufficiently demonstrate that in each and all particulars the great star-showers of the present century do most perfectly answer to the sacred prophecy concerning them. There can be, therefore, no question but that this celestial sign has occurred, and our Lord's words are fulfilled. (*The Great Consummation* 270)

Similarly, in his book *The Revelation of Bahá'u'lláh*, Adib Taherzadeh mentions the 1866 star-fall as a 'literal fulfilment of the prophecies of old'. However, he goes on to explain that the 'real significance' of Matthew 24:29 lies in what it symbolizes.[124] It appears that, like the earthquake that followed the Báb's martyrdom,[125] the star-fall of 1866 may be seen as an effective and appropriate outward symbol of an inner spiritual truth. This understanding can also be applied to the other signs which Jesus prophesied, such as the darkening of the sun as we will see next.

The Darkening of the Sun

Like meteor showers, this phenomenon has occurred on many occasions throughout history. Today we understand this event to be the result of an eclipse, that is, it occurs when the moon passes directly between the sun and our planet. In ancient times, people often regarded such an event as a portent of doom. The people witnessing it generally did not realize that they were simply in a shadow that was quickly moving across the earth and

124. See *The Revelation of Bahá'u'lláh*, Adrianople 1863-68, vol. II, 270-2. Taherzadeh also includes an Appendix on European reactions to the 1866 star-fall (422-6).
125. See Appendix I: Meaning and Metaphor.

that people in other regions were unaffected and probably unaware of its occurrence. Naturally, with our present knowledge, we know that such eclipses have occurred many times since Matthew recorded the prophecies of Jesus; and even though eclipses are sufficiently infrequent to be regarded as special, they have, nevertheless, heralded many rather inauspicious occasions. Therefore, if we interpret Jesus' prophecy literally as a reference to an eclipse, we are left with no real way to determine which particular eclipse had, or will have, any special importance. Apart from its symbolic significance, it is hard to see how an eclipse could be thought to have an effect on human affairs.

In order to understand the symbolism of Matthew 24:29, it is essential to understand the way in which the physical world is used as a metaphor to represent the spiritual world. Paul discusses what has come to be known as 'general Revelation', the concept that creation itself manifests the signs and evidences of God (Rom. 1:20). Revelation can thus be understood in two ways: (1) special Revelation, that is the Word of God as spoken through the Prophets, and (2) general Revelation, God's signs as revealed in creation.

The natural world is a metaphor for the spiritual world. For example, the sun, or light, is symbolic of truth. Physical light enables us to see our way in the world so that we will not injure ourselves by colliding with other objects. Spiritual light (truth) enables us to find our way in the world morally so that we do not bring harm to our souls. Thus Christ stated, 'As *long as I am in the world*, I am the light of the world' (John 9:4-5, emphasis added). Bahá'u'lláh teaches that this type of metaphorical relationship between material reality and spiritual reality is at the heart of the imagery in Jesus' prophecy:

> By the terms 'sun' and 'moon', mentioned in the writings of the Prophets of God, is not meant solely the sun and moon of the visible universe. Nay rather, manifold are the meanings they have intended for these terms. In every instance they have attached to them a particular significance. Thus, by the 'sun' in one sense is meant those Suns of Truth Who rise from the dayspring of ancient glory, and fill the world with a liberal effusion of grace from on high. These Suns of Truth are the universal Manifestations of God in the worlds of His attributes and names, even as the visible sun that assisteth, as decreed by God, the true One, the Adored, in the development of all

> earthly things, such as the trees, the fruits, and colours thereof, the minerals of the earth, and all that may be witnessed in the world of creation, so do the divine Luminaries, by their loving care and educative influence, cause the trees of divine unity, the fruits of His oneness, the leaves of detachment, the blossoms of knowledge and certitude, and the myrtles of wisdom and utterance, to exist and be made manifest. (*Certitude* 33-4)

From this explanation, the darkening of the sun, which physically occurs by the simple phenomenon of an eclipse, can also be understood as a symbol for the obscuring of the 'light' of truth, that is, of God's Word or Revelation. The development of a religion can be likened to the passage of the day. The early life of a new religion is like the morning. As the religion grows and influences large numbers of people, day becomes evident. After a long period of time, day begins to pass into night, that is, people gradually obscure the original teachings and turn away from its message. Thus Jesus said, 'I am the light of the world', but qualified His words with 'As long as I am in the world' (John 9:5). Thus, Scripture refers to the time of Christ's appearance as the 'Day' of the Lord (Acts 2:20).

The Moon Will Not Give Its Light

After the setting of the sun, the brightest luminary in the night sky is the moon. Bahá'u'lláh explains that the moon, like other symbols, can have different meanings. He explains the moon as being a symbol both for religious leaders and for the laws of God. He expounds on Matthew 24:29 with these words:

> 'the sun shall be darkened, and the moon shall not give her light, and the stars shall fall from heaven' is intended the waywardness of the divines, and the annulment of laws firmly established by divine Revelation. (*Certitude* 41)

This explanation indicates that Jesus' words are prophesying the end of Christianity's spiritual influence prior to and during Christ's return. In *The Book of Certitude*, Bahá'u'lláh explains that the darkening of the moon is when the teachings 'cease to exert their influence' and when the 'learning of a former Dispensation' has 'darkened and set' (*Certitude* 41-2).

The Stars Will Fall From Heaven

As explained above, the time of Christ's appearance and the period of His influence on earth can be likened to day. During this time, one could turn to Christ and find the light of guidance. But with Christ's ascension and the gradual obscuring of His message, the 'sun' set and people had to find their way during the 'night'. To do so they had to look up to heaven (the night sky) and rely on the stars to navigate by. Bahá'u'lláh says that the 'heaven' referred to in Scripture is sometimes used to represent religion, while the 'stars' are used to symbolize the pious and spiritually-minded among the clergy or religious leaders who act as guides in that religion. This use of 'stars' as a metaphor for wise leaders goes back to the Book of Daniel (Dan. 12:3). When Christ said the 'stars will fall from heaven', He was indicating that the leaders of the Christian religion would cease to be spiritual guides for the believers.

In *The Book of Certitude*, Bahá'u'lláh refers to the stars mentioned in Matthew 24:29 as 'the stars of understanding and utterance' and in another passage as 'the Stars of divine wisdom' (66). He indicates that the falling of the stars can symbolize the failure of the leaders of previous religions to recognize the new Manifestation (ibid. 36). In a Tablet especially addressed to Christians, Bahá'u'lláh writes:

> O concourse of bishops! Ye are the stars of the heaven of My knowledge. My mercy desireth not that ye should fall upon the earth. My justice, however, declareth: 'This is that which the Son hath decreed.' And whatsoever hath proceeded out of His blameless, His truth-speaking, trustworthy mouth, can never be altered. (*Tablets of Bahá'u'lláh* 14)

According to this explanation, the prophecy recorded in Matthew 24:29 indicates that the signs heralding Christ's return will be the decline of spiritual leadership and religious practice. Corruption in the Church, confusion among Christian believers, opposition to and rejection of Bahá'u'lláh, and other similar occurrences, are all aspects of prophecy unfolding in this day.

The Bahá'í view suggests that the signs described in Matthew 24:29 will characterize that stage of the tribulation which heralds the Second Advent. When the Second Advent is upon us 'the sun will be darkened, and the moon will not give its light; the stars will fall from heaven, and the powers of the heavens will be shaken'. These signs symbolize the final outcome of the tribulation: the obscuring of the religious guidance of Christ, the abandonment of religious practice, and the downfall of religious institutions.

When Bahá'u'lláh speaks of the tribulation, He states that its occurrence precedes and accompanies the appearance of every Manifestation (*Certitude* 31). This assertion and the symbolic nature of these signs are supported by the testimony of the Bible. All of the events prophesied in verse 29 of Jesus' Olivet Discourse were also prophesied in the Old Testament.[126]

From a Bahá'í point of view, the Old Testament prophesied that Jesus' First Advent would be accompanied by the darkening of the sun and moon, by the stars falling from heaven, and by Jesus Himself coming on the clouds of heaven. It is possible to argue that these signs also refer to the Second Advent, but it cannot be denied that they refer to the First Advent because their fulfilment is clearly indicated in the New Testament.

Peter proclaimed to the people of Judaea that Jesus had fulfilled prophecies very much like those whose fulfilment Christians await today. As Peter proclaimed the appearance of Jesus, he said, 'this is what was spoken by the prophet Joel'. He then quotes a prophecy containing this verse:

> The sun shall be turned into darkness, and the moon into blood, before the coming of the great and notable day of the LORD. (Acts 2:16, 20. See also Joel 2:28-32)

The way in which Christian commentators have tried to explain this verse is very interesting. Matthew Henry, for example, recognizes that Peter clearly interprets this prophecy as referring to the First Advent of Christ, but his attempt to understand this literally is quite problematic. Verse 20, he states, refers literally to the destruction of Jerusalem:

> Secondly, the terrible presages of that destruction are here foretold: There shall be wonders in heaven above, the sun turned into darkness and the moon into blood; and signs too in the earth beneath, blood and fire. Josephus, in his preface to

126. Cf. Deut. 30:4; Isa. 13:10, 27:13, 34:4; Ezek. 32:7; Dan. 7:13,14; Joel 2:10; Hag. 2:6.

> his history of the wars of the Jews, speaks of the signs and prodigies that preceded them, terrible thunders, lightnings, and earthquakes; there was a fiery comet that hung over the city for a year, and a flaming sword was seen pointing down upon it. The fire and vapour of smoke literally came to pass in the burning of their cities, and towns, and synagogues, and temple at last. (*Matthew Henry's Commentary*, vol. VI, 21)

Notice how Henry has attempted to prove the literal fulfilment of Joel's prophecy, yet the literal events which he cites are quite unlike those spoken of by Joel. Other commentators have argued that 'the sun shall be turned into darkness' refers to the 'darkness' that fell 'over all the land' when Jesus was crucified (Matt. 27:45; Luke 23:44-5). However, these attempts to establish such literal fulfilment of Joel's prophecy during the time of Christ do not seem very persuasive. There appear to be no historical records of such literal signs. If they existed, the people found them too unimpressive to remember, although surely at least the Apostles, or later Christians, would have wanted to record them.

If these signs did not occur literally, then Joel's prophecy was symbolic, and we therefore have good cause to interpret Matthew 24:29 symbolically also. If Joel's prophecy was fulfilled in an outwardly literal way, then we know that the signs will be so unremarkable as to be unrecognized or easily forgotten. If this is the case, then we should not expect everyone to recognize them or to know what such signs signify.

Another similar prophecy can be found in the Book of Daniel where it is written:

> I was watching in the night visions,
> And behold, one like the Son of Man,
> Coming on the clouds of heaven!
> He came to the Ancient of Days,
> And they brought Him near before Him. (Dan. 7:13)

Here, Daniel may be speaking of the Second Advent. However, during His ministry, Jesus already indicates that He came from heaven (see John 3:13; 6:38-42). Moreover, Bahá'u'lláh's explanation of the symbolism of the tribulation and the signs, such as stars falling, describes circumstances equally evident at the time of Christ - that is, the light of the Mosaic

Revelation had become obscured, the true meaning of the Scriptures was not understood (2 Cor. 3:14), and corrupt religious leaders had authority over the congregations (Matt. 16:1-12; and ch. 23). As Bahá'u'lláh says, these signs occur in every dispensation before, and accompany, the appearance of a Prophet or Manifestation of God.

In the next verse Jesus speaks of the culmination of these signs, the actual advent of the Son of Man.

HE WILL COME IN THE CLOUDS OF HEAVEN

> 30 *And then shall appear the sign of the Son of man in heaven: and then shall all the tribes of the earth mourn, and they shall see the Son of man coming in the clouds of heaven with power and great glory.*

COMMENTARY (24:30)

A Sign in the Heavens

This verse has two main parts, the first being a prophecy referring to a 'sign' that will appear in heaven. This singular 'sign', Bahá'u'lláh explains, is a star. The star has both a literal meaning and a symbolic one. Addressing the outward meaning first, He writes that by ' "heaven" is meant the visible heaven'. He states that:

> a star will appear in the heaven, heralding unto its people the advent of that most great light. (*Certitude* 62)

Bahá'u'lláh demonstrates this point by referring to stories of stars that heralded previous Prophets.[127] In this way, He conveys the idea that it is reasonable to accept that the 'sign' prophesied in Matthew 23:30 is the same kind of sign that heralded Messengers of God in former ages.

127. See Appendix VI: Jewish Legends.

Bahá'u'lláh then explains that there is a symbolic parallel between the appearance of a star in the visible heaven and a person sent to announce the new Manifestation of God. He indicates that the visible heaven symbolizes the invisible heaven, that is, religion:

> In like manner, in the invisible heaven a star shall be made manifest who, unto the peoples of the earth, shall act as a harbinger of the break of that true and exalted Morn. These twofold signs, in the visible and the invisible heaven, have announced the Revelation of each of the Prophets of God, as is commonly believed. (*Certitude* 62)

When Bahá'u'lláh states that the such twofold signs are 'commonly believed' to have heralded 'each of the Prophets', it should be noted that this is commonly believed in the East.[128] The Bible itself does not recount such signs except for those referring to Christ. In the case of Christianity, Bahá'u'lláh writes:

> when the hour of the Revelation of Jesus drew nigh, a few of the Magi, aware that the star of Jesus had appeared in heaven, sought and followed it, till they came unto the city which was the seat of the Kingdom of Herod. The sway of his sovereignty in those days embraced the whole of that land.
>
> These Magi said: 'Where is He that is born King of the Jews? for we have seen His star in the east and are come to worship Him!' When they had searched, they found out that in Bethlehem, in the land of Judaea, the Child had been born. This was the sign that was manifested in the visible heaven. (Ibid. 64)

This account is, within certain limits,[129] historically plausible, inasmuch as the star may have been a visible phenomenon such as a comet. Some have argued that the appearance of the star of Bethlehem may have been the

128. See Appendix VI: Jewish Legends.

129. Scripture often employs symbolism even in narratives which on the surface appear to be purely historical accounts. Scripture is not merely history but sacred history. The use of symbolism in such instances is essential to reveal and convey the actual significance of what took place, truths that would otherwise be imperceptible in an objective account. People often mistakenly criticize Scripture by analyzing and evaluating it according to limited historical or 'scientific' standards which are inapplicable to symbols.

appearance of Halley's Comet in 12 BC, or a configuration of planets in 7 BC.[130] If we take the New Testament story of the Magi in a strictly literal sense, which is a very problematic thing to do, these theories suggest that Jesus was born earlier than traditionally thought.[131] Of course, with the freedom to speculate, it can be argued that the star appeared early enough to enable the Magi to arrive in time for Christ's birth.[132]

In considering such phenomena, it should be noted that comets appear periodically and that not every comet heralds a Prophet or even an auspicious event. Scientists class comets in various categories of size and in orbits of different lengths of time. Presently, there are believed to be about 450 comets in orbit within our solar system, some taking as long as two million years to complete their circuits. There are sixteen comets that are in the same class as Halley's Comet and which return in less than two hundred years.[133] Comets are sufficiently rare to be regarded as unique phenomena but common enough to appear more often than do true Prophets.

Therefore, the significance of such 'signs' does not lie in the material reality of the comets themselves but in what they symbolize. This holds equally true for planetary configurations and novae. In other words, comets

130. D. Hughes, *The Star of Bethlehem Mystery*, ch. 10.

131. Ibid. 6, 47-84. Hughes attempts to arrive at probable dates based on a literal understanding of the text.

132. It is difficult, though not impossible, to theorize how the Magi could have understood the appearance of a star to be evidence of a Messiah among the Jews. It is also problematic to accept that a spectacular star could remain in the sky long enough to guide the Magi from the East to Bethlehem yet escape being mentioned in all other early (non-Christian) records. Scientific criticism of the narrative yields little of value except further cause to view the star's appearance symbolically rather than literally. There is no reason to reject the idea of an uncommon 'star' appearing at that time which could have been regarded as a 'sign', but it seems reasonable to assume that the story also presents symbolic imagery intended to convey a number of specific spiritual points that are true about the significance of Jesus' appearance. It draws parallels with the accounts of Moses, both in the Bible and in tradition. In a broad sense, it illustrates that it was the Gentiles, not the Jews, who sought out Christ It points out that wise men were able to see the signs indicating the truth of Christ and that extraordinary signs heralded an extraordinary Prophet. The Magi looked to the stars for signs whereas an angel appeared to the Jewish shepherds. This suggests that God guides people according to the language and ways that are best suited to their respective cultures. The Magi inquired of the Jews about the Messiah and found no answer, which suggests that those who should be guides are often unacquainted with the truth. Despite this, the Magi found Christ. These and many other spiritual points can be gleaned from this remarkable story of the Magi. See *Matthew Henry's Commentary*, vol. V, 10ff. In early Christian tradition there were a number of legends about the identity of the Magi. Some believed that they were from Persia and had come because the Prophet Zoroaster had prophesied Jesus' birth. Clement of Alexandria, in his *Stromata*, Book 1, Ch. 15, wrote of 'the Magi of the Persians, who foretold the Saviour's birth and came into the land of Judea guided by a star'. And according to *The Arabic Gospel of the Infancy*, it is written: 'And it came to pass when the Lord Jesus was born at Bethlehem of Judah, in the time of Herod the King, behold Magi came from the east to Jerusalem, as Zerdusht [Zoroaster] had predicted: and they had with them gifts' (Harris B. Cowper, *The Apocryphal Gospels* 176, clarification added).

133. Nigel Calder, *The Comet is Coming!* 54.

or stars are further visible metaphors for spiritual realities. They are used in Scripture metaphorically to signify the appearance of a divine Star in the spiritual heaven of guidance (i.e. religion). By pointing out such phenomena in the visible heaven, Scripture suggests the special and periodic occurrence of a unique Messenger from 'heaven'.

Following His recounting of the story of the star of Bethlehem, Bahá'u'lláh then recounts the story of John the Baptist to illustrate how this outward sign is fulfilled spiritually, in the 'invisible heaven':

> As to the sign in the invisible heaven - the heaven of divine knowledge and understanding - it was Yahyá, son of Zachariah, who gave unto the people the tidings of the Manifestation of Jesus. Even as He hath revealed: 'God announceth Yahyá to thee, who shall bear witness unto the Word from God, and a great one and chaste.'[134] By the term 'Word' is meant Jesus, Whose coming Yahyá foretold. Moreover, in the heavenly Scriptures it is written: 'John the Baptist was preaching in the wilderness of Judaea, and saying, Repent ye: for the Kingdom of heaven is at hand.' By John is meant Yahyá.[135] (*Certitude* 64-5)

This symbolic explanation is so appropriate that it was recognized in early Christian times.[136] Bahá'u'lláh goes on to point out that such signs in the 'visible' and 'invisible heaven' were also fulfilled in the time of Muhammad:

> Likewise, ere the beauty of Muhammad was unveiled, the signs of the visible heaven were made manifest. As to the signs of the invisible heaven, there appeared four men who successively announced unto the people the joyful tidings of the rise of that divine Luminary. Rúz-bih, later named Salmán, was honoured by being in their service. As the end of one of these approached, he would send Rúz-bih unto the other, until the fourth who, feeling his death to be nigh, addressed Rúz-bih saying: 'O Rúz-bih! when thou hast taken up my body and buried it, go to Hijáz

134. Bahá'u'lláh here quotes from the Qur'án (3:39). The Qur'án recounts the birth narrative of Jesus several times. See Sura (chapter) 19, entitled 'Mary' (Maryam) and Sura 3, 'The House of Imran'.
135. The origin of the Arabic 'Yahyá' is uncertain but it may have originated from Christian sources in Syria, e.g., the Syriac Yohannan, signifying John. See Geoffrey Parrinder, *Jesus in the Qur'án* 55-6.
136. See Appendix VI: Jewish Legends.

> for there the Day-star of Muhammad will arise. Happy art thou, for thou shalt behold His face!' (Ibid. 65)

Records show that a comet made a close appearance to earth in AD 607, which is only three years before Muhammad's mission is believed to have begun. Other sightings occurred in AD 613, which is the year Muhammad first publicly proclaimed His mission.[137] Either comet could be regarded as a star heralding the appearance of Muhammad's Revelation.

The presence of Rúz-bih and the appearance of a star demonstrate that the Revelation of Muhammad was heralded by a two-fold sign, fulfilling the prophecy of Matthew 24:30. Moreover, by recounting these stories, Bahá'u'lláh again illustrates that prophecy speaks of spiritual signs and truths that accompany the advent of every Manifestation of God. Prophecy has a universal or archetypal nature and an eternal quality that takes it beyond the limits of singular historic events. Even the outward sign of the unusual star in the visible heaven is periodic and symbolic of the special nature of the appearance of each of God's Messengers.

Bahá'u'lláh concludes this series of illustrations by showing that, in this age, the prophecy of Matthew has been fulfilled with the advent of the Bahá'í Revelation. He writes:

> And now concerning this wondrous and most exalted Cause. Know thou verily that many an astronomer hath announced the appearance of its star in the visible heaven. (Ibid. 65)

This account is equally verifiable. In the nineteenth century there appeared what is referred to as the 'Great Comet', or the 'Great March Comet'.[138] In 1845-6, another comet became visible. This comet was named Biela because it divided into two distinct comets. This was the first comet that modern scientists have observed to divide.[139] This may be

137. Nigel Calder, *The Comet is Coming!* 17-18.

138. In a book on prophecies, the Christian writer D.T. Taylor relates this interesting bit of paranoia concerning the Great March Comet: 'Prof. Proctor, who before his death in a public paper entitled *The Menacing Comet*, announced his belief that the vast comet of 1880, identical with that of 1843 and 1668, will, as the English astronomer Mr. Marth had calculated, return in 1897, and falling into the sun, cause an intense heat that will destroy all the higher forms of life on our earth' (*The Great Consummation*, 407). Taylor's book was copyrighted in 1891.

139. Ibid. 66-8. The Bahá'í author William Sears argues that this comet was a herald of the Bahá'í Faith. See *Thief in the Night* 194-7.

regarded as significant, because the Bahá'í Faith was similarly heralded by two individuals in the invisible heaven. After referring to the star, Bahá'u'lláh adds:

> Likewise, there appeared on earth Ahmad and Kázim, those twin resplendent lights - may God sanctify their resting-place! (Ibid. 65)

'Ahmad' and 'Kázim' refer to two individuals, Shaykh Ahmad (1753-1831) and Siyyid Kázim (1793-1843), who taught in the early nineteenth century that the time of the end was approaching. These individuals appeared within the Muslim world and, according to Bahá'í teachings, were heralds of the Bahá'í Revelation.[140] In Persia many responded to their teachings and later accepted the Bahá'í Faith.

Bahá'u'lláh concludes His explanation of Matthew 24:30 with these words:

> From all that We have stated it hath become clear and manifest that before the revelation of each of the Mirrors reflecting the divine Essence, the signs heralding their advent must needs be revealed in the visible heaven as well as in the invisible, wherein is the seat of the sun of knowledge, of the moon of wisdom, and of the stars of understanding and utterance. The sign of the invisible heaven must needs be revealed in the person of that perfect man who, before each Manifestation appeareth, educateth, and prepareth the souls of men for the advent of the divine Luminary, the Light of the unity of God amongst men. (Ibid. 66)

Each of the instances we have examined, that is, the references to the sun, the moon, and the stars have plausible spiritual meanings. Rather than providing a merely literal understanding, these interpretations reveal a message more relevant to the religious life. Viewing the following verse in a religious context also reinforces this same consistent spiritual message.

140. Accounts of their ministries are recorded in Nabíl's *The Dawn-Breakers*. See chs. 1-2.

All the Tribes of the Earth Shall Mourn

With reference to, 'And then shall all the tribes of the earth mourn' (Matt. 24:30), Bahá'u'lláh explains:

> These words signify that in those days men will lament the loss of the Sun of the divine beauty, of the Moon of knowledge, and of the Stars of divine wisdom. (*Certitude* 66-7)

This passage indicates that by 'mourn' is meant the suffering experienced with the decline of religion and spiritual truth. This interpretation, like most of Bahá'u'lláh's interpretations, is spiritual in nature. It emphasizes a meaning deeply involved with the state of our souls and describes the circumstances heralding the advent of all Prophets. Its meaning is not bound by reference to a particular historical event.

In the above excerpt, Bahá'u'lláh explains Matthew 24:30 with reference to Muhammad.[141] However, the universality of its spiritual message is further affirmed when Bahá'u'lláh presents the prophecy with reference to His own Revelation, as He does in a letter to Napoleon III, the Emperor of France.[142] Bahá'u'lláh writes that it is 'in these days' that:

> all the tribes of the earth have mourned, and the foundations of the cities have trembled, and the dust of irreligion hath enwrapped all men, except such as God, the All-Knowing, the All-Wise, was pleased to spare. (*Epistle* 46)

The Appearance of the Son of Man

All the signs mentioned thus far can be explained by physical events which are entirely within the realm of possibility and require no alteration of natural laws. But, progressively, the signs Jesus speaks of become more extraordinary. First He speaks of wars, famines and other disasters which are physical events that have occurred throughout history. He then speaks

141. Some Muslim commentators reject the authority of the New Testament. In defence of the Gospel, Bahá'u'lláh argues that Matthew presents prophecies that are clearly applicable to the Revelation of Muhammad. His explanations of Matthew, which form a large portion of the first part of *The Book of Certitude*, also provide the essential features of the Bahá'í approach to interpretation.

142. Bahá'u'lláh wrote to all the major powers of the nineteenth century. To Napoleon III Bahá'u'lláh wrote: 'Commotions shall seize all the people in that land, unless thou arisest to help this Cause, and followest Him Who is the Spirit of God [Jesus Christ] in this, the straight Path. Hath thy pomp made thee proud? By My Life! It shall not endure; nay, it shall soon pass away' (*Proclamation* 21, clarification added). This prophecy was fulfilled not long afterwards.

of rarer signs in heaven, but even these signs may have plausible explanations if we assume that the stars falling are meteors and that the sun and moon can be darkened by eclipses or by atmospheric conditions. Then, however, He speaks of the Son of man coming in the clouds of heaven. This great event has no parallel in the world of natural phenomena.

Such an event could take place only in the divine realm and only as a result of radical interference with the course of nature. This type of symbolic imagery appropriately gives emphasis to the divine nature of Jesus' return - it conveys that it is an event which reveals God actively working in history. It reinforces the distinction between the human realm and the divine, between human knowledge and the special act of revelation. Signs such as the tribulation involve the decline of religion, a development which originates from within the human world; but the appearance of a Manifestation of God, such as Moses, Christ, and now Bahá'u'lláh, is a unique spiritual event originating from God.[143] This unique and special relationship between the divine world and the appearance of a Manifestation of God is also evident in other statements made by Jesus. For example, Jesus said:

> no man hath ascended up to heaven, but he that came down from heaven, even, the Son of man which is in heaven. (John 3:13, KJV)

In this verse Jesus clearly states that He is from heaven. But since He also says He is in heaven - even as He stands on the ground - we have here an indication that heaven is not literally the physical sky or space above us. The same observation can be applied to Jesus' statement concerning the Second Advent, that is, that the appearance of the Son of Man in the 'clouds of heaven' does not mean the clouds of the physical sky.

These verses suggest that 'heaven' is used here to symbolize the exalted, holy nature and origin of His station. It emphasizes His relationship to God. The physical heaven above us is not the reality of heaven but is used in Scripture to symbolize the reality of the spiritual

143. Many Christians will argue that this uniqueness is applicable to Jesus alone, a view which they commonly cite John 14:6 to support: 'I am the way, the truth, and the life. No one comes to the Father except through Me'. From a Bahá'í point of view, this exclusiveness refers to His station, the station of One who manifests the attributes of God, and His role as One who acts as a Mediator for humankind - a station and a role which Bahá'ís believe embrace all Manifestations (e.g., Moses, Buddha, Christ, Muhammad and Bahá'u'lláh).

world. To assume that the 'heaven' Jesus speaks of is the sky above us is to confuse the symbol for the reality.

On another occasion Christ again asserted that He had come from heaven:

> For I have come down from heaven, not to do My own will, but the will of Him who sent Me. (John 6:38)

Believing that by heaven was intended the literal heaven above us, the Jews who heard Him could not understand His message:

> The Jews then murmured against Him, because He said, 'I am the bread which came down from heaven.' And they said, 'Is not this Jesus, the son of Joseph, whose father and mother we know? How is it then that He says, "I have come down from heaven"?' (John 6:41-2)

Despite such instances, which demonstrate the symbolic nature of heaven, many Christians await Jesus' return, expecting Him to appear in the sky. Even as the Jews interpreted Jesus' words literally and misunderstood them, Christians have interpreted the story of the resurrection of Jesus into heaven and the prophecies of His return in the same manner. Both these occurrences are factual and necessary truths with regard to the spiritual reality that they represent, but the circumstances of these events are described symbolically in the Scriptures and therefore it follows that they should not be taken literally. It is important not to confuse a symbol with the reality it represents.

Some people, failing to understand the value and necessity of symbolism, argue that if the resurrection is not literal then it did not happen and it is therefore a lie. However, if this were an accurate appraisal of symbolism, Jesus' statement that He came down from Heaven (John 6:38ff) would also have to be considered a lie. This would equally apply to many other statements by Jesus, and to other portions of the Bible as well. As we have previously seen in the introduction, Bahá'u'lláh directly addresses this issue in this claim concerning Himself:

> He, verily, hath again come down from heaven, even as He came down from it the first time. Beware lest ye dispute that

> which He proclaimeth, even as the people before you disputed His utterances. (*Tablets of Bahá'u'lláh* 11)

From the Bahá'í point of view, Jesus' prophecy concerning the Son of Man coming in the clouds of heaven has been fulfilled in the Person of Bahá'u'lláh. This is understood to be true quite simply because the life and teachings of Bahá'u'lláh indicate that He is from God. The recognition of this is, of course, the most important point and purpose of Jesus' Olivet Discourse for our time. Naturally, there are many who dispute this claim, even as the people before disputed Jesus' claims. But as we have already seen, and will see, these claims are entirely compatible with, and are supported by, Scripture.

The Meaning of 'Clouds'

Matthew's Gospel is rendered in English to read that the Son of Man will come 'in the clouds of heaven' (24:30 KJV). Mark records, 'in the clouds' (13:26) and Luke's version says 'in a cloud' (21:27).

In the Bahá'í writings, the clouds mentioned in Scripture are understood to have a symbolic or metaphorical meaning. They represent anything that obscures our vision and prevents us from recognizing the truth. This can cover a wide range of things. For instance, a person may reject Bahá'u'lláh because he or she disagrees with His teachings. Bahá'u'lláh writes:

> And now regarding His words, that the Son of man shall 'come in the clouds of heaven'. By the term 'clouds' is meant those things that are contrary to the ways and desires of men. (*Certitude* 71)

Using a slightly different emphasis, 'Abdu'l-Bahá writes:

> the cloud referred to in the Gospel is the human body, so called because the body is as a veil to man, which, even as a cloud, preventeth him from beholding the Sun of Truth that shineth from the horizon of Christ. (*Selections from the Writings of 'Abdu'l-Bahá* 168)

'Abdu'l-Bahá's explanation may pertain both to the human body of the individual who is confronted with a decision of faith and to the human body of the Manifestation (Bahá'u'lláh). This is possible because people's own physical desires are often the reason they reject the religious teachings of God, while the human nature of Bahá'u'lláh prevents some from recognizing His divinity. The crucifixion, for example, prevented many people from perceiving Jesus' divinity. They believed that if He were the Messiah it would not be possible to kill Him (Matt. 27:40-2). The symbolism of 'clouds' refers to those things which, like the crucifixion in the case of Christianity, were a 'stumbling block' over which the majority of the Jews fell, thereby failing to accept Christ (1 Cor. 1:23).

The Rapture

The Bahá'í writings not only provide an explanation of 'clouds' but also address the issue of the Rapture. Many conservative Christians believe that when Christ returns 'in the clouds' as prophesied in Matthew, the believers will be raised up to meet Him in the air. This concept is known as the 'Rapture'. Christians who regard the resurrection of Jesus as a literal event believe that it constitutes proof that Jesus can and will also raise His followers from the dead when He returns. The verses cited most often to support the belief in the Rapture are found in 1 Thessalonians 4:16-17. Paul writes:

> For the Lord Himself will descend from heaven with a shout, with the voice of an archangel, and with the trumpet of God. And the dead in Christ will rise first. Then we who are alive and remain shall be caught up together with them in the clouds to meet the Lord in the air.

Christians have traditionally interpreted this passage literally, but the Bahá'í writings clearly indicate that its terminology is symbolic and its meaning spiritual. Bahá'u'lláh writes:

> The shout hath been raised, and the people have come forth from their graves, and arising, are gazing around them. Some have made haste to attain the court of the God of Mercy, others have fallen down on their faces in the fire of Hell, while still others are lost in bewilderment. The verses of God have been revealed, and yet they have turned away from them. His proof hath been manifested, and yet they are unaware of it. And when they behold the face of the All-Merciful, their own faces are saddened, while they are disporting themselves. They

> hasten forward to Hell Fire, and mistake it for light. Far from God be what they fondly imagine! Say: Whether ye rejoice or whether ye burst for fury, the heavens are cleft asunder, and God hath come down, invested with radiant sovereignty. All created things are heard exclaiming: 'The Kingdom is God's, the Almighty, the All-Knowing, the All-Wise'. (*Gleanings* 41-2)

There are many other references in the Bahá'í writings which indicate the spiritual nature of the Rapture. In one passage, 'Abdu'l-Bahá tells the believers that 'through the power of the Word of God ye will bring to life the dead now buried in the graves of their sensual desires' (*Selections from the Writings of 'Abdu'l-Bahá* 37). In another passage, 'Abdu'l-Bahá says that the believers 'have risen upward to the refreshing skies of love' (ibid.). This last phrase is similar to a passage by Bahá'u'lláh that was specifically addressed to Christians:

> Blessed is the man who hath detached himself from all else but Me, hath soared in the atmosphere of My love . . . and hath shone forth from the horizon of divine knowledge engaged in My praise and glorification. (*Tablets of Bahá'u'lláh* 17)

From a Bahá'í point of view, the meaning of Paul's depiction of Christ's return and the Rapture lies in the symbolism of such terms as 'heaven', 'clouds', 'dead in Christ' and 'air'. An interpretation of 1 Thessalonians 4:16-17 may be as follows: The 'dead in Christ' signifies those 'dead in unbelief' (*Certitude* 114), those who have fallen away from the religious life. The 'dead in Christ will rise first' indicates that, in a general sense, many of the first to believe in Bahá'u'lláh will be those who have died spiritually because they have abandoned religious life.

Following these verses, Paul says, 'Then we who are alive and remain shall be caught up together with them in the clouds to meet the Lord in the air'. This appears to refer to those who are still faithful to Christ and who await His return. These would be the next to embrace the Revelation of Bahá'u'lláh and to be caught up in the 'clouds of knowledge' (*Gleanings* 45), that is, the next to have their lives changed and raised up spiritually by the divine teachings and laws (*Certitude* 71-2).

Based on this interpretation, the promised Rapture has already taken place. The Bahá'ís constitute the 'dead' and 'living' who have been raised up into the clouds of heaven. Bahá'u'lláh writes:

> Speed out of your sepulchres. How long will ye sleep? The second blast hath been blown on the trumpet. On whom are ye gazing? This is your Lord, the God of Mercy. (*Gleanings* 44)

And in the words of 'Abdu'l-Bahá:

> The light hath shone forth, and radiance floodeth Mount Sinai, and a gentle wind bloweth from over the gardens of the Ever-Forgiving Lord; the sweet breaths of the spirit are passing by, and those who lay buried in the grave are rising up - and still do the heedless slumber on in their tombs. (*Selections from the Writings of 'Abdu'l-Bahá* 14)

Thus far we have seen how the Bahá'í writings provide an understanding of the symbolic meanings of Christ's return in the clouds and of the Rapture of the believers. But it would be a great omission not to note and explain the specific character of this appearance in the clouds. Jesus states that the Son of Man will come on the clouds of heaven 'with power and great glory'.

The Meaning of 'With Power and Great Glory'

Christ's return in 'glory' is a theme which is central to the prophecies of the Old Testament (e.g. Ezek. 43:1-2; Isa. 35:2, 40:5), the prophecies of the New Testament (e.g. Mark 8:38, 13:26; Rev. 21:23), and to Bahá'u'lláh's claims. Addressing Christians, Bahá'u'lláh writes:

> Day and night ye have been calling upon your Lord, the Omnipotent, but when He came from the heaven of eternity in His great glory, ye turned aside from Him and remained sunk in heedlessness. (*Tablets of Bahá'u'lláh* 9)

In stating that He has come 'from the heaven of eternity in His great glory', Bahá'u'lláh indicates that His appearance is the fulfilment of Jesus' prophecy that 'the Son of Man' will come 'on the clouds of heaven with power and great glory' (Matt. 24:30).

The glory of Christ is seen by many Christians in the Resurrection because it represents Christ's triumph over death, but they believe that

Christ's glory will be especially revealed at the time of His return. Traditionally, many Christians have believed that when Christ returns at the end of the age, He will be opposed by the forces of evil in an epic battle of unparalleled carnage, which some regard as the battle of Armageddon mentioned in Scripture.[144] Jesus' triumph in this battle is supposed to reveal His power and glory.

According to conservative Christian belief, Satan's human agent, the beast, will gain the allegiance of 'the kings of the earth' and will lead them into battle against Christ and His hosts. This is based on the Book of Revelation, chapter 19:

> And I saw the beast, the kings of the earth, and their armies, gathered together to make war against Him who sat on the horse and against His army. Then the beast was captured, and with him the false prophet who worked signs in his presence, by which he deceived those who received the mark of the beast and those who worshipped his image. These two were cast alive into the lake of fire burning with brimstone. And the rest were killed with the sword which proceeded from the mouth of Him who sat on the horse. (Rev. 19:19-21)

According to Scripture, Christ and His hosts are victorious and Satan[145] is bound for 'a thousand years' (Rev. 20:2). The beast is believed by some Christians to be a totalitarian world ruler.[146]

From a Bahá'í point of view, these biblical passages have an inward spiritual significance. The battle is a spiritual battle and the victory is the triumph of Bahá'u'lláh's Faith over those who opposed Him and over the evil in the world which stands in opposition to the truth of His Cause.

Therefore, the power of the Second Advent is, in fact, revealed

144. The war mentioned in Revelation 19:17-21 is linked by some Christians to the term Armageddon, which appears only once in the Bible (Rev. 16:16). Ezekiel 39:1-4, among others, is also believed by some Christians to be a description of the same battle of Armageddon.

145. The word Satan, in Greek 'satanas', comes from the Hebrew meaning opponent, adversary, arch enemy of good. It can signify any arch enemy of the Prophet or the tendency within anyone to oppose God's will, especially in the sense of creating conflict, adversarial relations and disunity.

146. As already mentioned in the commentary on Matt. 24:15, 'Abdu'l-Bahá explains that the beast mentioned in the eleventh chapter of the Book of Revelation refers to evil individuals of the Umayyad dynasty who usurped power in the Faith of Islam (see *Some Answered Questions* chs. 11 and 13), and seriously damaged the development of Islam. The war against the 'two witnesses' (Rev. 11:7) is correlated with the Umayyads wrongfully opposing 'the religion of Muhammad' and 'the reality of 'Alí', the rightful successor of Muhammad (see *Some Answered Questions* 60). The symbolism of the Book of

David Roberts' nineteenth-century depiction of 'Akká. Bahá'u'lláh, along with His family and a few followers, arrived here as exiles in the late afternoon of 31 August 1868. Many years later, Bahá'u'lláh's son, 'Abdu'l-Bahá, remarked, 'It is difficult to understand how Bahá'u'lláh could have been obliged to leave Persia, and to pitch His tent in this Holy Land, but for the persecution of His enemies, His banishment and exile'. (As quoted in *God Passes By*.)

through the persecutions and afflictions Bahá'u'lláh suffered. His suffering reveals His power because the truth of His words and the spirituality of His life could not be overcome and destroyed by His persecutors and adversaries. His power is, therefore, manifest in His spiritual invincibility. His glory is evident in His triumph over the persecution He suffered.[147] The triumph of His Cause and its spiritual transformation of the people who accept His teachings is another sign of His victory over the forces of evil.

Revelation and many of the characteristics of Islam bear out 'Abdu'l-Bahá's interpretation. Moreover, it is entirely reasonable that the rise of a major world religion (i.e., Islam) in the Holy Land would be mentioned and figure prominently in John's vision. 'Abdu'l-Bahá sees the course of Islam (*Some Answered Questions*, chs. 11, 13), the unfolding of the Bahá'í Faith (*Selections from the Writing of 'Abdu'l-Bahá* 12-13), and some current world events all revealed in the Book of Revelation (see *Tablets of the Divine Plan* 45). The symbolism of the Book of Revelation and many of the characteristics of Islam support 'Abdu'l-Bahá's interpretations and provide us with a basis for understanding how later sections might relate to the opposition which Bahá'u'lláh encountered and over which He ultimately triumphed. The beast and false prophet described in these later chapters of Revelation are likely to be symbolic of individuals, such as Siyyid Muhammad and Mírzá Yahyá, who opposed Bahá'u'lláh and did so much to inflict harm upon Him and His followers. See Shoghi Effendi, *God Passes By*, esp. ch. 10.

147. This understanding is also conveyed in the Bahá'í writings with regard to Christ. 'Abdu'l-Bahá writes: 'Bahá'ís say that the sovereignty of Christ was a heavenly, divine, everlasting sovereignty, not a Napoleonic sovereignty that vanisheth in a short time. For well nigh two thousand years this sovereignty of Christ hath been established, and until now it endureth, and to all eternity that Holy Being will be exalted upon an everlasting throne' (*Selections from the Writings of 'Abdu'l-Bahá* 45-6).

A recent photo of the interior of the cell where Bahá'u'lláh was imprisoned. Bahá'u'lláh chose to designate this prison the 'Most Great Prison'. (*Photo courtesy of the Bahá'í World Centre, Audio-Visual Department.*)

His power and glory are not concerned with a temporal victory such as a military general seeks but are, rather, seen in His spiritual victory - His triumph despite the rejection and persecution He suffered. He does not come in the glory of men but, as it says in the Scriptures, in 'the glory of the Father' (Mark 8:38).

God's 'glory' is perceived in the revelation of God's spiritual presence and divine attributes. The significance and appropriateness of Bahá'u'lláh's name, which means 'the glory of God', is made evident by the divine nature of His Person and Revelation. His life reveals that real glory does not depend on material property, the support of popular opinion or temporal victories. Real glory - spiritual glory - is revealed in the triumph of the religious life. It is a glory attainable even to those who are among the poorest of the poor or who are, to all outward appearances, defeated even to the point of death.

'Abdu'l-Bahá explains that the teachings for which Bahá'u'lláh has suffered are the real means by which people 'may attain to glory':

> if man lives up to these divine commandments, this world of earth shall be transformed into the world of heaven, and this

> material sphere shall be converted into a paradise of glory. It is my hope that you may become successful in this high calling so that like brilliant lamps you may cast light upon the world of humanity and quicken and stir the body of existence like unto a spirit of life. This is eternal glory. (*Promulgation* 470)

On a different occasion, He stated:

> Man must be lofty in endeavour. He must seek to become heavenly and spiritual, to find the pathway to the threshold of God and become acceptable in the sight of God. This is eternal glory - to be near to God. (Ibid. 186)

The validity of the Bahá'í understanding of 'power and glory' can be seen in the biblical teachings about the sacrifice of Christ. The Bible indicates that Christ's suffering was not a sign of humiliation, powerlessness or defeat. Paul states that to the spiritually minded this suffering reveals the power and wisdom of God:

> For Jews request a sign, and Greeks seek after wisdom; but we preach Christ crucified, to the Jews a stumbling block and to the Greeks foolishness, but to those who are called, both Jews and Greeks, Christ the power of God and the wisdom of God. (1 Cor. 1:22-4)

Another passage which affirms this understanding can be found in the Book of Revelation:

> Worthy is the Lamb who was slain to receive power and riches and wisdom, and strength and honour and glory and blessing! (Rev. 5:12)

This message is also apparent in Bahá'u'lláh's words concerning His oppressors, 'They are, however, oblivious of the fact that abasement in the path of God is My true glory' (*Epistle* 125).

Therefore, from a Bahá'í point of view, Christians who are awaiting the fulfilment of Matthew 24:30 - the coming of Christ with power and glory - should not look for an epic military battle at the time of the end but, rather, should look to the power and glory already revealed in the suffering and imprisonment of Bahá'u'lláh. They should look to the victory that is attained by all those who truly know Bahá'u'lláh and practise His teachings.

HE WILL SEND FORTH HIS ANGELS

> 31 *And he shall send his angels with a great sound of a trumpet, and they shall gather together his elect*[148] *from the four winds, from one end of heaven to the other.*

COMMENTARY (24:31)

The Meaning of Angels

Christians who believe that Jesus' Olivet Discourse is not about the return of Christ but about the coming victory of Christ through the establishment of the Church, believe that the 'gathering together of the elect' refers to the missionary outreach of the Church. That is, it represents the process of Christians (angels) travelling throughout the earth and converting (gathering together) new persons (His elect) to the cause of Christ.

The more commonly-accepted view argues that the gathering together of the elect refers to angels of Christ bringing together all the true Christians at the time of Christ's return. This view coincides with Bahá'u'lláh's explanation:

> And now, concerning His words: 'And He shall send His angels . . .' By 'angels' is meant those who, reinforced by the power of the spirit, have consumed, with the fire of the love of God, all human traits and limitations, and have clothed

148. The 'elect' is from the Greek '*eklektos*' and literally signifies those picked out or the ones chosen.

> themselves with the attributes of the most exalted Beings and of the Cherubim.[149] (*Certitude* 78-9)

This passage indicates that angels signify, or can refer to, persons living in this world whose lives are completely sanctified. In a later passage, He adds:

> And now, inasmuch as these holy beings have sanctified themselves from every human limitation, have become endowed with the attributes of the spiritual, and have been adorned with the noble traits of the blessed, they therefore have been designated as 'angels'. (*Certitude* 79-80)

In other references, Bahá'u'lláh indicates that this prophecy concerning angels has been fulfilled in this day:

> This is the Day whereon the All-Merciful hath come down in the clouds of knowledge, clothed with manifest sovereignty. He well knoweth the actions of men. He it is Whose glory none can mistake, could ye but comprehend it. The heaven of every religion hath been rent, and the earth of human understanding been cleft asunder, and the angels of God are seen descending. (*Proclamation* 98)

These passages suggest that Matthew 24:31 involves the appearance of Christ, who, upon His return, sends His followers out to proclaim His appearance and gather those who are receptive to His message into one common Faith. Bahá'ís recognize that this is exactly what Bahá'u'lláh has done. He has sent out His followers to proclaim and teach His Cause:

> Arise thou to serve the Cause of thy Lord; then give the people the joyful tidings concerning this resplendent Light whose revelation hath been announced by God through His Prophets and Messengers. (*Tablets of Bahá'u'lláh* 242)

149. In the Bible the term 'Cherubim' signifies beings who are possibly of a high order of angels and who, in some instances, accompany the Presence of God. Figures of Cherubim were part of the symbolism wrought into the mercy seat of the Temple's Holy of Holies. See, e.g., Exod. 25:18-22, and also Ps. 80:1, 99:1. However, some passages suggest a greater distinction from angels. For a discussion of their symbolism and origins see James Strong, *The Tabernacle of Israel* 80-90, 132-3.

> Verily, We behold you from Our realm of glory, and shall aid whosoever will arise for the triumph of Our Cause with the hosts of the Concourse on high and a company of Our favoured angels. (*Synopsis and Codification* 16)

> They that have forsaken their country for the purpose of teaching Our Cause - these shall the Faithful Spirit strengthen through its power. A company of Our chosen angels shall go forth with them, as bidden by Him Who is the Almighty, the All-Wise. (*Gleanings* 334)

Today Bahá'u'lláh's message has been spread to all nations, and millions of souls have embraced His Faith throughout the entire world. They represent individuals from all the world's religions. Thus the elect have been and are being gathered together 'from one end of heaven to the other'. 'Abdu'l-Bahá states:

> Array yourselves in the perfection of divine virtues. I hope you may be quickened and vivified by the breaths of the Holy Spirit. Then shall ye indeed become the angels of heaven whom Christ promised would appear in this Day to gather the harvest of divine planting. This is my hope. This is my prayer for you. (*Promulgation* 7)

The Sound of the Trumpet

Other passages in the Bahá'í writings also indicate that the 'great sound of the trumpet' has been heard through the proclamation of Bahá'u'lláh:

> Arise, and proclaim unto the entire creation the tidings that He Who is the All-Merciful hath directed His steps towards the Ridván and entered it. Guide, then, the people unto the garden of delight which God hath made the Throne of His Paradise. We have chosen thee [His pen] to be our most mighty Trumpet, whose blast is to signalize the resurrection of all mankind. (*Gleanings* 31, clarification added)

Trumpets are used to announce the approach of a King or the proclamation of a decree, or announcement. The trumpet symbolizes Bahá'u'lláh's

Revelation, which calls people to God and announces the Glad-Tidings of God's word amongst humankind. The meaning of Jesus' words (Matt. 24:31) is essentially about the proclamation of the Faith of God. When Bahá'u'lláh states, 'We have chosen thee to be our most mighty Trumpet', He is referring to His Revelation and calling upon the believers to carry His message to the people of the world.

PART IV

THE COMMAND TO WATCH

THE PARABLE OF THE FIG TREE

[32] *Now learn a parable of the fig tree; When his branch is yet tender, and putteth forth leaves, ye know that summer is nigh:*
[33] *So likewise ye, when ye shall see all these things, know that it is near, even at the doors.*

COMMENTARY (24:32-3)

The Spiritual Life of Mankind

In this parable of the fig tree, we have an analogy applicable to the changes that will take place in the spiritual life of humankind and in the institutions of religion. Like the seasons, our spiritual life has cycles. This type of decline and renewal is seen in the life of the nation Israel as portrayed in the Old Testament. Most significantly, the transformation brought about by Moses can be likened to a spiritual Springtime. The appearance of Christ is another example of a Divine Springtime in the history of the world. 'Abdu'l-Bahá specifically points out the appropriateness of this analogy, of one season following upon another, to suggest the progressive and organic nature of humankind's spiritual life, the course and evolution of religion:

> The spiritual world is like unto the phenomenal world. They are the exact counterpart of each other. Whatever objects appear in this world of existence are the outer pictures of the world of heaven. When we look upon the phenomenal world, we perceive that it is divided into four seasons; one is the season of spring, another the season of summer, another autumn and then these three seasons are followed by winter.

> When the season of spring appears in the arena of existence, the whole world is rejuvenated and finds new life. The soul-refreshing breeze is wafted from every direction; the soul-quickening bounty is everywhere; the cloud of mercy showers down its rain, and the sun shines upon everything. Day by day we perceive that the signs of vegetation are all about us. Wonderful flowers, hyacinths and roses perfume the nostrils. The trees are full of leaves and blossoms, and the blossoms are followed by fruit. The spring and summer are followed by autumn and winter. The flowers wither and are no more; the leaves turn grey and life has gone. Then comes another springtime; the former springtime is renewed; again a new life stirs within everything.
>
> The appearances of the Manifestations of God are the divine springtime. When Christ appeared in this world, it was like the vernal bounty; the outpouring descended; the effulgences of the Merciful encircled all things; the human world found new life. Even the physical world partook of it. The divine perfections were upraised; souls were trained in the school of heaven so that all grades of human existence received life and light. Then by degrees these fragrances of heaven were discontinued; the season of winter came upon the world; the beauties of spring vanished; the excellences and perfections passed away; the lights and quickening were no longer evident; the phenomenal world and its materialities conquered everything; the spiritualities of life were lost; the world of existence became life unto a lifeless body; there was no trace of the spring left.
>
> Bahá'u'lláh has come into this world. He has renewed that springtime. The same fragrances are wafting; the same heat of the Sun is giving life; the same cloud is pouring its rain, and with our own eyes we see that the world of existence is advancing and progressing. The human world has found new life. (*Promulgation* 10)

In the parable of the fig tree, 'these things' refers to the putting forth of leaves, which happens in the springtime, and that which is 'near' is summer. Christ states that 'when you see these things, know that it is near'. But it is not clear which of the things Christ has spoken of in His discourse is being likened to the putting forth of leaves. Is it the tribulation (v. 29), the sign that is to appear in heaven (v. 30), and/or the sending forth of His angels (v. 31)? And what does He mean by 'it' is near? Is 'it' the tribulation, the appearance of Christ, or the establishment of the Kingdom of God on earth?

From the general applicability of the parable, it could represent any of these things. The truth of the message is quite simple: events must and will precede one another according to an appropriate and divinely pre-ordained plan. Spiritual decline will lead to tribulation and then the Son of Man will appear to deliver the believers. His appearance, similarly, precedes the sending forth of His 'angels' and the establishment of His Kingdom.

In many passages, the Bahá'í Scriptures recall this parable of the fig tree, inasmuch as the appearance of Bahá'u'lláh's Revelation is likened to a divine springtime. Bahá'u'lláh proclaims the 'Divine Springtime is come' (*Gleanings* 27). In one passage He writes:

> O friends! It behoveth you to refresh and revive your souls through the gracious favours which in this Divine, this soul-stirring Springtime are being showered upon you. The Day Star of His great glory hath shed its radiance upon you, and the clouds of His limitless grace have overshadowed you. How high the reward of him that hath not deprived himself of so great a bounty, nor failed to recognize the beauty of his Best-Beloved in this, His new attire. (Ibid. 94)

This divine springtime is experienced in the effect the Revelation of God - Bahá'u'lláh's appearance and teachings - has on the personal life of the believer, and in the effect this experience has, in turn, on the world around us. 'Abdu'l-Bahá explains:

> If you abide by the precepts and teachings of the Blessed Perfection [Bahá'u'lláh], the heavenly world and ancient Kingdom will be yours - eternal happiness, love and everlasting life. The divine bounties are flowing. Each one of you has been given the opportunity of becoming a tree yielding abundant fruits. This is the springtime of Bahá'u'lláh. The

> verdure and foliage of spiritual growth are appearing in great abundance in the gardens of human hearts. (*Promulgation* 9, clarification added)

Jesus' use of metaphors and symbols, such as the fig tree putting forth leaves, provided His followers with references to natural phenomena which could serve as continual reminders of His assurances and teachings. In every instance, we have seen that such symbolism appears to be an integral part of Jesus' discourse. It gives every statement numerous spiritual meanings which go beyond ordinary and limited contexts. Yet, despite this use of symbolism, Jesus' words have frequently been interpreted in a very limited manner, even to the extent that some people have assumed He was mistaken in what He was saying. This is the case with the next verse.

ALL THESE THINGS WILL BE FULFILLED

> 34 *Verily I say unto you, This generation shall not pass, till all these things be fulfilled.*
> 35 *Heaven and earth shall pass away, but my words shall not pass away.*
> 36 *But of that day and hour knoweth no man, no, not the angels of heaven, but my Father only.*

COMMENTARY (24:34-6)

The Meaning of 'This Generation'

The words 'this generation shall not pass, till all these things be fulfilled' have caused great difficulty for Christians who interpret 'all these things' as a reference to the events following the tribulation, or preceding it, or both. Similarly, 'this generation' has been understood to mean those who were living at the time of Christ or those living at the end time. Some have also argued that 'this generation' has a more elastic meaning embracing the Jewish or Christian peoples.[150] These points and other related ones have been heavily debated. Some even assert that Christ Himself mistakenly thought His return would come within His generation. Others have argued that the verse was added later and is not part of Jesus' discourse. This theory, for example, is based on the assertion that the author misunderstood Jesus and believed these prophecies would take place very soon.[151]

If we interpret 'this generation' as the generation living at the time of Christ, then 'all these things' cannot refer to the Second Advent. In biblical language, a generation would probably be understood as forty years (e.g., Ps. 95:10). This would mean we could then know that Christ would have returned in roughly forty years. As we have seen in the prophecies of Daniel, the Bible does give guidance which seems to indicate clearly when the appearance of Christ would take place, as well as when His return would occur. These interpretations, however, can only be verified by comparing them with the timing of the first and second appearances inasmuch as Christ is most emphatic that 'of that day and hour no one knows, no, not even the angels of heaven' (Matt. 24:36). With this verse in mind, it must be accepted that the only sure way to verify that an interpretation is correct is by the fulfilment of the prophecy. To argue that we know when Christ was to return based on our understanding of the phrase 'this generation' is to fail to balance our interpretation with the statements Christ made. Similarly, it cannot be argued that Christ Himself, or those who recorded His statements, misunderstood when the Second Advent was to occur - that is, that Christ or the writer of Matthew 24 believed it would take place within a generation of the end of Christ's first ministry - since the parables that follow, in Chapter 25, contain strong suggestions of a delayed return.

Therefore, if 'this generation' refers to those living at the time of Christ, 'all these things' must have meant all these things which He stated would inaugurate 'the beginning of sorrows' (Matt. 24:8); that is, the emergence of false teachers and their laying of the foundation for future

150. Ryrie writes, 'the Greek word can mean "race" or "family", which makes good sense here; i.e., the Jewish race will be preserved, in spite of terrible persecution, until the Lord comes' (*The Ryrie Study Bible* 52). This view has a host of supporters including Lange, Alford, Stier, Calovius, Auberlen, Dorner, Riggenbach, Jansen, Storr, Heubner, Hebart, Scofield, Gaebelein, Petingill, Morgan, Wordsworth, Torrey, Blackstone and Mackintosh. Others such as Ellicott, Olshausen, Meyer and Godet maintain that this verse simply refers to the generation living at the time of Christ, the signs being fulfilled then.

151. See G.R. Beasley-Murray, *Jesus and the Future* 2-3 ff.

strife in the Church. It could also include the actual destruction of the Jerusalem Temple in AD 70 and the symbolic destruction of the Temple represented in the crucifixion and the fleeing of the Apostles (Matt. 26:56).

If Jesus is referring to the generation living in the 'end times', it can easily be argued that His words were fulfilled. The generation of Bahá'u'lláh's contemporaries saw, from a Bahá'í point of view, the tribulation, the coming of the Son of Man with great power and glory, and the sending forth of His angels. Also, the generation which persecuted Bahá'u'lláh was in spirit the same as the generation which persecuted Christ, and in this sense they were the return of the generation of Christ's time. This understanding is suggested by Bahá'u'lláh in His explanation of the meaning of return.[152] If, however, we understand the passage in a broader sense, that is, as a reference to the whole community of Christ's followers, the Church throughout the ages, this too is consistent with history.

His Words Will Not Pass Away

Reinforcing Christ's assurance that His prophecies will take place are His words that 'Heaven and earth shall pass away, but my words shall not pass away'. As we have already noted, Bahá'u'lláh has affirmed that:

> whatsoever hath proceeded out of His [Christ's] blameless, His truth-speaking, trustworthy mouth, can never be altered. (*Tablets of Bahá'u'lláh* 14)

Bahá'u'lláh teaches that the divinity of God's Manifestations is eternal. Thus Christ's sovereignty - that is, His Lordship for example - is eternal. Even though Lordship is manifested outwardly through rulership of others, the Lordship of the Manifestations exists because of the spiritual and divine reality of their nature and is not dependent on outward dominion. In other words, it is possible to affirm clearly that Christ, Muhammad, Bahá'u'lláh, or any Manifestation of God, are Lord by the evidence of their rule over the hearts of their followers. However, this does not mean that the Manifestations would not have any Lordship if they had no followers or no dominion in this world. This is because, unlike worldly rulers such as kings,

152. See *Certitude* 158ff. This would explain the prophecy which states that when Christ returns, everyone will see Him, including 'they also who pierced Him' (Rev. 1:7), meaning the Roman soldier who put a spear into the side of Christ while He was on the Cross (John 19:34).

the Manifestations do not owe their power to those whom they rule. The station of the Manifestations comes from, and is a reflection of, God's eternal sovereignty.

The verse, 'Heaven and earth shall pass away, but my words shall not pass away', clearly suggests the eternal nature of the truth of Jesus' words, the Gospel. However, if we interpret the words 'heaven' and 'earth' in accordance with explanations Bahá'u'lláh provides in *The Book of Certitude*, we can find added understanding which reinforces this verse's clear meaning. If the word 'heaven' is understood as religion and 'earth' as human understanding, then the verse, 'Heaven and earth shall pass away', may be a way of saying that the institution of Christianity and the believers' understanding of the religion will pass away, but that the Gospel itself, both the actual Book and the eternal truth expressed in it, will never pass away.

The Unknown Hour

Even though Christ assures the disciples that all these things He has prophesied will take place and that His word will not pass away, He tells them that the hour in which these things will occur is unknown to all except God: 'But of that day and hour knoweth no man, no, not the angels of heaven, but my Father only'. The word 'hour' is from the Greek 'hora' and means, primarily, any period of time. In the context of verse 36 it probably does not mean a particular hour but, rather, the 'Day of the Lord'. Matthew Henry writes:

> But as to that day and hour which will put a period of time, that knoweth no man, v. 36 . . There is a certain day and hour fixed for the judgment to come; it is called the day of the Lord. (*Matthew Henry's Commentary*, vol. V, 361)

Jesus states that not even the angels of heaven know the hour, only God. In Mark it is written, 'not even the angels in heaven, nor the Son, but only the Father' (Mark 13:32).[153]

153. Matthew Henry comments on this inclusion of 'nor the Son': 'But it [v. 32] follows, neither the Son; but is there anything which the Son is ignorant of? There were those in the primitive times, who taught from this text, that there were some things that Christ, as man, was ignorant of; they said, "It was no more absurd to say so than to say that his human soul suffered grief and fear". Christ, as God, could not be ignorant of anything; but the divine wisdom which dwelt in our Saviour, did communicate itself to his human soul, according to the divine pleasure, so that his human nature might sometimes not know some things; therefore Christ is said to grow in wisdom (Luke 2:52)' (*Matthew Henry's Commentary*, vol. V, 544).

In an obvious reference to the hour of which Jesus spoke, Bahá'u'lláh proclaims to the Christian world:

> The Hour which We had concealed from the knowledge of the peoples of the earth and of the favoured angels hath come to pass. (*Tablets of Bahá'u'lláh* 11)

Bahá'u'lláh follows this proclamation with the words:

> Say, verily, He hath testified of Me, and I do testify of Him. Indeed, He hath purposed no one other than Me. Unto this beareth witness every fair-minded and understanding soul. (Ibid. 11)

These words demonstrate the Messianic nature of Bahá'u'lláh's claims and emphasize that, from the Bahá'í point of view, the concealed hour spoken of in Matthew 24:36 and in Mark 13:32 concerns the end of the age. In another Tablet Bahá'u'lláh writes:

> The mysteries of Resurrection and the events of the Last Hour are openly manifest, but the people are sunk in heedlessness and have suffered themselves to be wrapt in veils. (Ibid. 40-1)

Bahá'u'lláh adds:

> By the righteousness of God! The Dawn hath truly brightened and the light hath shone forth and the night hath receded. Happy are they that comprehend. Happy are they that have attained thereunto. (Ibid. 41)

Naturally, Christians during the nineteenth century were confronted by the difficulty that while they believed the prophecies were being fulfilled in a way clearer and surer than ever before, nevertheless the New Testament stated that 'no one knoweth the hour'. This issue was therefore taken up by many commentators. H.G. Guinness, for example, believed that some elements of prophecy built up to a culmination in history, and therefore, 'It can be no wonder that, as the page of history has unrolled itself, greater accuracy should have been attained, than it was possible for earlier students to possess' (*Approaching End of the Age* 130). For many Christians, this reasoning explained why Christians in earlier centuries did not seem to understand the prophecies as clearly. Elaborating on the progressive nature of the Christian understanding of prophecy, Guinness writes:

> The glory of God is declared by every prophecy. His foreknowledge is one of his highest attributes. His people are comforted, and their faith is strengthened, when they find that the experiences through which they are passing, the troubles that are befalling them, or the difficulties that they encounter, have been foreseen and foretold by their God. But there are some things which it is better for God's people not to know beforehand; as for instance the true length of the present period of the absence of Christ from his church. Divine wisdom and love judged it best, as we have seen, to conceal from the early church the foreordained duration of this Christian age, and to allow every generation of Christians to live in the expectation of the speedy return of their Lord. 'Known unto God are all his works from the beginning of the world.' He of course knew that over eighteen centuries would elapse before the second coming of Christ, and could very easily have revealed this in plain words to the church. He did not do so, as is proved by the fact that the early generations of Christians expected the return of Christ in their own day. If then God, for the guidance of his people especially during its later stages, wished to reveal the events of this period, without revealing its duration, He must needs adopt a style of prediction, which would reveal while concealing and conceal while revealing, the truth. This is exactly what He has done. The revelations granted to Daniel and John, relating to the events of this dispensation, are not couched in ordinary language, or made in plain terms, which admit of no second meaning. They are embodied in mysterious symbolic forms, which require to be translated before they can be understood. They are not incomprehensible; very far from that! Incomprehensible prophecy could answer no conceivable object. But prophecy which would be obscure for a time, and clear only after the lapse of ages, would answer the object

> supposed above, of concealing from one generation that which it would not be desirable for it to know, while revealing it to a succeeding one, to which the knowledge was indispensable. (*Approaching End of the Age* 294-5)[154]

However, this only hints at an answer to the question arising from the statement 'no one knoweth the hour'. Some, therefore, were compelled to argue that this passage simply indicated that the literal day and hour could not be known, but that 'prophecy reveals the *proximate* period when it will take place' (Shimeall, *The Second Coming* 304, emphasis added). History would agree that the literal day and hour remained unknown prior to its dawning, but the actual Greek does not necessitate such a strict literal reading. Jesus' emphatic statement that no one knows this hour is therefore believed by many to bring into question all attempts to calculate the time of Christ's return. It seems a direct contradiction that, on the one hand, no one knows the hour, and on the other, many Bible scholars who interpreted Scripture indicate the hour as the year 1844. For some who reject that the Second Advent occurred in 1844, verse 36 appears an added confirmation that their rejection is sound. In actuality, verse 36 should be a warning to the critics that they cannot be certain that the predicted 'hour' - that is, 1844 - was not the right hour.

To those who accept that 1844 was the 'hour' foretold in the Scriptures, 'no one knows' must at least suggest the uncertainty of human knowledge and human interpretations of Scripture - even though they may later prove right. Scripture, therefore, demands humility from the believer. The most important point is this: no one can say with certainty what date was foretold and then assert that Christ has failed to fulfil the promise of Scripture. Nor can the critic say with certainty that the scholars and believers who calculated the date 1844 were wrong.

Certain knowledge of this 'hour' lay with God alone. The Scriptures provided indications of the times for both the First and Second Advents of Christ; yet no one could be certain of an interpretation without Christ's appearance to confirm it. The Book of Daniel itself states, 'the words are

154. In more recent times, this view has been reaffirmed in the words of Le Roy Froom: 'Indeed, only as history actually unrolled the prophetic scroll through fulfilment, could its intent be perceived. To have unfolded clearly in unveiled terminology the spreading span of the intervening ages would doubtless have been to shake or crush the faith of the harassed martyr church. Yet for the prophets not to have spoken thus would have left God without this matchless predictive witness, and would have deprived later generations of the certainties of such prophetic declarations' (*The Prophetic Faith of Our Fathers*, vol. 1, 242).

closed up and sealed till the time of the end', and that 'none of the wicked shall understand, but the wise *shall* understand' (Dan. 12:9-10, emphasis added).

The proof, or truth, of a Prophet is not dependent on our fallible interpretations of Scripture but, rather, is made evident through His own perfections and divine teachings. The phrase 'no one knows' addresses the arrogance of rejecting a Prophet owing to demands that Scripture be fulfilled according to *our* expectations!

IT WILL BE AS IN THE DAYS OF NOAH

> 37 *But as the days of Noe*[155] *were, so shall also the coming of the Son of man be.*
> 38 *For as in the days that were before the flood they were eating and drinking, marrying and giving in marriage, until the day that Noe entered into the ark,*
> 39 *And knew not until the flood came, and took them all away; so shall also the coming of the Son of man be.*
> 40 *Then shall two be in the field; the one shall be taken, and the other left.*
> 41 *Two women shall be grinding at the mill; the one shall be taken, and the other left.*

COMMENTARY (24:37-41)

The Archetypal Nature of the Story of Noah

The Bahá'í teachings view the accounts of both the ark and the flood as symbolic.[156] When understood symbolically, these accounts provide a

155. The Old English rendering of 'Noah'.
156. This point is addressed in a letter written on behalf of Shoghi Effendi (the Guardian of the Bahá'i Faith) to an individual believer, October 28, 1949. See *Bahá'í News*, No. 228, February 1950, p. 4., or Helen Hornby, *Lights of Guidance* 378.

conceptual framework that is applicable to the ministry of every Prophet and the spiritual quest of every believer. For this reason, Jesus is able to use the story of Noah in relationship to His future return.

An examination of the Old Testament passages concerning Noah reveals the following essential characteristics: God sends a Messenger who warns the people that they must obey God's covenant to gain eternal life. The people ignore the warnings and are destroyed by the consequences (symbolized by the flood) which are brought on by their own disobedience (Gen. 6:6-7). Those who respond to the Prophet's message (i.e. enter into the ark) are saved. Entering the ark symbolizes entering into agreement with God, which essentially means accepting, and abiding by, God's covenant. Thus, Noah's ark has the same spiritual significance as the ark of the covenant (Deut. 10:8).

Most commentators connect Jesus' words 'as the days of Noah' to 'the days that were before the flood'. With this emphasis they argue that Jesus' message about the days of Noah is intended to draw a parallel between the time of the end and the sinfulness that brought on the flood. This interpretation is entirely plausible, but it should be noted that the emphasis provided by Jesus is not on any specific sins but on ordinary living: 'they were eating and drinking, marrying and giving in marriage, until the day that Noah entered the ark' (Matt. 24:38). Jesus says 'marrying', not fornicating and sinning.[157]

Jesus' warning may include a moral parallel, but the emphasis appears to be in the context of verse 36, which states, 'of that day and hour no one knows'. Thus, the people went on with their lives, failing to heed the warnings of Noah, 'and did not know until the flood came and took them away, so also will the coming of the Son of Man be' (Matt. 24:39).

Jesus' narration suggests that the people will not see the warnings, that while they are going about their personal business, as in the days of Noah, the returned Christ (the Son of Man) will have already led the faithful into the ark of deliverance. Their heedlessness of God's new Revelation will then bring about their inundation with suffering. This description aptly fits the unfolding of the world's response to Bahá'u'lláh's message, and the consequences which subsequently swept over the world.[158]

157. The account in Genesis clearly suggests that the flood was brought on because of 'the wickedness of man' (Gen. 6:5).

158. At the beginning of World War II, Shoghi Effendi, in a book entitled *The Promised Day Is Come*, outlined the world's sufferings in relationship to its rejection of Bahá'u'lláh and His teachings.

It is significant that in Luke's account Jesus prefaces the story of the flood with these words:

> But first He must suffer many things and be rejected by this generation. (Luke 17:25)

This passage is generally interpreted to mean that Jesus must suffer many things at the hands of the 'generation' then living, that is, the generation that crucified Him. Some Christians assume that Jesus will return and conquer His enemies militarily, therefore they argue that Jesus will not suffer when He returns. From this point of view, it appears that Luke 17:25 cannot refer to His Second Advent. However, from a Bahá'í point of view, the assumptions underlying this interpretation do not hold because God's victory, triumph and glory are not based on the concept of a material victory on a battlefield. Rather, God's victory is the triumph of His Word over sin. Hence, Jesus returns and defeats His enemies with a sword which comes out of His mouth (Rev. 19:21; Eph. 6:17). As stated earlier, this victory is realized in the triumph of the Revelation of Bahá'u'lláh over sin, over His oppressors, and in its spread throughout the world. Thus, Jesus' words that 'first He must suffer many things and be rejected by this generation' are also applicable to His return. 'This generation' refers to the generation living in the time of the end, the time of Bahá'u'lláh.

This interpretation of Luke 17:25 offers a framework for viewing the subsequent references to the days of Noah. Bahá'u'lláh must suffer and be rejected even as Noah suffered and was rejected. Then, heedless of His message, many are 'left', (i.e. brought down in the spiritual crises of this age) while others accept His Faith and are 'taken' (Matt. 24:40).

Modern Criticism of the Flood Story

Many modern critics have noted that different versions of the flood account appear in ancient myths and even extant myths among primitive cultures today. One of the most famous versions of the flood story is recounted in the Epic of Gilgamesh which is believed to predate the writing of Genesis. The parallels have led some to discount the validity or divine inspiration of the traditional biblical account. Some view it as simply an adaptation of an ancient myth. There are, however, several crucial differences between the story as it appears in the Epic of Gilgamesh and in the Book of Genesis. In the Gilgamesh version, the flood is the product of a quarrel between the gods, but in the Genesis account the story takes a moral direction and is cast in the context of humankind's relationship to God. The flood is thus divine retribution for the sinfulness of humankind. Salvation is ensured for those who respond to and are faithful to God's covenant.

The Genesis account uses the symbolism of the ancient flood story to demonstrate spiritual truths. An evaluation based solely on the relationship of the symbols to actual ancient historical floods, or on an explanation of how the symbol originated, is secondary to the account's message. The truth of the account does not rest upon the occurrence of a literal flood but on the internal evidence of our personal moral lives and our acceptance of God's teachings.

The flood story is a beautiful example of how the Prophets and authors of the Scriptures conveyed their inspiration. Even as God is symbolically described as forming man from clay and breathing into his nostrils the breath of life (Gen. 2:7), God breathed life into the words and accounts used in the Scriptures through the inspiration given to the writers of the Bible.

THE DAY OF JUDGEMENT

42 *Watch therefore: for ye know not what hour your Lord doth come.*

43 *But know this, that if the goodman of the house had known in what watch*[159] *the thief would come, he would have watched, and would not have suffered his house to be broken up.*

44 *Therefore be ye also ready: for in such an hour as ye think not the Son of man cometh.*

45 *Who then is a faithful and wise servant, whom his lord hath made ruler over his household, to give them meat in due season?*

46 *Blessed is that servant, whom his lord when he cometh shall find so doing.*

159. NKJV translates the Greek '*phulake*' as *hour* instead of *watch*.

47 *Verily I say unto you, That he shall make him ruler over all his goods.*
48 *But and if that evil servant shall say in his heart, My lord delayeth his coming;*
49 *And shall begin to smite his fellow servants, and to eat and drink with the drunken;*
50 *The lord of that servant shall come in a day when he looketh not for him, and in an hour that he is not aware of,*
51 *And shall cut him asunder, and appoint him his portion with the hypocrites: there shall be weeping and gnashing of teeth.*

COMMENTARY (24:42-51)

The Faithful Servant

In His writings, 'Abdu'l-Bahá suggests that those who have accepted Bahá'u'lláh are accounted as those who 'watched' and, thus, were ready when the Son of Man came upon them:

> Praise ye the Lord of Hosts for He, riding upon the clouds, hath come down to this world out of the heaven of the invisible realm, so that East and West were lit by the glory of the Sun of Truth, and the call of the Kingdom was raised, and the heralds of the realm above, with melodies of the Concourse on high, sang out the glad tidings of the Coming. Then the whole world of being did quiver for joy, and still the people, even as the Messiah saith, slept on: for the day of the Manifestation, when the Lord of Hosts descended, found them wrapped in the slumber of unknowing. As He saith in the Gospel, My coming is even as when the thief is in the house, and the goodman of the house watcheth not.
>
> From amongst all mankind hath He chosen you, and your eyes have been opened to the light of guidance and your ears attuned to the music of the Company above; and blessed by abounding grace, your hearts and souls have been born into new life. Thank ye and praise ye God that the hand of infinite bestowals hath set upon your heads this gem-studded crown, this crown whose lustrous jewels will

> forever flash and sparkle down all the reaches of time. (*Selections from the Writings of 'Abdu'l-Bahá* 35)

In this passage 'Abdu'l-Bahá links biblical prophecies with the appearance of Bahá'u'lláh and the faith of His followers. Bahá'u'lláh is identified as the Lord of Hosts (Ps. 24:10) who, in turn, 'Abdu'l-Bahá indicates is the Son of Man come in the clouds of Heaven (Matt. 24:30). The people who have failed to recognize Bahá'u'lláh are identified with those who did not follow Christ's instruction to watch for His coming (Matt. 24:42-3). The meaning of Jesus' promise to make the faithful servant who watches 'ruler over all his goods' is expressed by association with another biblical prophecy. 'Abdu'l-Bahá's words appear to refer to Peter's statement:

> when the Chief Shepherd appears, you will receive the crown of glory that does not fade away. (1 Pet. 5:4)

Thus, 'Abdu'l-Bahá may be suggesting that 'ruler over all his goods' (v. 47) is equivalent in meaning to attaining the 'crown of glory'. The reward is embodied in the spiritual life bestowed by the Lord of Hosts, who is the Chief Shepherd and Son of Man. Both promises express spiritual sovereignty, one with the word 'ruler' (v. 47) and the other with the word 'crown' (1 Peter 5:4). This rulership expresses the power of faith and the glory of spiritual victory which belong to those who recognize Bahá'u'lláh. In a letter to an individual, 'Abdu'l-Bahá wrote:

> Praise thou God that in this age, the age of the dispensation of Bahá'u'lláh, thou hast been awakened, hast been made aware of the Manifestation of the Lord of Hosts. All the people of the world are buried in the graves of nature, or are slumbering, heedless and unaware. Just as Christ saith: 'I may come when you are not aware. The coming of the Son of Man is like the coming of a thief into a house, the owner of which is utterly unaware.' (*Selections from the Writings of 'Abdu'l-Bahá* 198-9)[160]

It has been suggested that the main message of these verses (v. 42-50) is that the believer who wishes to be ready for Christ's return must remain

160. Cf. Rev. 3:3, 16:15; Luke 12:39; 1 Thes. 5:2, 4; 2 Pet. 3:10

faithful to His teachings.[161] This requires both watching for the signs of His appearance and following the religious life.

The story is about a servant and his master, but it is clear that it represents the believer - that is, the Christian - who awaits Christ's return. The parable implies that, for many, there is a moral deterrence in not knowing at what hour Christ will return. This is seen in the suggestion that, had the servant expected a quick return, he would have guarded himself against committing evil. Hence Scripture is intentionally cryptic and ambiguous concerning when the Second Advent will occur. Nevertheless, the story of the evil servant does hint at a long wait.

The evil servant surmises that his lord is delaying his return and, thus, the servant decides to take advantage of his master's absence to commit evil acts. The fact that the servant abuses his responsibility as guard of his master's household has led some to believe that the servant represents the clergy, who oversee the well-being of the congregation.

Christ concludes the story with the master returning and catching the evil servant whom he then punishes severely. The Messiah comes as judge, and judgement is meted out. Bahá'u'lláh writes:

> We have a fixed time for you, O peoples. If ye fail, at the appointed hour, to turn towards God, He, verily, will lay violent hold on you, and will cause grievous afflictions to assail you from every direction. How severe, indeed, is the chastisement with which your Lord will then chastise you! (*Gleanings* 214)

In verse 24:51, Christ states that the master cuts 'him asunder': literally, 'shall cut him in pieces' (ASV) or 'will cut him to pieces' (NIV). It has also been translated as 'will scourge him till his flesh is cut' (ML), but all these versions have obviously troubled some translators, and so we also find, 'will punish him' (RS).

The story should not be taken as literally describing what will actually befall the unwatchful and disobedient in the final hour. Understood symbolically, the story suggests that the disobedient will be separated from, or denied, the rewards of the believers. The message reflects Psalm 37:

> For evildoers shall be cut off;
> But those who wait on the LORD,

161. William Hendriksen, *New Testament Commentary* 871-4.

> They shall inherit the earth. (Ps. 37:9)

This theme is picked up again in verse 22:

> For those who are blessed by Him shall inherit the earth,
> But those who are cursed by Him shall be cut off.

Matthew Henry writes, 'His Lord shall cut him asunder, "he shall cut him off from the land of the living", from the congregation of the righteous, shall separate him unto evil' (*Matthew Henry's Commentary*, vol. V, 366).

Carson views the non-literal interpretation as unconvincing. 'Here, however, the wicked servant is not cut off from anything; he is cut in pieces - a most severe and awful punishment - and joins the hypocrites in weeping and grinding of teeth' (*Expositor's Bible Commentary*, vol. 8, 511).

Carson may have the meaning right with regard to the intended imagery of the story, but the literal imagery must be understood as only the story's form. The recognition of the Bahá'í Faith as fulfilment of the Olivet Discourse completely rules out a literal interpretation. Judgement in the end times does not pertain to a bloodbath for evil doers but, rather, should be understood spiritually. Every soul is called to judgement at the time of decision between belief and unbelief. That decision, like all choices, is followed by the consequences it warrants. The Bahá'í concept of judgement can be seen in 'Abdu'l-Bahá's commentary on Revelation 11:18:

> 'And the time of the dead, that they should be judged' means that the time has come that the dead - that is to say, those who are deprived of the spirit of the love of God and have not a share of the sanctified eternal life - will be judged with justice, meaning they will arise to receive that which they deserve. He will make the reality of their secrets evident, showing what a low degree they occupy in the world of existence, and that in reality they are under the rule of death. (*Some Answered Questions* 59)

Bahá'u'lláh writes:

> By the terms 'life' and 'death', spoken of in the scriptures, is intended the life of faith and the death of unbelief. (*Certitude* 114)

Thus, from a Bahá'í point of view, the judgement of 'life' or 'death', in this day, the end times, is decided by the act of belief or disbelief in the truth of Bahá'u'lláh's Revelation. It is a deeply personal experience characterized by each believer's relationship with God and acceptance of His Mediator. It is the decision that separates those who disbelieve from those who partake of the benefits of Bahá'u'lláh's Revelation and participate in the long-awaited establishment of the Kingdom of God on earth. Bahá'u'lláh writes:

> Blessed is the man that hath, on the wings of longing, soared towards God, the Lord of the Judgement Day. (*Epistle* 94)

EPILOGUE

EPILOGUE: AFTER THE NIGHT

'But the day of the Lord will come as a thief in the night'
St Peter (2 Pet. 3:10)

As many of the books cited in this commentary suggest, the beginning of the nineteenth century was a period in which many Christians were preoccupied with the study of prophecy. The Bible still carried enormous authority and Christianity stood as a powerful force in society. Many leaders of thought adhered firmly to a literal understanding of Scripture. Missionaries were engaged in evangelizing nations in all parts of the globe as the hope of Christ's return was being preached from pulpits and expounded in books throughout the Christian world. The extraordinary technological progress transforming society and the material prosperity of Western nations was frequently identified as the natural outcome of Christian belief. However, by the end of the century the prestige of Christianity, confidence in traditional beliefs, and Christian influence in government and education were all being rapidly eroded.

Developments both in science and religious scholarship completely changed how the generality of educated people perceived the Bible. The publications of scientists such as Sir Charles Lyell and Charles Darwin, and religious scholars like Schleiermacher, Mohler and Strauss led many to distrust or even abandon their belief in the inspiration of the Bible and the divinity of Christ.

Despite these trends there remained a substantial number of conservative Christians who continued to adhere to traditional views about the meaning of the Bible and who firmly believed that Christianity would be vindicated by the literal fulfilment of biblical prophecy. As the century drew to a close and it seemed that their interpretations of prophecy had been misguided, Christian scholars and preachers were confronted with having to admit they had been wrong about the Scriptures at a time when many of their followers were already beginning to doubt the Bible's reliability. The seeming lack of fulfilment following upon such high hopes at a time of such heavy criticism was a crushing blow to mainstream Christianity. Thereafter, a process of secularization gained a momentum that Christian leaders have never been able to halt.

While people were beginning to reject the inspiration of the Bible and to view prophecy with scepticism, the Faith of the Báb had successfully heralded the appearance of Bahá'u'lláh. This period, which came to be known by historians of Christianity as the 'Great Disappointment', had, in the lands of the Bible, witnessed the triumph of Bahá'u'lláh's Faith, despite severe persecution, and the beginnings of its steady spread throughout the world.

Its significance was as under-appreciated by the world as were the early beginnings of Christianity, but its birth and growth had not gone by unnoticed. Christian missionaries set forth accounts and appraisals of circumstances in foreign lands that were widely published and read. Slowly the emergence of the Bahá'í Faith began to be reported in books and missionary journals. All of the most well-known missionaries in Persia, men such as Dr George W. Holmes, P.Z. Easton, Dr Shedd, The Revd James W. Hawkes, The Revd J.N. Wright, The Revd J.L. Potter and many others, noted the early beginnings and emergence of the Faith and sent reports back to the West.

These reports, often clouded by extreme prejudice, were largely inaccurate and misinformed due to reliance on hostile sources of information or, in some cases, because their missionary authors were eager to gather converts and feared the competition of a religion that was having dramatic success. For Christian missionaries, this success presented a disconcerting contrast to the failure Christian missions were experiencing in Muslim countries, a failure that was both long-standing and well known.[162] But the extremely successful spread of the Bábí and later Bahá'í Faith more than hinted that their negative accounts could not be fair evaluations of a movement capable of inspiring so many people to such great levels of self-sacrifice. These new believers were so transformed by

162. As one missionary wrote, 'We fear the Babis will get hold of some of our young men [to convert them]. Many of the Jews in Teheran have become Babis, some of our Moslem friends we believe to be such' (Speer, *Missions and Modern History* 155, clarification added).

their conviction of the truth they had found that, in the face of extremely violent persecution, they willingly renounced their lives rather than recant their faith.

Nevertheless, even the most biased missionary reports bore witness to the powerful and vital spirit animating this new-born Faith.[163] Dr Shedd, a missionary in Persia, reported that only a few years after the Báb had begun His ministry, the Bábí Faith had caught the attention of Christians then living there: 'When the Báb passed through Urumia in 1850 on the way to his execution, the missionaries watched the excitement with great interest. The crowds of people were ready to receive him as the long expected Imám, even the water in which he bathed was regarded as holy water.'[164] In 1897 the Board of Foreign Missions of the Presbyterian Church of the United States writes with regard to the situation in Persia: 'During the last thirty years the whole body of Moslems has been convulsed by the new religion of the Báb'.[165] In 1899 one observer recounted, in a history of the Church Missionary Society, that the Bábís were 'a remarkable sect which, in the past half-century, has spread in Persia with extraordinary rapidity. The whole story of this strange and in many respects hopeful religious movement is of extreme interest. Thousands of Bábís were cruelly put to death in the late Sháh's reign, and others fiercely persecuted; "but the more they afflicted them the more they multiplied and grew".'[166] The same publication acknowledges that the 'Bábís' hold the Bible 'in great reverence' and are 'most friendly to Christians' whom they regard as 'brethren'.

Robert Speer, the secretary of the Foreign Missions of the Presbyterian Church, reported that the new Faith had 'shaken a whole nation' and was 'one of the most remarkable movements of our day'.[167] In the same article he notes the significant beginning of the new Faith in 1844: 'The date of the Manifestation and of the first disciple's conversion was May 23, 1844'. He even points out that this occurred 'almost exactly 1,000 years' after the

163. For an extensive survey of early encounters with the Bábí and Bahá'í Faiths see *The Babí and Bahá'í Religions, 1844-1944, Some Contemporary Western Accounts*, ed. Moojan Momen.
164. Ibid. 180.
165. Board of Foreign Missions of the Presbyterian Church U.S.A., *Historical Sketches of the Missions* 242.
166. Eugene Stock, *The History of the Church Missionary Society*, vol. III, 753.
167. Speer, *Missions and Modern History* 121. Like most of the others Mr Speer failed to arrive at a favourable appraisal of the Bahá'í Faith; however, rather than exploit the few misguided acts of some Bahá'ís and Bábís as many missionaries did, he fairly acknowledged that 'To charge the burden of such views on Babism and the Bab would be, however, as wrong as to charge the Inquisition upon Christianity and Christ' (ibid. 146).

disappearance of the Twelfth Imám, an event which occurred in AH 260 and to which the 1,000 years brings to AH 1260 of the Islamic calendar, a date which some Christian scholars had already noted as corollary to the prophetic 1844.

Many people, among them Gratten Guinness, were close observers of the missionary enterprise and were keenly aware of the prophetic significance of such dates as 1844 and its correspondence to the Islamic 1260. However, there is no existing evidence that he or anyone else set aside their literal expectations long enough to think there might be a connection between the ministry of the Báb and Bahá'u'lláh and these biblical prophecies. The belief that Christ's return would take place in the literal heavens, that His rule would be of an immediate and visible nature, was too strong for any of these observers to recognize that what they had so fervently anticipated had actually taken place.

Moreover, the perception of many Christians was deeply embedded in the Victorian mentality of the time and there was, therefore, a strong aversion to many of Bahá'u'lláh's progressive teachings. Church institutions were struggling to combat scientific knowledge in order to maintain their positions of authority, Christians were divided by growing nationalistic movements, others openly engaged in racism, and the social order was ruled by a male hierarchal power structure. The common ground shared by the world's different religious systems was only beginning to be dimly perceived. Hence, Bahá'u'lláh's teachings concerning the harmony of science and religion, His call for an international tribunal for the arbitration of international disputes, for the adoption or creation of a world language, the elimination of all forms of prejudice, the recognition of the oneness of humankind, and the establishment of the equality of men and women, were all too radical for many Christians. It was, therefore, the more liberal Christians such as The Revd Dr T.K. Cheyne,[168] The Revd R.J. Campbell, The Revd Dr John Kelman, The Revd A.B. Robb, and the well-known Russian writer and Christian mystic Leo Tolstoy, among many others, who took the greatest interest in, and showed the most sympathy for, the emerging world religion of Bahá'u'lláh. And, as history eloquently testifies, many open-minded individuals gradually came forward and clearly recognized the revitalizing and inspiring nature of Bahá'u'lláh's teachings.

168. 'If there has been any prophet in recent times, it is to Bahá'u'lláh that we must go. Character is the final judge. Bahá'u'lláh was a man of the highest class - that of prophets' (Appreciations of the Bahá'í Faith 18, excerpted from Revd T.K. Cheyne, *The Reconciliation of Races and Religions*, [1914]).

The Seat of the Universal House of Justice, supreme governing body of the Bahá'í world community, located on Mount Carmel, Haifa, Israel. The first members of the Universal House of Justice were elected in 1963. In 1954, the appointed Guardian of the Bahá'í Faith, Shoghi Effendi, wrote, 'The final establishment of this seat of the future Bahá'í World Commonwealth will signalize at once the proclamation of the sovereignty of the Founder of our Faith and the advent of the Kingdom of the Father repeatedly lauded and promised by Jesus Christ' (*Messages to the Bahá'í World* 75). (*Photo courtesy of the Bahá'í World Centre, Audio-Visual Department.*)

These believers often left their homes and devoted their lives to spreading the new message.

Today some Christian scholars, both liberal and conservative, still speculate on and debate the meaning and authenticity of biblical prophecies such as those contained in Jesus' Olivet Discourse. However, in the years since Bahá'u'lláh proclaimed their fulfilment, the Bahá'í Faith has steadily spread over the world, establishing itself in 164 independent countries; translating its literature into 727 languages; and attracting adherents representing more than 2,100 indigenous races, tribes and ethnic groups.[169]

169. These figures are gathered from *The Seven Year Plan: 1979-86, Statistical Report* 41, 61, 116.

APPENDICES

APPENDIX I

MEANING AND METAPHOR

When we wish to express or communicate the presence of some reality that is not perceptible to the senses, we use symbols. For example, knowledge is not a perceptible reality, whereas the sun is. Typically we say knowledge is light, but in reality light is merely being used as a symbol and is not what is literally meant. However, the fact that light is just a symbol does not mean that what it symbolizes does not exist.

There are many examples of the use of symbolism in the Bible. In some instances, however, it is not always apparent that symbols are being used, while a symbolic meaning may not always preclude a possible literal meaning as well. For example, according to the Gospel of Matthew, when Jesus yielded up His spirit on the cross 'the earth quaked' (Matt. 27:51), but there are no known accounts from this period, other than Matthew's, which record such a phenomenon. In fact, none of the other accounts of the Gospel mention it. This does not mean that it did not happen, but it does at least suggest the strong possibility that Matthew is using the phrase 'the earth quaked' as a symbol or metaphor intended to suggest the force of the crucifixion on human affairs.

Matthew's account of the Resurrection provides another example of the same symbolism. Again, in all the accounts of Jesus' resurrection, only Matthew records an earthquake. However, the account does not indicate that the earthquake served any purpose. It did not cause the stone blocking Jesus' tomb to move; rather, the angel 'came and rolled back the stone' (Matt. 28:2). It was not the cause of the guards' fear, for they 'shook for fear of him [i.e. the angel]' (Matt. 28:4). The earthquake appears to have only symbolic significance. This significance can be understood as the impact that the Resurrection - which is symbolic of the establishment of the Church - had on history. The raising up of the Church after the crucifixion was an act which struck down the authority of Judaic institutions and eventually overturned the religion and much of the barbarism of the Roman Empire.

If we turn to the Bahá'í accounts of the early history of the Bahá'í Revelation, we find a further example of this type of symbolism. In Nabíl's account, *The Dawn-Breakers*, he does not speak of an earthquake occurring at the time of, or immediately after, the Báb's martyrdom. However, Nabíl writes,

> The very moment the shots were fired, a gale of exceptional severity arose and swept over the whole city. A whirlwind of dust of incredible density obscured the light of the sun and blinded the eyes of the people. The entire city remained enveloped in that darkness from noon till night. (*Dawn-Breakers* 515)

Even though Nabíl's words appear to be intended literally, there is cause to suspect that they are, at least in part, symbolic. Nabíl's description is very similar to the account found in the synoptic Gospels which states that when Christ was put on the cross 'there was darkness over all the land' (Matt. 27:45; Mark 15:33; and Luke 23:44). At the time of the Báb's martyrdom the people were so engulfed by evil that the light of the sun - that is, God's Revelation - was completely obscured. The symbolism is apt. They thought the death of the Báb represented His defeat. This belief was like dust in their eyes (i.e. their understanding), obscuring the light of the sun (i.e. the truth and true power of the Báb's Revelation). Nabíl, like the writers of the accounts of the Gospel, is recording actual history but at the same time, again like the Apostles, he is preaching a message of salvation which objective historical facts alone are insufficient to convey. For this reason symbolic language is used.

This does not mean, however, that historical fact has been embellished with fiction - quite the contrary. Symbols are used to convey spiritual facts which otherwise would not be evident in the mere description of the event. Thus, it is actually less accurate to omit such symbols than to include them.

As mentioned, Nabíl does not record that an earthquake occurred when the Báb was martyred. But 'Abdu'l-Bahá's portrayal of the Báb's life clearly suggests the appropriateness of such symbolism:

> This illustrious Soul arose with such power that He shook the

> supports of religion, of the morals, the conditions, the habits and the customs of Persia, and instituted new rules, new laws and a new religion. Though the great personages of the State, nearly all the clergy, and the public men arose to destroy and annihilate Him, He alone withstood them and moved the whole of Persia. (*Some Answered Questions* 30)

Shoghi Effendi, on the other hand, does write of an actual earthquake occurring after the Báb's martyrdom:

> Nor was this all. The very moment the shots were fired a gale of exceptional violence arose and swept over the city. From noon till night a whirlwind of dust obscured the light of the sun, and blinded the eyes of the people. In Shíráz an 'earthquake', foreshadowed in no less weighty a Book than the Revelation of St John [Rev. 11:13],[170] occurred in 1268 AH which threw the whole city into turmoil and wrought havoc amongst its people, a havoc that was greatly aggravated by the outbreak of cholera, by famine and other afflictions. (*God Passes By* 53-4)

Shoghi Effendi not only speaks of an earthquake but provides a date - 1268 AH[171] - which indicates that this earthquake was an actual material phenomenon, and records confirm its occurrence.[172] However, there is reason to believe that Shoghi Effendi would not have regarded the literal event as the exclusive meaning intended by the Revelation of St John. This literal earthquake takes its significance from its symbolic and metaphorical value. Shoghi Effendi is probably using literal history, first to illustrate metaphorically the spiritual impact of the Báb's sacrifice and, also, as a symbol of God's retribution to a people who rejected His Messenger.

170. See *Some Answered Questions* 55.

171. The Báb was martyred 'at noon on Sunday, the twenty-eighth of Sha'bán, in the year 1266 AH' (*Dawn-Breakers* 517). This date corresponds to 9 July, 1850. The earthquake that struck Shíráz, the city where the Báb first proclaimed His mission, occurred several years later.

172. The Persian historian Hasan-e Fasá'í (1821/2-1896/7) writes, 'In the night of 25th Rajab of that year [May 3, 1853] . . . a heavy earthquake occurred at Shiraz. Several hundred houses were ruined and several thousand damaged. Several thousand people died under the ruined buildings. Most of the mosques and madrasahs were destroyed, all of them needed repair' (*History of Persia Under Qajar Rule* 305).

Revelation 11:13 thus provides an interesting example of Bahá'í interpretation because it is among a number of prophecies which Bahá'ís regard as having been fulfilled literally. Nevertheless, its significance does not come from its literal reality alone but, primarily, from the reality it symbolizes. In the opinion of this writer, this is an extremely important point with regard to interpretation. It suggests that physical reality can act as a symbol for spiritual reality. Symbols are used in prophecies to express events of great spiritual significance which will occur in the future. But they can also find an outward fulfilment in history. The outward and seemingly literal fulfilment is not the actual fulfilment in itself, but rather is used as a symbol of the spiritual fulfilment.

Therefore, it can be argued that the literal earthquake in Shíráz is not in itself what Revelation 11:13 prophesied but, rather, it is a tangible symbol of the spiritual reality that the Book of Revelation did prophesy. Without the appearance of the Báb, the earthquake would have had no more significance than any other earthquake. This point should be kept in mind when reading Scripture in general.

APPENDIX II

A BRIEF HISTORY OF CHRISTIAN MILLENNIAL VIEWS

In order to understand Christian beliefs about the millennium, it is useful to have some knowledge of the historical ideas and circumstances that influenced the interpretation of prophecy. Since early times, Christians have struggled both to understand how the millennium fits into the sequence of events described in prophecy and to define its nature. This struggle was affected most by the early persecution of the Church, Augustine's revision of Christian interpretations after the acceptance of Christianity by the Roman emperor Constantine, the antagonisms between Roman Catholics and Protestants and, in the nineteenth century, by the ideas of Bible expositors like William Miller who perceived a connection between the year 1844 and the prophecies of the Bible.

The picture of the future described in the prophecies contains three prominent features which Christians have ordered according to the above mentioned influences: (1) The 'tribulation', which involves the appearance of an evil world power that persecutes the true believers. This power is represented symbolically as the Beast or referred to as the (or an) Antichrist. (2) The eventual triumph of good over evil and the establishment of the millennial Kingdom of God. (3) The Second Advent of Christ.

That the 'tribulation', or persecution of the righteous, was to occur before the establishment of the millennium, or Kingdom of God, has essentially been accepted throughout the history of Christian interpretation. However, when Christ was to return in relation to these events has remained an issue of dispute. Some Christians argued, and still do, that Christ will return after the Christians have themselves established the Kingdom of God on earth. This view is known as 'post-millennialism', that is, Christ will return after the establishment of the millennial Kingdom. Others maintained that when Christ returns He will establish the Kingdom Himself. This view is known as 'pre-millennialism'.

Early Christian writings from the second and third centuries of the Christian era indicate that Christians expected both the persecutions to worsen and the 'tribulation' to take place in the near future. However, some Christians during this period may have anticipated later generations by regarding the severe persecutions they were already suffering under the Roman rulers Nero, Decius and Diocletian as the prophesied tribulation. Cyprian (c. AD 200/10-258), Bishop of Carthage, for example, believed the persecutions of his time were in fact prophesied by Christ.[173] However, whether or not Christians believed they were living during the tribulation, almost all the early Church Fathers were pre-millennialist. When the Roman emperor Constantine embraced Christianity, many Christians accepted the view that the tribulation was essentially over, that the apocalyptic visions of the Bible were largely fulfilled, and that the time for building the Kingdom of God on earth had arrived. But inasmuch as the Kingdom had arrived without the appearance of Christ, the old pre-millennial interpretations of the Church Fathers needed replacing with a new understanding. This task was most successfully undertaken and accomplished by the great Christian writer Augustine of Hippo (AD 354-430), who set forth the basis for the post-millennial interpretation in his book *The City of God*.[174]

From this time on, the prophecies of the Bible appeared to be fulfilled and, therefore, they began to receive less attention from the mainstream, or orthodox, Bible expositors. This point has been noted by the historian Shirley Jackson Case:

> During the fourth century Christianity made such rapid progress that it became the legal religion of the Roman Empire, thus making it possible for Augustine in the first quarter of the fifth century to write his famous treatise describing the church as the city of God on earth. The millennium was now no longer a desideratum; it was already a realization. Working from this point of view, Augustine lays the ghost of millennialism so effectively that for centuries thereafter the subject is practically ignored. (*The Millennial Hope* 179)

173. The Epistles of Cyprian. See Revd Alexander Roberts, *The Ante-Nicene Fathers*, vol. V, 347.
174. See especially ch. 20ff.

Nevertheless, the Church continued occasionally to interpret some apocalyptic prophecies in the light of contemporary events, such as the emergence of Islam in the seventh century. But it was not until around the year AD 1000 that millennial expectations began to appear again in force. This prophetic understanding was, in part, prompted by the simple, though weak, equation of the millennium's length[175] (Rev. 20:2) to the numerical equivalent in the date AD 1000, and by the growing discontent with the corruption existing in the monasteries and hierarchy of the Church.[176] This idea was also useful to those who questioned the authority and practices of the existing Church. Not surprisingly, the re-emergence of millennial interpretations of prophecy grew alongside the discontent that eventually gave birth to the Protestant Reformation.

The protests against the abuses of the Roman Catholic Church, which led to the establishment of the various denominations of Protestant Christianity, had a major impact on the interpretation of prophecy. Many Protestants firmly believed that the corruptions they perceived in the Roman Catholic Church were clearly set forth in the prophecies and, in time, they came to believe that these were signs indicating the approach of the Second Advent. As interest in the prophecies grew, various Protestants in the nineteenth century wrote polemical histories outlining the interpretation of prophecy.

Gratten Guinness[177] (1835-1910), for example, attempts to show the dominant views as they took form during the Reformation period, the impact they had up to that time, while at the same time attempting to discredit Roman Catholic views.[178] His historical account follows a pattern typical of other writers and acquaints us not only with the main opposing views as they

175. The word 'millennium' is derived from the Latin '*milli*', meaning *a thousand*. The Latin was, of course, the translation of the Greek '*chilioi*' found in Revelation; hence, the alternative term to Millenarians is the Chiliasts, a term frequently used in nineteenth-century literature.

176. The tendency to use millennial interpretations against the Papacy develops more clearly in the thirteenth century. Joachim of Flore (d. 1202) composed several works dwelling upon the ages of the world and speculated that their consummation would begin in the year 1260. Although Joachim did not oppose the Pope, he believed that the Anti-christ would eventually assume the title and various books attributed to Joachim, the authenticity of which is doubted, turn elements of Joachim's views into an anti-Papacy polemic. See Schaff, *History of the Christian Church* vol. V, 374-5n.

177. Guinness was ordained an evangelist (1857) and preached in both Europe and America. He was the author of many books and founder of the East London Institute for training missionaries.

178. Another, longer and more detailed history was written by The Revd Richard Cunningham Shimeall entitled *The Second Coming of Christ*. This book was printed and bound into one volume together with a reprint of Shimeall's Reply to an Article on Eschatology which responds to The Revd. Prof. Shedd's article on eschatology published in his *History of Christian Doctrines*. Shedd's article was

existed up till the nineteenth century, but allows us to see first hand the antipathy of Protestants for Catholics during that period. The view he explains at greatest length is the one of which he himself is a proponent, which he refers to as the 'historic Protestant view' of the prophecies:

> which considers them to predict the great events to happen in the world and in the church, from St. John's time to the coming of the Lord; which sees in the Church of Rome, and in the Papacy, the fulfilment of the prophecies of Babylon and of the Beast, and which interprets the times of the Apocalypse on the year-day system. (*The Approaching End of the Age* 94)

The entire elaboration that follows suggests the extent to which the antagonism between Protestants and Catholics influenced the interpretation of prophecy:

> This view [the 'historic Protestant view' summarized above] originated about the eleventh century, with those who even then began to protest against the growing corruptions of the Church of Rome. It grew among the Waldenses, Wickliffites, and Hussites, into a consistent scheme of interpretation, and was embraced with enthusiasm and held with intense conviction of its truth, by the Reformers of the sixteenth century. In their hands it became a powerful and formidable weapon, to attack and expose the mighty apostasy, with which they were called to do battle. From this time it spread with rapidity that was astonishing, so that ere long it was received as a self evident and fundamental truth among Protestant churches everywhere. It nerved the Reformers in England, France, Germany, Switzerland, Denmark, and Sweden, and animated the martyrs of Italy and Spain; it decided the conscientious and timid adherents of the Papacy to cross the Rubicon, and separate from the so called Catholic Church; and it has kept all the Reformed churches since, from attempting reunion with Rome.
>
> It was held and taught by Joachim Abbas, Walter Brute,

clearly an inadequate and inaccurate historical overview of Christian eschatology which prompted a number of Christian expositors to write responses. Shimeall's response is perhaps the most thorough and includes what he calls an 'Authentic History of Chiliasm' (ch. 3, 53-117).

> Luther, Zwingli, Melanchthon, Calvin, and the rest of the Reformers; by Bullinger, Bale, and Foxe; by Brightman and Mede, Sir Isaac and Bishop Newton, Vitringa, Daubuz and Whiston, as well as by Faber, Cunningham, Frere, Birks and Elliott; no two of these may agree on all questions of minor details, but they agree on the grand outline, and each one has added more or less to the strength and solidity of the system, by his researches. During the last seven centuries this system has been deepening its hold on the convictions of the Christian church, and has been embraced by some of her wisest and best guides and teachers. It originated with martyrs and confessors, exerted a sanctifying and strengthening influence over those who received it; it tended to revive the hope of the premillennial coming of the Lord, which had long lain in abeyance, leading naturally to many false anticipations of the event, which have been disproved by time, as well as to many very remarkable approximations to the truth, as to the time of other events. It met of course with intense and bitter opposition from the church it branded as Babylon, and the power it denounced as Antichrist, and to this day is rejected by all who in any way maintain or defend these, as well as by some who do neither. (Ibid. 94-5)

Guinness explains two alternative views, both of which he presents as Roman Catholic counter-responses to the 'historic Protestant view'. One view, he says:

> considers these prophecies to have been fulfilled in the downfall of the Jewish nation and the old Roman empire, limiting their range thus to the first six centuries of the Christian era, and making Nero Antichrist.
>
> This scheme originated with the Jesuit Alcazar towards the end of the sixteenth century; it has been held and taught under various modifications by Grotius, Hammond, Bossuet, Eichhorn and other German commentators, Moses Stuart, and Dr Davidson. It has few supporters now. (Ibid. 93)

It seems doubtful that this view can be attributed to the sixteenth-century

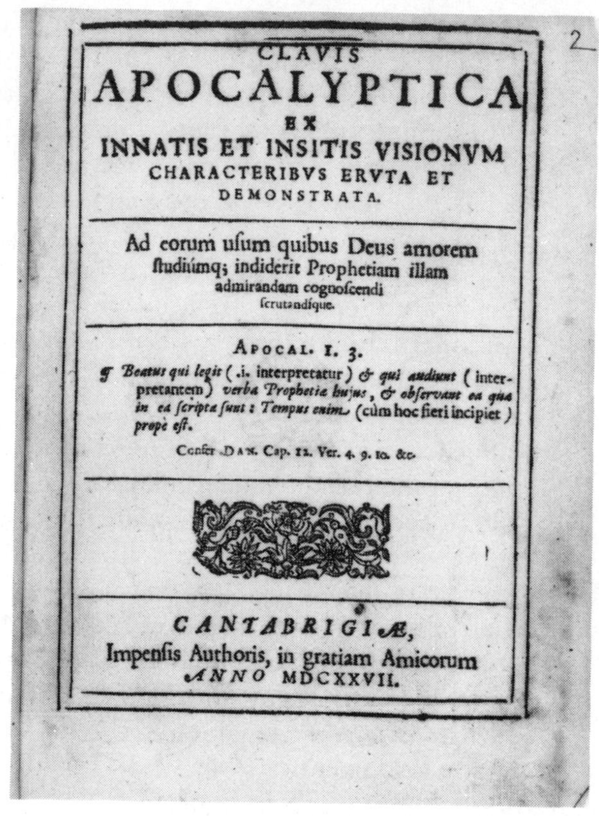

CLAVIS
APOCALYPTICA
EX
INNATIS ET INSITIS VISIONVM
CHARACTERIBVS ERVTA ET
DEMONSTRATA.

Ad eorum uſum quibus Deus amorem ſtudiúmq; indiderit Prophetiam illam admirandam cognoſcendi ſcrutandique.

APOCAL. I. 3.

¶ *Beatus qui legit* (.i. interpretatur) *& qui audiunt* (interpretantem) *verba Prophetiæ hujus, & obſervant ea quæ in ea ſcripta ſunt: Tempus enim* (cùm hoc fieri incipiet) *propè eſt.*

Confer DAN. Cap. 12. Ver. 4. 9. 10. &c.

CANTABRIGIÆ,
Impenſis Authoris, in gratiam Amicorum
ANNO MDCXXVII.

Title page of Joseph Mede's *Clavis Apocalyptica* (*Key to the Apocalypse*, 1627, 1643). Considered one of the greatest biblical scholars produced by England, his *Apocalyptica* supported the day/year theory and was a major and enduring force in the shift to the premillennial interpretation of prophecy. The text was translated from the Latin several times in the nineteenth century. (*Reproduced with permission from the Bodleian Library, University of Oxford. Shelfmark: KK.42 Th.(2).*)

Jesuit Alcazar since aspects of the writings of the early Church Fathers and Augustine's revision of early premillennial thinking would have naturally led to this line of interpretation. Gratten Guinness is probably linking these ideas to Roman Catholicism in order to discredit the view as merely anti-Protestant propaganda. The other view he refers to as the 'Futurist view':

> which teaches that the prophetic visions of Revelation, from chapters iv to xix, prefigure events still wholly future and not to take place, till just at the close of this dispensation. (Ibid. 95)

Guinness points out that the 'Futurist view', like the other Catholic interpretation, has some elements that are clearly evident in the writings of the early Church Fathers. However, he adds:

> In its present form . . . it [the futurist view] may be said to have originated at the end of the sixteenth century, with the Jesuit Ribera, who, moved like Alcazar, to relieve the Papacy from the

> terrible stigma cast upon it by the Protestant interpretation, tried to do so, by referring these prophecies to the distant future, instead of like Alcazar to the distant past. (Ibid. 95)

Guinness, however, admits that this interpretation is not found exclusively among Roman Catholics:

> For a considerable period this view was confined to the Romanists, and was refuted by several masterly Protestant works. But of late years, since the commencement of this century, it has sprung up afresh, and sprung up strange to say among Protestants. It was revived by such writers as the two Maitlands, Burgh, Tyso, Dr Todd, the leaders of the 'brethren'[179] generally, and by some Puseyite[180] expositors also. It is held by extremist parties; by those who though Protestants, are ashamed of the Reformation, speak of it as an unwarrantable Schism, and verge as closely on Rome as is possible; and by those, who though Protestants, deem the glorious Reformation to have stopped grievously short of the mark, and see so much of Babylon still, in the Reformed churches, that they refuse to regard them as having come out of Babylon, or as victors over Antichrist. (Ibid. 95-6)

Thus not all Christians, not even all Protestants, saw Christendom divided into two camps, one signifying the good and the other representing the worst evils foreshadowed in the Bible. The Church had been in need of reform and even Catholics admitted this by launching their own reform efforts (the Counter Reformation). But, however needed the reforms may have been, the Protestant Reformation also represented schism, which was clearly condemned in the Bible (1 Cor. 12:25-7).[181] Protestants had cause to think the Church had drifted into error but they were wrong in

179. The 'Brethren' seems to refer to the 'Plymouth Brethren', a movement trying to return to the simplicity of apostolic times and reacting against the sectarianism that characterized the beginning of the nineteenth century. See Douglas, *New International Dictionary of the Christian Church* 789.

180. Guinness uses the term 'Puseyite' to identify followers of the high church movement. It was a common term derived from the name of the Anglican theologian and professor active in the Oxford Movement, Edward Bouverie Pusey (1800-82). The Oxford Movement was both conservative and reactionary.

181. Shoghi Effendi comments on the Reformation in a letter written on his behalf: 'What contribution the Reformation did really make was to seriously challenge, and partly undermine, the edifice which the Fathers of the Church had themselves reared, and to discard and demonstrate the purely human origin of

magnifying the errors of the Catholics while overlooking their own.

Nevertheless, it seems indisputable that the Roman Catholic Church saw the growing Protestant movement as a major challenge to its political dominion and that this challenge gave impetus to the numerous campaigns of persecution in which thousands were put to death. The century from 1550 onwards was characterised by warfare between Catholic and Protestant monarchs, and in some realms (e.g., France) by civil war between Protestant and Catholic. Generally Catholic institutions had to retreat, and the process culminated in the abolition of the Holy Roman Empire and the loss of the Pope's remaining temporal power in the nineteenth century.

Protestants were so embittered by these persecutions that, not surprisingly, they thought these trials to be no less than what had been prophesied in the Scriptures. What developed was a simple interpretation that was to have a lasting effect. They argued that the 'tribulation' (Matt. 24:29) was what they had suffered at the hands of the Pope, whom they regarded as the Antichrist. Moreover, such dark events, they reasoned, could be nothing less than evidence that they were living in the end times and that the Second Advent must be fast approaching. As Guinness has pointed out, the advocates of this interpretation revived the pre-millennial hopes which had characterized Christian thinkers in the early centuries before Augustine wrote his *City of God*.

Not all Protestants, however, accepted that these events suggested the imminent return of Christ, nor would some of the previous interpretations of the Bible be abandoned quickly. Many remained ardent proponents of the post-millennial theory. Consequently, numerous books took up this subject for debate. Perhaps one of the most noteworthy and influential nineteenth-century books in this debate was Dr David Brown's *Christ's Second Coming, Will it be Premillennial?* (1876).[182] Even though the debate was never entirely resolved, towards the end of the nineteenth century popular support had clearly shifted to the side of the pre-millennialist.

While Christian scholars and ministers continued to dispute these issues, they also continued to preach about prophecies in general. It was a time in which people everywhere were filled with anticipation. The belief

the elaborate doctrines, ceremonies and institutions which they had devised. The Reformation was a right challenge to the man-made organization of the Church, and as such was a step in advance. In its origins, it was a reflection of the new spirit which Islam had released, and a God-sent punishment to those who had refused to embrace its truth' (See Helen Hornby, *Lights of Guidance* 373).

182. See also James H. Snowden, *The Coming of the Lord: Will It Be Premillennial?* For many, these books completed the argument begun by Joseph Mede (1586-1638) with his scholarly *Apocalyptica* (1627, 1643).

that they were living in the end times dominated popular religious thought. These beliefs were reinforced during the early 1800s by the extraordinary changes and developments that were occurring. The European nations were expanding both technologically and intellectually. Through the use of this new technology and learning, these nations sought, and were able to secure, other parts of the world as colonies. Explorers sought new territories for their monarchs, and missionaries sought new souls to convert from among the so-called 'heathen' races. As this process of colonization grew, a few European nations envisioned control of the whole world.

At this time, the people of Europe thought of their nations as 'Christian', and many believed that their new-found power and technological supremacy in the world was ordained by God. They compared themselves with other parts of the world and concluded that they were superior, the spreaders of Christian civilization. With this outlook, some Christians breathed new life into the concept that Christians would themselves build the Kingdom of God on earth, after which Christ would return. Thus the post-millennial view was temporarily reinforced. This view was especially popular in Britain where it remained a major force until World War I. The devastating results of the war shattered the optimistic view that the 'tribulation' had occurred sometime in the past and that the world was going to improve progressively until Christ returned. Before the more pessimistic and modern outlook took hold, however, the advocates of post-millennialism interpreted many verses as very symbolic and extremely allegorical. As strange as it might seem, some even believed that the spread and establishment of Christian colonialism actually represented the return of Christ spoken of in Scripture.

However, the pre-millennialists pointed out that 'Christian' Europe was not at this point united or at peace. Moreover, Roman Catholicism was spreading throughout the colonies even as Protestantism was. To the Protestants, it appeared increasingly as if the nations were being gathered by the 'beast', mentioned in the Book of Revelation, to wage war with Christ when He returned. Consequently, they reacted against the very popular post-millennial view. Unfortunately, they also reacted strongly to the allegorical interpretations of the post-millennialists. They advocated a strict literal approach to the Scriptures, building upon the views espoused by Martin Luther when he broke with the Roman Catholic Church.[183]

183. This approach did not always preclude symbolic interpretations. Some passages in Daniel and the Book of Revelation are inescapably symbolic and this was recognized. However, strict literalism was re-

Spurred on by the bitterest anti-Roman Catholic feelings, Protestants searched the Scriptures for confirmation of their point of view. This endeavour shaped their interpretation of prophecy - especially Daniel's prophecies concerning the 2,300 and 1,260 days - from the eleventh century to the twentieth. These prophecies, along with Matthew 24:15 and Revelation 11:1-14, occupied the special attention of many expositors because it was widely believed that such verses referred to the condition of the Church, if not to the actual time of Jesus' return.

In 1701, an English Protestant, Robert Fleming, published a book that asserted that the French monarchy would soon crumble. At first this book went largely unnoticed, but eventually it provided a great deal of popular momentum to the study of prophecy. Fleming argued that the '1,260 years' referred to a period of corruption in the Church. Building upon ideas that went back as far as Joachim of Flora (c. 1135-1202), Fleming asserted that the corruption foretold was attributable to the rule of the Papacy. However, he faced the familiar difficulty of ascertaining the year in which the 1,260-year period would begin. Assuming that the rise of Papal temporal authority could be dated from AD 552, 606 or 758, he calculated that the 1,260-year period should terminate in the years 1794, 1848 or 2000. Since France was the strongest European power supporting the Pope, Fleming asserted that the monarch's fall would be included in this scenario. When the French revolution overthrew the monarch some ninety years later, it appeared to many that Fleming's interpretations were correct.[184]

However, apart from the monarch's fall, it was difficult to see how the violent revolutionaries and their reign of terror fitted in with Fleming's 'angels' who were to overthrow religious corruption. This prompted other Christian expositors to come forward to refute Fleming's views.[185] Many, using the same methods, offered their own interpretations and chronological outlines of events they saw foretold in the Scriptures. Others maintained

reflected in the tendency to interpret everything literally that the Scripture did not specifically indicate to be symbolic, such as dreams and visions. Thus, for example, Jesus returning in the clouds was taken to be literal by most pre-millennialists.

184. The French Revolution cannot be set at one single date. Rather, it covers a period roughly from 1789 to 1805. During this time, a number of signal events occurred. It should be noted that amongst the stages outlined by Fleming, he emphasized the 606 date as the possible beginning of the 1,260-year period. This prompted the republishing of his book in 1848 in anticipation of the next stage of the Pope's downfall or decline in power.

185. E.g., Benjamin Wills Newton published a paper in which he attempted to refute the standard methodology used by Fleming. More significantly, he also pointed out many of the inconsistencies between the French Revolution and the imagery of biblical prophecy. He also rejected the idea that the Pope was the Antichrist. This paper was later included in *Newton's Aids to Prophetic Enquiry* 170.

that the French Revolution was the terminus, but reinterpreted it to fit into other aspects of prophecy.[186]

By this time there were Christians in almost every western nation who argued that the Second Advent of Christ would take place around the years 1843-7. They based their arguments on the prophecies of Daniel and on a well-known allegorical interpretation of the 'Seventh Day'.[187] The more vocal and organized advocates of these beliefs were frequently referred to as 'Adventists'.

This controversy about prophetic dates provides one of the most interesting pages in Christian history. Ironically, the storm would eventually centre around a pious, self-educated farmer from Vermont. This farmer, who in 1833 had become a Baptist preacher, was a man by the name of William Miller. After a period of Bible study lasting over a decade, Miller felt certain that, according to Scripture, Christ would return in 1843-4. His arguments were convincing enough to capture the attention of other ministers and, eventually to receive publicity in some leading newspapers.

As we will see, Miller's beliefs also attracted the interest of numerous critics and he became the object of much scathing ridicule. He was a person of humble origin and, as such, he was perfectly suited to the task of taking this message to the masses. It seems unlikely that Miller would have gained so much attention and attracted so many supporters except for the circumstances of his day and the coherence of his arguments. Of all the Adventists, none has left a more enduring impact, inspired so many admirers or provoked so many critics.

Miller is often credited with founding the Adventist movement. However, this seems to be a misjudgement inasmuch as, in earlier times, many preachers and Bible commentators had argued the same or similar points. The basic core of Adventism, especially its pre-millennial outlook, can even be found among the Church Fathers: Polycarp, Ignatius, Justin Martyr and many others. In later centuries, other aspects of

186. The inclusion of the French Revolution in later interpretations of prophecy is clearly evident in the works of many expositors. It also remained in the thinking of Seventh-Day Adventists.

187. The statement that there were six days of creation followed by a seventh on which God rested had been traditionally interpreted as an allegory representing the whole of human history from Adam to the end of the millennium. Each day signified a thousand years of human history, the sixth day of which was followed by the thousand-year Kingdom of God on earth. Nineteenth-century Christians, relying on biblical chronology alone, typically calculated 6,000 years from the time of Adam to roughly the middle of the nineteenth century. Despite the symbolic nature of biblical numerology, this allegorical interpretation was traditionally tied to a literal interpretation of Genesis and, therefore, it collapsed under the weight of modern knowledge about the age of the earth and the length of human history. See Appendix III: The Seventh Day.

Miller's views were to be found among the Taborites, the Anabaptists and others. Even Isaac Newton (1642-1717), remembered for his formulation of the law of gravity, was one of many who studied the Bible intently and made his own contribution to Adventist ideas. More correctly, it can be said that William Miller's ministry was instrumental in the events that led to the establishment of several new Christian denominations which emphasized the 'end times', such as the Seventh-Day Adventists and other related splinter groups.[188]

OBSERVATIONS
UPON THE
PROPHECIES
OF
DANIEL,
AND THE
APOCALYPSE
OF
St. JOHN.

In Two Parts.

By Sir ISAAC NEWTON.

DUBLIN:
Printed by S. POWELL,
For George Risk, at the Shakespear's-Head, George Ewing, at the Angel and Bible, and William Smith, at the Hercules, in Dame's-street, Booksellers, M. DCC. XXXIII.

Title page of Sir Isaac Newton's *Observations Upon the Prophecies*. (*Reproduced with permission from the Bodleian Library, University of Oxford. Shelfmark: 1093 e. 254.*)

Most significantly, from a Bahá'í point of view, it can be said that Miller was one of the great Christian Adventists who taught that Christ would return in the year 1844 - the year that marks the beginning of the Bahá'í era. Miller was instrumental in shifting attention from the 1,260 years (Dan. 12:7; Rev. 11:2-3) to the 2,300 years (Dan. 8:14). According to Miller and many others, these two periods began at different times in history but culminated at the same point with

188. Apart from different adventist Churches that sprang up, other new religious movements, such as the Church of Jesus Christ of the Latter-Day Saints (more commonly known as the Mormon Church), as well as the more recent Jehovah's Witnesses, were also influenced by these interpretations. Joseph Smith, for example, who founded the Mormon church, not only believed that he was living in the latter-days (i.e., end times) but went so far as to write, 'I was once praying very earnestly to know the time of the coming of the Son of Man, when I heard a voice repeat the following: Joseph, my son, if thou livest until thou art eighty-five years old, thou shalt see the face of the Son of Man; therefore let this suffice, and trouble me no more on this matter' (Joseph Smith, *Doctrines and Covenants* 238, from a selection dated April 2, 1843). Joseph Smith was born in 1805 but was murdered before the *terminus a quo* in 1890. It is inconceivable that he was unaware that the date he described was within the period considered by his contemporary Bible expositors to be the one most likely to see the Second Advent. Moreover, he obviously shared their convictions and hopes about Jesus' return.

the Second Advent. Miller was not an innovator; rather, as recent historians have noted, he simply took a method of calculation that had been acknowledged for centuries and drew it to its logical conclusion.

It was in 1836 that Miller first made his views concerning the Second Advent known in the publication *Evidence From Scripture and History of the Second Coming of Christ About the Year 1843*. He had been very cautious about expressing his views but this publication generated an intense response that soon called him to a life of Adventist preaching.[189]

From this time onwards, the expectation of Jesus' Second Advent was spread far beyond the writings of religious academics, isolated preachers and Bible commentators. Miller gained the support and encouragement of more prominent preachers who provided him with the opportunity to spread these views to other American states. Miller and his supporters were very confident and an immense sense of expectation was generated; so when the expected date of 1843 passed, he and some other devoted Adventists reconsidered the opinions of those who had argued that 1844 was the more accurate date. The Adventist scholar Le Roy E. Froom recounts the transition from the 1843 to the 1844 date:

> for over a decade before the actual Jewish year '1843' began, Miller realized that the prophesied 2300th year would not end until sometime in the common, civil, calendar year 1844, for he reckoned '1843' to be on the basis of the 'Jewish sacred year', which he understood extended from spring to spring. This he calculated as approximately from equinox to equinox, or March 21, 1843, to March 21, 1844. However,it was not until Miller's 'Jewish year 1843' ran out (in the spring of 1844) that the great majority of the Millerites began to pay serious heed to a few insistent voices in their midst. These had been trying to demonstrate that 2300 years from 457 BC would terminate over in the Jewish year '1844', not within the year '1844'. (*The Prophetic Faith of Our Fathers*, vol. IV, 790-1)

189. In that book he wrote, 'In presenting these Lectures to the public, the writer is only complying with the solicitations of some of his friends, who have requested that his views on the prophecies of Daniel and John [Revelation] might be made public' (op. cit. 3).

Eventually the last of the anticipated dates passed and Christ still had not appeared - at least, the Second Advent did not occur in the literal way the Adventists had expected. As mentioned, the failure of their literal expectations has come to be known as 'the great disappointment'.

With the passing of the expected dates, Miller's critics intensified their attacks. Writers depicted the Millerites as irrational fanatics characterized by sensational and extreme types of behaviour, such as waiting on their rooftops wearing ascension robes, and going mad when their predictions appeared to have failed. Scholars today have shown that no evidence exists to warrant such images and allegations.[190] Nevertheless, many Christians who know about this period in history look upon it with embarrassment or would, at least, prefer to forget it.

Miller gave up the movement, but others were disinclined to give up what seemed to them to be a clear prophecy. They advocated that something had happened - but not on earth - and that Christ's return was still to come later. The main idea was that the prophesied 'cleansing of the sanctuary' (Dan. 8:13) had occurred in heaven rather than on earth. This view was put forth and illustrated in Seventh-Day books such as *Bible Readings*. It was the individuals who accepted these later views who went on to found the group known today as Seventh-Day Adventists.

The methods of interpretation, such as the 'day/year theory', which had been so popular among Christians for centuries and which were central to Adventist thinking, are today regarded as erroneous by most Christian scholars, both liberal and conservative. However, because these calculations also accurately reveal the time of Jesus' First Advent, some Christian apologists still accept them.[191] To the knowledge of this writer, there was no movement among Christians which understood that the Second Advent in 1844 was literal, that is, that 'the Son of Man' would,

190. See, e.g., Francis D. Nichol, *Midnight Cry* 321-498. Even the conservative Christian writer, Walter Martin, who devoted considerable energy to attacking the faith of Seventh-Day Adventists, writes: 'Lest anyone reading the various accounts of the rise of "Millerism" in United States come to the conclusion that Miller and his followers were "crackpots" or "uneducated tools of Satan", the following facts should be known: The great advent awakening movement which spanned the Atlantic from Europe was bolstered by a tremendous wave of contemporary biblical scholarship. Although Miller himself lacked academic theological training, actually scores of prophetic scholars in Europe and the United States had espoused Miller's views before he himself announced them. In reality, his was only one more voice proclaiming the 1843/1844 fulfilment of Daniel 8:14, or the 2,300 day period allegedly dating from 457 BC and ending in 1843-1844.' Martin further admits, 'If we condemn him, we must also condemn a large number of internationally known scholars who were among the most highly educated men of their day' (*Kingdom of the Cults* 412-13).

191. See, e.g., Josh McDowell, *Evidence that Demands a Verdict* 171-5.

physically and historically, manifest Himself on earth, but that the signs spoken of in the prophecies were symbolic - as the Bahá'ís believe.

APPENDIX III

THE SEVENTH-DAY

Apart from the day/year interpretation of such verses as Daniel 8:14 and Revelation 11:3, there also existed a day/thousand-year equation that was applied to the seven-day creation account in the Book of Genesis and which presented a millennial prophecy. The origins of this allegorical (or typological) understanding appear to go back to pre-Christian times. For example, in the late nineteenth century, several Slavonic recensions of an interesting and long-misplaced book, *The Secrets of Enoch*,[192] were discovered and translated. This book appears to have been known to early Christian writers and it may even have existed in pre-New Testament times.[193] Following a reference to the seventh day upon which God rested, as mentioned in the Book of Genesis, the writer of the Enoch account adds:

> And I appointed the eighth day also, that the eighth day should be the first-created after my work, and that the first seven revolve in the form of the seventh thousand, and that at the beginning of the eighth thousand there should be a time of

192. This work is attributed to Enoch who is mentioned in the Bible. See Gen. 5:24; Heb. 11:5. Another version, the Ethiopic Book of Enoch, is more well known and is regarded as canonical by the Ethiopian Christians (Coptic Church). This Ethiopic version is quoted in the New Testament in the Epistle of Jude. Cf. Jude 1:14-15; Book of Enoch, book 1, verse 9. See also Charlesworth, *The Old Testament Pseudepigraphia* 13-14.

193. In *De Principiis*, Origen (AD 180-253) writes, 'in that little treatise called *The Pastor or Angel of Repentance*, composed by Hermas, we have the following: "First of all, believe that there is one God who created and arranged all things to be; who Himself contains all things, but Himself is contained by none". And in the book of Enoch also we have similar descriptions.' See Roberts, *The Ante-Nicene Fathers*, vol. IV, 252. R.H. Charles points out that this statement by Origen 'cannot be justified from the Ethiopic Enoch'. This suggests some other literary source attributed to Enoch, a point which he finds confirmed in the Enoch version now only preserved in Slavonic, 'for in *The Book of the Secrets of Enoch* 'we have an elaborate account of the creation, 24-9:3, and an insistence on the unity of God, 33:8, 36:1.' See also Hastings, *A Dictionary of the Bible*, vol. I, 708ff., esp. 711.

> not-counting, endless, with neither years nor months nor weeks nor days nor hours. (33:1)[194]

The phrase 'the first seven revolve in the form of the seventh thousand' means 7,000 years. Here the days of creation are interpreted in the light of the biblical equation 'a thousand years in Thy sight are but as yesterday' (Ps. 90:4; cf. 2 Pet. 3:8). The eighth day is depicted as a day which does not end. This may be corollary to the canonical Book of Revelation, which describes how, after the thousand-year Kingdom of God on earth, Satan is let loose for a short time before being cast into a lake of fire for ever (Rev. 20:7-10). It is not necessary to take up the issue of whether or not *The Secrets of Enoch* contains any canonical merit or inspiration. It is sufficient simply to note that this kind of interpretation and chronological understanding existed before and during New Testament times.[195] If this information is correct, we can assume that such an outlook would not have been alien either to the author of the Book of Revelation or, possibly, to the author of the earlier Book of Daniel.

Another early text containing this allegory is the *Epistle of Barnabas* (not to be confused with the later forgery known as the Gospel of Barnabas), which states:

> Of the sabbath He speaketh in the beginning of the creation; And God made the works of His hands in six days, and He ended on the seventh day, and rested on it, and He hallowed it. Give heed, children, what this meaneth; He ended in six days. He meaneth this, that in six thousand years the Lord shall bring all things to an end; for the day with Him signifieth a thousand years; and this He himself beareth me witness, saying; Behold, the day of the Lord shall be as a thousand

194. See Rutherford H. Platt, *The Forgotten Books of Eden* 98. This passage is in essential agreement with Rev. 20:7-10, assuming the eighth day is the time following the thousand year period described in verse 7.

195. 'Bishop Russel [*Discourse on the Millennium*, 39] says there is "no room for doubt that the notion of the millennium preceded by several centuries the introduction of the Christian Faith". Rabbi Elias, a Jewish doctor of high celebrity, whose opinion is called by the Jews "a tradition of the house of Elias", and who flourished about 200 years before Christ, taught that the world would be "2000 years void of the law; 2000 years under the law; and 2000 years under the Messiah". He limited the duration of the world to 6000 years, and held that in the seventh millenary, "the earth would be renewed" ' (Shimeall, Reply to an Article on Eschatology 59-60, reprinted and attached to *The Second Coming of Christ*).

> years. Therefore, children, in six days, that is in six thousand years, everything shall come to an end. And He rested on the seventh day. This He meaneth; when His Son shall come, and shall abolish the time of the Lawless One, and shall judge the ungodly, and shall change the sun and the moon and the stars, then shall He truly rest on the seventh day. (J.B. Lightfoot, *The Apostolic Fathers* 284)

The *Epistle of Barnabas* is believed to have been written around AD 70-9, which places it slightly earlier than the writing of the Book of Revelation, thought to have been composed around AD 80-90. The thousand-year length of the 'seventh-day' corresponds to the Book of Revelation, which speaks of the thousand-year Kingdom of God. Another consistency between the *Epistle of Barnabas* and the canonical Books can be seen in the reference to Christ changing 'the sun and the moon and the stars', which essentially corresponds to Jesus' own words in Matthew 24:29. These points suggest a common and accepted terminology and allegorical understanding which existed at that time.

Within the New Testament itself there is also mention of the seventh-day rest which the believers are encouraged to reach:

> If Joshua had led them into this place of rest, God would not later on have spoken so much of another day. There must still be, therefore, a place of rest reserved for God's people, the seventh-day rest, since to reach the place of rest is to rest after your work, as God did after his. We must therefore do everything we can to reach this place of rest, or some of you might copy this example of disobedience and be lost. (Epistle to the Hebrews 4:8-11, trans.: *The Jerusalem Bible*)

The prophetic understanding of the seven days of creation and the seventh-day rest continued to be passed down to later thinkers. Augustine, for example, writes:

> 'And God rested on the seventh day from all His works which He had made. And God blessed the seventh day, and sanctified it; because that in it He had rested from all His work which God began to make [Gen. 2:2-3].' For we shall ourselves

> be the seventh day, when we shall be filled and replenished with God's blessing and sanctification. (*City of God* 618)

Shortly thereafter he adds:

> This Sabbath shall appear still more clearly if we count the ages as days, in accordance with the periods of time defined in Scripture, for that period will be found to be the seventh. The first age, as the first day, extends from Adam to the deluge; the second from the deluge to Abraham, equalling the first, not in length of time, but in the number of generations, there being ten in each. From Abraham to the advent of Christ there are, as the evangelist Matthew calculates, three periods, in each of which are fourteen generations - one period from Abraham to David, a second from David to the captivity, a third from the captivity to the birth of Christ in the flesh. There are thus five ages in all. The sixth is now passing, and cannot be measured by any number of generations, as it has been said, 'It is not for you to know the times, which the Father hath out in His own power' [Acts 1:7]. After this period God shall rest as on the seventh day, when He shall give us (who shall be the seventh day) rest in Himself. But there is not space to treat of these ages; suffice it to say that the seventh shall be our Sabbath, which shall be brought to a close, not by an evening, but by the Lord's day, as an eighth and eternal day. (Ibid. 618)

This 'seventh day' interpretation continued to the nineteenth century, most believing that, according to biblical chronology, it would terminate in the mid-nineteenth century. The 6,000-year understanding of biblical chronology, the 1,260 days and the 2,300 days prophesied by Daniel, together filled Christians with confidence and expectation.

In time, however, the seventh day interpretation emphasized less and less because of modern scientific findings. A literal interpretation of Genesis and an acceptance that the earth was roughly 6,000 years old prevailed among interpreters of chronological prophecy. When geological science soundly refuted the literal interpretation of Genesis, this understanding of prophecy was gradually abandoned and, for the most part, has now been forgotten.

The account in Genesis cannot be literal but it obviously has many deep metaphorical meanings which testify to its inspiration, and it may even be symbolic of the beginning of a specific age. Nineteenth-century Christian interpreters failed to consider the possibility that biblical chronology, as it actually appears in the sacred texts, was intended to be more a prophetic time scale than an accurate record of literal history. Although biblical chronology is established to be historically accurate in many cases, anyone who examines the occurrences and corresponding significance of certain numbers, such as the 'forty days' so frequently mentioned in Scripture, will quickly detect a symbolic numerology and a type of 'sacred arithmetic'. But where actual history and symbol diverge and converge is not always clear, for in our own time when history is clearer, these numbers continue to unfold in the same pattern. Even Bahá'u'lláh's ministry, if calculated from His imprisonment in the Síyáh-Chál, encompassed forty years in true biblical fashion.

APPENDIX IV

THE KINGDOM OF GOD

Christians who interpret the Bible literally believe that the Kingdom of God signifies a material paradise wherein everything on earth is transformed, even, for example, carnivorous animals which, it is believed, will turn into herbivores. This view is based on a literal interpretation of the prophecy, 'the wolf also shall dwell with the lamb' (Isaiah 11:6).[196] Reflecting this view, the popular American evangelist Billy Graham writes, 'He [Jesus] will remove all deformities and handicaps. At that time there'll be no designated spots on parking lots, or graduated ramps on buildings, for the handicapped. There will be no blindness, deafness, muteness, paralysis - no need for eyeglasses, hearing aids, speech therapy, wheel chairs, crutches, or white canes' (*Approaching Hoofbeats* 261). The alternative Christian view asserts that the Kingdom of God pertains to a state of spiritual well-being involving the inner life of the believers, not a material paradise.

Bahá'í teachings support the second view. Some people objected to Bahá'u'lláh's messianic claims by pointing out that the paradise to be established in fulfilment of prophecy had not occurred. Rejecting the literal interpretation of such verses, Bahá'u'lláh indicated that the paradise promised in Scripture signifies the closeness to God that can be attained through the acceptance of His Revelation (*Epistle* 132). True paradise is not a material place where all the circumstances or tests of temporal existence have been removed. Some degrees of difficulty will always exist in this world inasmuch as they are essential for the development of such spiritual qualities as patience, forgiveness, charity and detachment. Paradise, therefore, is achieved through following the teachings of God which enable people to develop spiritual perfections and to live in peace even while many of life's difficulties continue.

196. Referring to the literal interpretation of the same verse (Isa. 11:6), Bahá'u'lláh writes, 'of what profit would it be to the world were such a thing to take place?' (*Certitude* 113).

Understood in this light it is clear that, even during the ministry of Christ, the Kingdom of God was established. This understanding is supported by the Scriptures inasmuch as it is stated that John the Baptist heralded the ministry of Christ by preaching 'Repent ye, for the Kingdom of heaven is at hand' (Matt. 3:1-2; *Certitude* 65). Moreover, Christ taught that 'the Kingdom of God is within you' (Luke 17:21). However, if Christ established the Kingdom of God during His ministry, why did He instruct His followers to pray for its appearance: 'Thy kingdom come. Thy will be done in earth, as it is in heaven' (Matt. 6:10)? Furthermore, why are there so many prophecies in the Book of Revelation referring to a future Kingdom?

The writings of Bahá'u'lláh indicate that every Messenger of God has been invested with all the attributes of God such as sovereignty and dominion (*Certitude* 104). This divine sovereignty signifies their Lordship over their dominion, which encompasses the hearts of the believers. This dominion can be understood as the Kingdom of God that is established and renewed in every age when a divinely-appointed Messenger of God appears. Hence, for example, 'Abdu'l-Bahá states:

> When Christ appeared He manifested Himself at Jerusalem. He called men to the Kingdom of God, He invited them to Eternal life and He told them to acquire human perfections. The Light of Guidance was shed forth by that radiant Star, and He at length gave His life in sacrifice for humanity. (*Paris Talks* 116-17)

Similarly, in another talk, 'Abdu'l-Bahá stated:

> Through His death and teachings we have entered into His Kingdom. His essential teaching was the unity of mankind and the attainment of supreme human virtues through love. He came to establish the Kingdom of peace and everlasting life. (*Promulgation* 5-6)

And again, He stated, 'His word conquered the East and the West. His Kingdom is everlasting' (*Paris Talks* 56). 'Abdu'l-Bahá explains that:

> Jesus Christ came to teach the people of the world this heavenly civilization and not material civilization. He

> breathed the breath of the Holy Spirit into the body of the world and established an illumined civilization. Among the principles of divine civilization He came to proclaim is the Most Great Peace of mankind. (*Promulgation* 11)

Later 'Abdu'l-Bahá added, 'Jesus Christ summoned all to the Most Great Peace through the acquisition of pure morals' (*Promulgation* 109).

Some might suppose that while Christ may have established the Kingdom of God within the hearts of His followers, this is not the same as the Kingdom of God that is to be established on earth. However, this point of view seems inconsistent inasmuch as this inner transformation, and thus the appearance of the Kingdom within, cannot take place without having some form of outward effect on the material world. Once Christians set about establishing charities, building Churches and uniting contending peoples into a common fellowship, they had already begun to establish, in a material way, the Kingdom of God on earth.

By following the teachings of Bahá'u'lláh and promoting them throughout the world, Bahá'ís believe they are in the process of establishing the Kingdom of God on earth in this age. Shoghi Effendi stated that the Bahá'í Faith is 'no less than the fulfilment of the Promise given by Jesus Christ, and the establisher of the Kingdom He Himself had prayed for and foretold' (*God Passes By* 318; see also *Advent* 73-4). At the dedication of the first Bahá'í Temple in America, 'Abdu'l-Bahá stated that the Temple's construction marked 'the inception of the Kingdom of God on earth' (*Citadel of Faith* 69). However, 'Abdu'l-Bahá's teachings suggest that He believed the Kingdom had already been established, that is, in the hearts of the believers, even before the occasion of the Temple dedication. Moreover, Bahá'u'lláh, referring to those who have accepted His Cause, wrote 'they who were not in the Kingdom have now entered it' (*Proclamation* 91). Therefore, it seems reasonable to assume that 'Abdu'l-Bahá, at the Temple dedication, was referring to the fact that the inner spiritual awakening and transformation that had already occurred was now manifesting itself outwardly in the construction of the Temple.

The Bahá'í teachings and beliefs about the establishment of the Kingdom do not appear, however, to preclude the idea that the Kingdom of God was established 'on earth' in the Christian era. That is, the Kingdom was established to the degree that Christ's teachings were followed and were able to bring about changes in the world at that time. The building of the first cathedrals in the Christian era, for example, could be regarded in a similar light as the construction of the first Bahá'í Temple on the North American continent.

The fact that biblical prophecy suggests the establishment of the Kingdom of God on earth to a degree unparalleled in human history can be attributed to the circumstances, maturity and capacity of the human race in this age. Whatever the accomplishments of the followers of former religions, no previous age possessed the necessary maturity or level of technological advance to permit the uniting of the whole human race or the establishment of peace throughout the entire globe. However, the followers of Bahá'u'lláh believe that, in this age, not only have the necessary divine teachings been provided, but the conditions exist which make it possible to bring about such dramatic and all-pervasive changes. This is the goal towards which Bahá'ís are working. It is within the context of this great transformation of human life that biblical prophecy suggests that no former age can be compared to this age. As Shoghi Effendi explains:

> If the Light that is now streaming forth upon an increasingly responsive humanity with a radiance that bids fair to eclipse the splendour of such triumphs as the forces of religion have achieved in days past; if the signs and tokens which proclaimed its advent have been, in many respects, unique in the annals of past Revelations; if its votaries have evinced traits and qualities unexampled in the spiritual history of mankind; these should be attributed not to a superior merit which the Faith of Bahá'u'lláh, as a Revelation isolated and alien from any previous Dispensation, might possess, *but rather should be viewed and explained as the inevitable outcome of the forces that have made of this present age an age infinitely more advanced, more receptive, and more insistent to receive an ampler measure of Divine Guidance than has hitherto been vouchsafed to mankind.* (*World Order* 60, emphasis added)

APPENDIX V

THE HOLY CITY

The Book of Revelation states that the holy city will be trodden 'under foot for forty-two months' (Rev. 11:2). 'Abdu'l-Bahá explains that this verse has an outer and an inner meaning. The outer meaning refers to the city of Jerusalem:

> 'And the holy city shall they tread under foot forty and two months' - that is to say, the Gentiles shall govern and control Jerusalem forty and two months, signifying twelve hundred and sixty days; and as each day signifies a year, by this reckoning it becomes twelve hundred and sixty years, which is the duration of the cycle of the Qur'án. (*Some Answered Questions* 46)

Although 1,260 years is exactly the number of Islamic years which transpired before the Bahá'í era began, the outward correlation 'Abdu'l-Bahá presents must be understood in general terms. The Muslims did not conquer and begin to govern Jerusalem until shortly after Muhammad's death. Thus, outwardly, Jerusalem was trodden under foot by the followers of Islam not for 1,260 years, but by a people whose era lasted 1,260 years. The literal treading under foot of Jerusalem was a later outward appearance of the treading under foot of the spiritual city that had already begun.

As previously mentioned, Christians in the West have commonly understood the Roman assault on Jerusalem to be what Jesus was speaking of when He said: 'But when you see Jerusalem surrounded by armies, then know that its desolation is near' (Luke 21:20). However, to the Christians in the East, the appearance of Islamic armies surrounding Jerusalem must have suggested another possible interpretation. After Jerusalem fell to the Muslims, it is reported that the head patriarch, upon seeing Muslims, in particular the Caliph Omar, in the Church of the Holy Sepulchre, stated it was the fulfilment of Daniel's prophecy concerning the Abomination of Desolation.[197]

However, if the patriarch intended this interpretation of Daniel literally, he failed to consider several obvious points. The Caliph was not setting up an idol in the Church of the Holy Sepulchre. He did not ask anyone to worship him or anything other than God, the same God of Judaism and Christianity. Moreover, he did not even require the Christians to become Muslims. As the historian Romilly Jenkins put it, 'wholesale and forcible conversion' was not part of the Muslim creed:

> Whereas the Byzantine [Christians] believed in 'compelling them to come in', since conquest necessarily implied conversion to orthodox Christianity in order to fit the conquered in the imperial scheme of one empire and one faith, the Arab [Muslim] was content to remain one of the dominant caste of the Faithful, to tax the infidel at a higher rate than himself, but to leave him otherwise free to worship as he chose. (*Byzantium: The Imperial Centuries* 33)

Omar had come to the Church of the Holy Sepulchre to show reverence for the sacred site. So it would be wrong to confuse the pious intention of Omar for an act of abomination. If Omar had committed an abomination, it was not his reverence for the Holy Sepulchre, it was his taking up the sword against 'the people of the Book'. The growing element of imperial greed that inspired some Muslims to conquest was one of the evidences of a growing abomination that was afflicting Islam. This, of course, caused many Christians to feel fear and revulsion towards the Faith of Muhammad.

197. See Romilly Jenkins, *Byzantium: The Imperial Centuries* 34.

APPENDIX VI

JEWISH LEGENDS

There are a number of stories recounted in the Bahá'í Scriptures which are not found in what is commonly regarded as the canonical Bible. Bahá'u'lláh's references to stars heralding Abraham and Moses are among such stories. Omission from the Bible is not reason in itself for arguing that such information is not historical. Much is not included in the Bible. For example, even the early years of Jesus' life between His childhood and the beginning of His ministry are not mentioned.

The authenticity and historicity of such non-biblical accounts is probably not a central or necessary point when considering the message Bahá'u'lláh is setting forth. For the benefit of His audience, Bahá'u'lláh is simply illustrating the reasonableness of His interpretation by referring to stories that are known and generally accepted in the East. The message is simple: Since ancient times, stories recount how stars appeared as 'signs' and heralds of Messengers of God such as Abraham, Moses and Christ. Such a star is, therefore, the likely meaning of Jesus' prophecy; that is, 'the sign' (Matt. 24:29) which Jesus says will appear in heaven as a herald to His return is physically a star and symbolically a saintly person.

This interpretation is so appropriate that the physical and symbolic meaning of the Star were accepted among Christians in early times. Ephraim Syrus (or Ephraim the Syrian, c. 300-73), in his 'Hymns For the Feast of the Epiphany' wrote:

> John cried,
> 'Who comes after me, He is before me:
> I am the Voice but not the Word;
> I am the torch but not the Light;
> the Star that rises before the Sun of Righteousness'.

And in a following verse:

> In the Height and the Depth the Son had two heralds. - The star of light proclaimed Him from above; - John likewise preached Him from beneath: - two heralds, the earthly and the heavenly.[198]

Bahá'u'lláh states that these signs 'have announced the Revelation of each of the Prophets of God'. He then adds, 'as is commonly believed' (*Certitude* 62). It should be remembered that Bahá'u'lláh originally wrote *The Book of Certitude* in the context of Middle-Eastern culture where Islamic commentaries about Abraham and Moses abound and such beliefs are popular.[199] These stories originate in Jewish legends which predate Islam and even Christianity.

For example, Bahá'u'lláh states:

> Among the Prophets was Abraham, the Friend of God. Ere He manifested Himself, Nimrod dreamed a dream. Thereupon, he summoned the soothsayers, who informed him of the rise of a star in the heaven. Likewise, there appeared a herald who announced throughout the land the coming of Abraham. (*Certitude* 62-3)

The following can be found in Jewish legend:

> When Abraham was born, a star appeared in the east so bright that all the stars around it paled in the sky. The royal star gazers came running to King Nimrod and said: 'Your Majesty, a son has been born to Terah who will destroy our gods and convert all the inhabitants of the earth to his beliefs. There is but one thing to do, and that is to destroy him before he grows up.' (Joseph Gaer, *The Lore of the Old Testament* 85)[200]

198. See Ephraim Syrus, 'Hymns For the Feast of the Epiphany' (1:9-17), *Nicene and Post-Nicene Fathers*, vol. 13, 265-6.

199. See, e.g., Charles D. Matthews, *Palistine - Mohammedan Holy Land*. Matthews provides translations of Islamic pilgrims' guides to Palestine. These guides recount stories of biblical personages connected with the shrines, including a version of Nimrod and the star heralding Abraham (48-9).

200. The details of such Jewish legends vary slightly. See Louis Ginzberg, *The Legends of the Jews*, vols. 1 & 5.

Apart from the omission of Nimrod's dream, this account presents virtually the same story provided by Bahá'u'lláh. Both refer to the star and depict Nimrod as a contemporary of Abraham. The story suggests a parallel between Nimrod, Pharaoh and Herod (see Matt. 2:1-7). Although Nimrod is mentioned in the Old Testament (Gen. 10:8-10; 1 Chron. 1:10; Mic. 5:6), this parallel is not provided in the Scriptures of the Bible. In the Qur'án the encounter between Nimrod and Abraham may be suggested:

> Hast thou not thought on him who disputed with Abraham about his Lord, because God had given him the kingdom? (*The Koran*, trans. J.M. Rodwell, 2:60, p. 367)[201]

The reference to 'him who disputed' has been commonly believed by Muslim commentators to be Nimrod.

Bahá'u'lláh relates a similar story about Moses, which also is not clearly seen in the Bible. He then states:

> To this testify the records of the sacred books. Were the details to be mentioned, this epistle would swell into a book. Moreover, it is not Our wish to relate the stories of the days that are past. God is Our witness that what We even now mention is due solely to Our tender affection for thee, that haply the poor of the earth may attain the shores of the sea of wealth, the ignorant be led unto the ocean of divine knowledge, and they that thirst for understanding partake of the Salsabil of divine wisdom. Otherwise, this servant regardeth the consideration of such records a grave mistake and a grievous transgression. (*Certitude* 63)

201. Rodwell includes a footnote indicating Nimrod. The Muslim commentator Yusuf 'Alí footnotes the following: 'The three verses 258-260 have been the subject of much controversy as to the exact meaning to be attached to the incidents and the precise persons alluded to, whose names are not mentioned. M.M.A.'s learned notes give some indication of the points at issue. In such matters, where the Qur'án has given no names and the Holy Apostle has himself given no indication, it seems to me useless to speculate, and still worse to put forward positive opinions. In questions of learning, speculations are often interesting. But it seems to me that the meaning of the Qur'án is so wide and universal that we are in danger of missing the real and eternal meaning if we go on disputing about minor points. All three incidents are such as may happen again and again in any prophet's lifetime, and be seen in impersonal vision at any time. Here they are connected with Mustafa's vision as shown by the opening words of verse 258' (*The Holy Qur'án*, trans. and comm. by Yusuf 'Alí, 104).

It is reasonable to assume that His statement 'To this testify the records of the sacred books' cannot mean the Qur'án or the Bible. Rather, the 'sacred books' most simply mean religious books, as distinguished from secular books.

Bahá'u'lláh does not state why a lengthy consideration of such records would be 'a grave mistake and a grievous transgression'. However, since His explanation is Revelation from God, it stands on its own spiritual merits. It is not a secular book and, hence, it would not be appropriate to rest its testimony on the extensive use of supporting secular evidence. These explanations are given because of His affection for us, not because God's Word stands in need of scholarly documentation.

APPENDIX VII

THE CHRONOLOGICAL PROPHECIES

In the Book of Daniel, five numerical prophecies are given. According to the principle that days signify years (cf. Num. 14:34), there is the 490 years concerning the appearance of Christ (Dan. 9:24-6); the 2,300 years concerning the time of the end (Dan. 8:13-14, 17); the 1,260 years concerning the abomination of desolation and the commencing of the cleansing of the sanctuary (Dan. 12:7, parallel to Rev. 11); the 1,290 years marking the end of the cleansing of the sanctuary (Dan. 12:11); and finally there is the 1,335 years concerning a great blessing that is to come (Dan. 12:12), a blessing the nature of which is probably alluded to in the next passage by the word 'rest' (Dan. 12:13), signifying the seventh-day rest which marks the world triumph of Bahá'u'lláh's Faith.

The first prophecy (Dan. 9:24-6) refers to the first appearance of Christ, while the last four all involve chronological predictions concerning the time of the end. Of these four chronological numbers, two - the 1,260 years and the 1,290 years - conform to the lunar calendar, and the remaining two - the 2,300 years and the 1,335 years - correspond to the solar calendar. Even though the western world was essentially divided into two dominate religious groups using two different calendars, solar (Christian) and lunar (Islamic), the prophecies still provide sufficient guidance for all because history has shown that either calendar could be used to arrive at the primary date initiating the new age. This is most clearly demonstrated in the exact correlation between the 2,300 solar years and the 1,260 lunar years. Nothing short of divine providence could have caused the 2,300 years - calculated from the edict (457 BC) which commences 490 years before Christ's ascension - to correspond so exactly to the 1,260-year date of the Islamic calendar, a date which also corresponds precisely to Qur'ánic verses (40:7, 32:4; cf. 2 Pet. 3:8) understood to refer to the 1,000 years that would pass after the disappearance of the Twelfth Imám (260 AH) before the coming of the Day of God.

In this way very clear guidance was provided to those who lived in the Middle East where the prophecies where first revealed and fulfilled, and to the Christian world in the West which would later prove more receptive to the new Revelation of God. Moreover, the dates were corollary to the prophecies found in the sacred Books of the Jews (the Book of Daniel), the Christians (the Book of Revelation), and the Muslims (the Qur'án). Christ had confirmed the prophecies of Daniel in His last major sermon (Matt. 24:15) and Muhammad had confirmed the Gospel in the Qur'án (5:49-50). Thus both the Christians and the Muslims could confidently refer to other religious Scriptures for guidance and, had they been willing, the followers of all these Faiths could have checked their understanding against the prophecies of each other's holy books and found additional and extraordinary confirmation.

The most significant failing of the Christian world was its lack of appreciation and understanding of Islam, for none of the dates associated with the 1,260, 1,290 and 1,335 years can be fully understood without an awareness of Islam. Each date commences at a significant moment in the history of Islam and ends with the advent of a similarly momentous date in the history of the Bahá'í Revelation. The 1,260 years is calculated from the beginning of the Islamic era, which is initiated with the Hegira. The Hegira marks the point where Muhammad's persecutors had so intensified their opposition that He moved residence from Mecca to Medina. These persecutors were the same persons who would later corrupt the Cause of Islam from within and thus bring in 'the abomination of desolation'. This date culminates with the beginning of the Bahá'í era, which marks the beginning of the cleansing of the sanctuary, that is, the removal of the abomination of desolation and the re-establishment of God's Faith without corruption. Nevertheless, both dates are parallel in that both mark the inception of a new era.

The commencing and culmination of the 1,290 years also corresponds to an important parallel. It begins with Muhammad's open proclamation of His divine claims three years after His ministry had begun (AD 613) and concludes with the year of Bahá'u'lláh's similar open proclamation of His ministry, a lunar year overlapping 1863-4 of the Gregorian calendar. Both Muhammad and Bahá'u'lláh kept their station concealed for a time before openly announcing them.

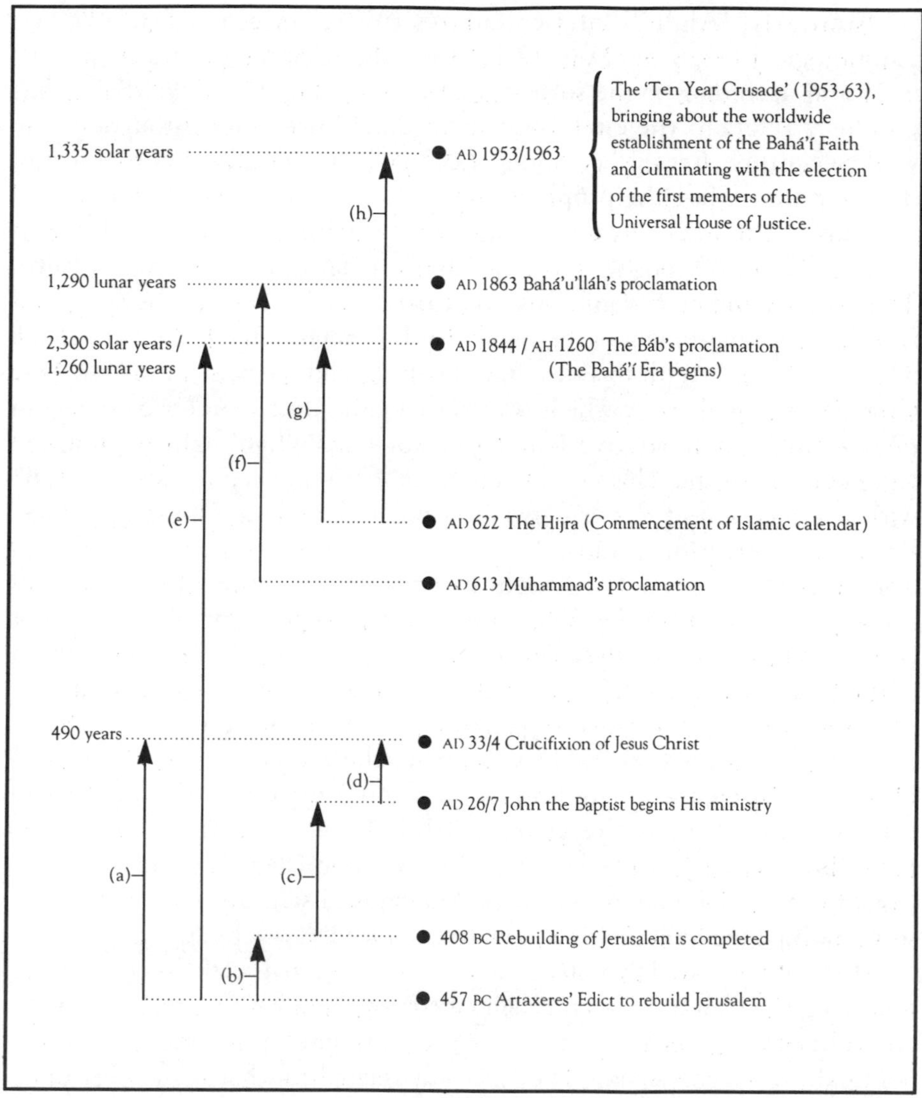

The chronological prophecies of the Book of Daniel and their relationship to Christianity, Islam and the Bahá'í Faith: Before the twentieth century nearly all Christian commentators agreed on calculation (a) and many also accepted (b), (c) and (d). After the twentieth century, most Christians began to reject such interpretations or at least ignore the issue, except for some conservative Christians who have continued to accept these same calculations, especially (a). During the nineteenth century many Christians also accepted calculations (e) and (f), although fewer accepted (f) and none fully understood its real significance - from the Bahá'í point of view. Calculations (g) and (h) are based on interpretations found only in Bahá'í writings.

Similarly, 'Abdu'l-Bahá calculates the 1,335 years, Daniel's last chronological prophecy (Dan. 12:12) from the beginning of the Hijra (AD 622) and according to the solar calendar. According to 'Abdu'l-Bahá, this prophecy refers to the establishment of Bahá'í teachings throughout the world a century after the beginning of Bahá'u'lláh's ministry. In other words, it is apparent that the prophecy refers to something great that would happen, and according to solar calculations, this would mean (622+1335=1957) roughly 100 years after the dawning of the Bahá'í Faith. The greatest and most significant event that would occur was the successful worldwide establishment of the Bahá'í Faith (Shoghi Effendi, *Citadel of Faith* 32, 50, 104-5).[202] With this in mind Shoghi Effendi launched the 'Ten Year Crusade', the purpose of which was to establish, 'on a world-wide scale, an unassailable administrative foundation for Bahá'u'lláh's Christ-promised Kingdom on earth'. This crusade began in 1953 and culminated in 1963 with the election of the first members of the Universal House of Justice. Before this election could take place, it was important for the Bahá'í community to spread throughout the world - the objective and accomplishment of the Ten Year Crusade. Although the prophecy does not correspond exactly with the *conclusion* of this period, marked by the election of the Universal House of Justice, it does culminate *in* this crucial period.

In addition to the above explanation, it is perhaps worth noting that if one simply counts back 1,335 years from the election of the Universal House of Justice and the end of the Ten Year Crusade (1963) the termination point is the year AD 628, the year of the Truce of al-Hudaybiyyah which marked an important stage in Islam's victory over idol-worship in Arabia and a time when Muhammad sent out messages to the surrounding kingdoms inviting them to embrace His teachings.

It should be noted that all of these dates are related solely to occurrences involving the Cause of God throughout the ages and have no relationship to any other events such as wars, natural catastrophes, scientific discoveries, political events and so on. They are only related to what is the overriding concern of all the Scriptures: God's Revelation and the spiritual redemption of humankind.

202. This suggests that precise calendar knowledge and mathematical precision is not necessary for the understanding and fulfilment of these prophecies. For additional references in the Bahá'í writings on the chronological prophecies see: 'Abdu'l-Bahá, *Some Answered Questions*, ch. 10; Shoghi Effendi, *God Passes By* 58, 95, 110-11, 139, 151, 155; *Messages to America* 88-9; *Messages to the Bahá'í World* 18, 44; and letters on behalf of the Guardian in *Lights of Guidance* 323-4.

ABBREVIATIONS

THE OLD TESTAMENT

Genesis	Gen.
Exodus	Exod.
Leviticus	Lev.
Numbers	Num.
Deuteronomy	Deut.
Joshua	Jos.
Judges	Jud.
Ruth	Ruth
1 Samuel	1 Sam.
2 Samuel	2 Sam.
1 Kings	1 Kings
2 Kings	2 Kings
1 Chronicles	1 Chron.
2 Chronicles	2 Chron.
Ezra	Ezra
Nehemiah	Neh.
Esther	Esther
Job	Job
Psalms	Ps.
Proverbs	Pro.
Ecclesiastes	Eccles.
Song of Solomon	Song of Sol.
Isaiah	Isa.
Jeremiah	Jer.
Lamentations	Lam.
Ezekiel	Ezek.
Daniel	Dan.
Hosea	Hosea
Joel	Joel
Amos	Amos
Obadiah	Obad.
Jonah	Jonah
Micah	Micah
Nahum	Nah.
Habakkuk	Hab.
Zephaniah	Zeph.
Haggai	Hag.
Zechariah	Zech.
Malachi	Mal.

THE NEW TESTAMENT

Matthew	Matt.
Mark	Mark
Luke	Luke
John	John
The Acts	Acts
Romans	Rom.
1 Corinthians	1 Cor.
2 Corinthians	2 Cor.
Galatians	Gal.
Ephesians	Eph.
Philippians	Philip.
Colossians	Col.
1 Thessalonians	1 Thess.
2 Thessalonians	2 Thess.
1 Timothy	1 Tim.
2 Timothy	2 Tim.
Titus	Titus
Philemon	Phil.
Hebrews	Heb.
James	James
1 Peter	1 Pet.
2 Peter	2 Pet.
1 John	1 John
2 John	2 John
3 John	3 John
Jude	Jude
Revelation	Rev.

BIBLES

American Standard Version	ASV
King James Version	KJV
The Modern Language Bible	ML
New International Version	NIV
New King James Version	NKJV
Revised Standard Version	RSV

BIBLIOGRAPHY

'Abdu'l-Bahá. *The Promulgation of Universal Peace: Talks Delivered by 'Abdu'l-Bahá During His Visit to the United States and Canada in 1912*. Comp. Howard MacNutt. Wilmette, Ill.: Bahá'í Publishing Trust, 1982.

---- *The Secret of Divine Civilization*. Trans. Marzieh Gail and 'Alí-Kuli Khan.Wilmette, Ill.: Bahá'í Publishing Trust, 3rd edn, 1975.

---- *Selections from the Writings of 'Abdu'l-Bahá*. Comp. Research Department of the Universal House of Justice, trans. Marzieh Gail and a Committee at the Bahá'í World Centre. Haifa, Israel: Bahá'í World Centre, 1982.

---- *Some Answered Questions*. Comp. and trans. Laura Clifford Barney. London: KeganPaul, Trench, Trubner and Co. Ltd., 1908. Rev. edn. London: Bahá'í Publishing Trust, 1981.

---- *Tablets of the Divine Plan*. Wilmette, Ill.: Bahá'í Publishing Trust, 1977.

---- *The Will and Testament of 'Abdu'l-Bahá*. Wilmette, Ill.: Bahá'í Publishing Trust, 1944, 1971.

Appreciations of the Bahá'í Faith. Wilmette, Ill: Bahá'í Publishing Trust, 1947.

Auberlen, Carl August. *The Prophecies of Daniel and the Revelation of St. John*. Edinburgh: T.& T. Clark, 1856. Contains an analysis of the different edicts concerning the restoration of Jews from the Babylonian captivity.

Augustine, St. *The City of God*. Chicago, Ill: University of Chicago, Encyclopedia Britannica, (Great Books of the Western World, vol. 18), 1952.

The Bahá'í World: An International Record. Vol. XVIII: 136-140 of the Bahá'í Era, 1979-1983. Haifa, Israel: Bahá'í World Centre, 1986.

Bahá'u'lláh. *The Book of Certitude (Kitáb-i-Iqán)*. Trans. Shoghi Effendi. Wilmette, Ill.: Bahá'í PublishingTrust, 1931, 3rd edn., 1974.

---- *Epistle to the Son of the Wolf*. Trans. Shoghi Effendi. Wilmette, Ill.: Bahá'í Publishing Trust, 1941, 3rd edn., 1976.

---- *Gleanings from the Writings of Bahá'u'lláh*. Trans. Shoghi Effendi. Wilmette, Ill.: Bahá'í Publishing Trust, 1939, 2nd edn., 1956.

---- *The Proclamation of Bahá'u'lláh*. Haifa, Israel: Bahá'í World Centre, 1972.

---- *Synopsis and Codification of the Laws and Ordinances of the Kitáb-i-Aqdas*. Trans. Shoghi Effendi. Haifa, Israel: Bahá'í World Centre, 1973.

---- *Tablets of Bahá'u'lláh revealed after the Kitáb-i-Aqdas*. Comp. ResearchDepartment of the Universal House of Justice, trans. Habib Taherzadeh and a Committee at the Bahá'í World Centre. Haifa, Israel: Bahá'í World Centre, 1978.

Balyuzi, H.M. *Muhammad and the Course of Islam*. Oxford, England: George Ronald, 1976.

Beasley-Murray. *Jesus and the Future*. London: MacMillan & Co., 1954. An excellent account of the evolution of critical writings concerning the Olivet Discourse (or Synoptic Apocalypse, Mark 13). Beasley-Murray writes from the conservative Protestant viewpoint.

Beckwith, I.T. *The Apocalypse of John*. New York: The Macmillan Company, 1919.

Bible Readings. Battle Creek, Mich.: Review and Herald Publishing Co., 1888. (Seventh-Day Adventist.) This book contains a list of contributors at the end, but omits to mention the editors or compilers.

The Holy Bible: *New King James Version*. Nashville, Tenn.: Thomas Nelson, 1982.

Blauw, Johannes (Secretary, Netherlands Missionary Council). *The Missionary Nature of the Church*. New York: McGraw-Hill Book Company, Inc., 1962.

Board of Foreign Missions of the Presbyterian Church U.S.A. Historical Sketches of the Missions. Philadelphia: 4th edn., 1897.

Bohnstedt, John W. *The Infidel Scourge of God, The Turkish Menace as Seen by German Pamphleteers of the Reformation Era*. Philadelphia: The American Philosophical Society, 1968.

Brown, Colin, ed. *The New International Dictionary of New Testament Theology*, vol. I. Grand Rapids, Mich.: Zondervan Publishing House, 1975.

Brown, Revd David. *Christ's Second Coming, Will It Be Pre-Millennial?* New York: Robert Carter and Brothers, 1876. One of many books which led to the re-establishment of pre-millenarianism. Guinness considered it the best and refers to it as 'that most able treatise ever penned against them [the post-millenarians]'.

Bush, L. Russ, ed. *Classical Readings in Christian Apologetics*, AD *100-1800*. Grand Rapids, Mich.: Academic Books, 1984.

Calder, Nigel. *The Comet Is Coming!* New York: Viking Press, 1980.

Calvin, John (1500-64). *Commentaries on the Book of the Prophet Daniel*, 2nd vol. Edinburgh: Printed for the Calvin Translation Society, 1853. 'Now First Translated from the Original Latin, and Collated with the French Version, With Dissertations, New Translation of the Text, and Copious Indices, by Thomas Myers, M.A., Vicar of Sheriff-Hutton, Yorkshire.' Later editions omit appendices which examine the day/year theory.

Campbell, James M. *The Second Coming of Christ*. New York: The Methodist Book Concern, 1919. This book is in its entirety a concise and interesting argument for the extreme position that the return of Christ is entirely spiritual and immaterial in nature.

Case, Shirley Jackson. *The Millennial Hope: A Phase of War-Time Thinking*. Chicago, Ill.: University of

Chicago Press, 1918. This book, as Marsden notes, (*Fundamentalism* 146), attempts to dismiss millennialism on historical grounds.

Charlesworth, James H. *The Old Testament Pseudepigraphia*, vol. 2. Garden City, New York: Doubleday & Company, 1985.

Clement of Alexandria. *The Stromata*. Grand Rapids, Mich.: Wm. B. Eerdman's Publishing Company, 1962. (See especially Book 1, ch. 15, *The Ante-Nicene Fathers.*)

Cohn, Norman. *The Pursuit of the Millennium*. New York: Harper Torchbooks, 2nd edn., 1961. Interesting history of millennial beliefs but does not provide documentation.

Cowper, Harris B., *The Apocryphal Gospels*. London: Frederic Norgate, 1881.

Cumming, Revd John (1807-81). *The Great Preparation*. New York: Rudd & Carleton, 1840. Cumming's works are frequently referred to by many millenarian writers.

---- *The Great Tribulation*. New York: Rudd & Carleton, 1840.

---- *Prophetic Studies: Lectures on the Book of Daniel*. Philadelphia: Lindsay and Blakiston, 1854.

Dante Alighieri. *The Divine Comedy of Dante Alighieri*. Trans. Charles Eliot Norton. Chicago, Ill: The University of Chicago, William Benton, Encyclopedia Britannica, (Great Books of the Western World, vol. 21), 1952.

A Debate on the Roman Catholic Religion. A transcript of a debate between Alexander Campbell and Rt. Revd John B. Purcell, Bishop of Cincinnati. Cincinnati: A. James & Co., 1837. Campbell attempts to connect a number of prophecies to the Pope and Catholicism, Purcell counters by arguing that they refer to 'Mahommedanism'. Campbell then argues that the prophecies do not fit Muhammad.

Douglas, J.D., gen. ed. *The New International Dictionary of the Christian Church*. Grand Rapids, Mich.: Zondervan Publishing House, rev. edn., 1978.

Durant, Will. *Caesar and Christ*. New York: Simon and Schuster, 1944.

Ellicott, John Charles (1819-1905). *Ellicott's Commentary on the Whole Bible*, vols. 2 & 3 (containing vols. 3, 4 & 5, 6). Grand Rapids, Mich.: Zondervan Publishing House, 1981.

Elwell, Walter A., ed. *Evangelical Dictionary of Theology*. Grand Rapids, Mich.: Baker Book House, 1987.

Ephraim Syrus. 'Hymns For the Feast of the Epiphany' (1:9-17) in *Nicene and Post-Nicene Fathers.*, vol. 13, 265-6. New York: The Christian Literature Company, 1898.

Eusebius (of Caesarea, c. 265-c. 339). *The History of the Church*. Trans. G.A. Williamson. Harmondsworth, England: Penguin Books, 1984.

Faber, George Stanley. *A Dissertation on the Prophecies*. London: Printed for F.C. and J. Rivington, 1814.

Fasá'í, Hasan-e. *History Of Persia Under Qajar Rule* (Farsnama-ye Naseri). Trans. Heribert Busse. New York: Columbia University Press, 1972. This book is especially significant for its contemporary accounts of some early persecutions of the Bábís.

Fleming, Robert, (d. 1716). *The Rise and Fall of Rome Papal*. London: Houlston and Wright, 1701, 1863. A very influential book during the nineteenth century. Fleming's writings are vehemently anti-Roman Catholic. His interpretations concerning biblical prophecy and the later French Revolution have continued to be accepted in modified forms even today by some Christians.

Fowler, Harold. *The Gospel of Matthew*. Joplin, Missouri: College Press Publishing Co., 1985.

Froom, Le Roy Edwin. *The Prophetic Faith of Our Fathers*, vols. I-IV. Washington, D.C.: Review and Herald, 1954. (Seventh-Day Adventist.) This four-volume set is probably one of the most detailed analyses of the history of the interpretation of prophecy available. This is especially true with regard to the day/year theory. Contains detailed bibliography.

Fry, Revd John. *Observations on the Unfulfilled Prophecies*. London: James Duncan, 1835. Contains appendix examining the prophetic year 1844 and briefly discusses Islamic messianic expectations.

Gaebelein, Frank E., ed. *The Expositor's Bible Commentary*, 12 vols. Grand Rapids, Mich.: Zondervan Publishing House, 1984.

Gaer, Joseph. *The Lore of the Old Testament*. Boston: Little Brown, 1951.

Gibbon, Edward (1737-1794). *The Decline and Fall of the Roman Empire*. New York: Harcourt, Brace and Company, abr. edn., 1960. Nineteenth-century Protestant writers commonly referred to Gibbon as the 'infidel historian'. Nevertheless, they often relied upon his work as an authoritative history of the early Church.

Gilbert, Martin. *Jerusalem, Rebirth of a City*. Viking Penguin Inc., 1985.

Gill, John (1697-1771). *An Exposition of the New Testament*, vol. I. Philadelphia: William W. Woodward, 1811. Gill was a Baptist minister and biblical scholar. His views were especially Calvinistic. Gill's work ranked high among expositions of the Bible, both for its inclusion and analysis of diverse opinions and his knowledge of Rabbinical learning.

Ginzberg, Louis. *The Legends of the Jews*, vols. I & V. Philadelphia: The Jewish Publication Society of America, 1968.

Govett, Robert (1813-1901). *The Prophecy on Olivet*. Miami Springs, Florida: Conley and Schoettle Publishing Co., Inc., 1985. Govett preached in the Church of England until resigning over a disagreement concerning infant baptism. He then became pastor of a non-denominational church. His writings show an emphasis on eschatology and were respected for their scholarship. This book was originally published in 1881 and focuses on refuting the idea that the Roman destruction of the Temple was the meaning of the 'abomination of desolation'.

Graham, Billy. *Approaching Hoofbeats*. New York: Avon Books, 1983.

Guinness, Henry Grattan (1835-1910). *The Approaching End of the Age*. London: Hodder and Stoughton, 11th edn., 1892. An evangelical writer and strong missionary advocate, he founded the East London Institute for training missionaries. This book contains a variety of arguments supporting the day-year theory and an explanation of 'progressive revelation' as it relates to the gradual unfolding of prophecy. Guinness believed, and offers documentary evidence, that the time of the Gentiles had been fulfilled in 1844. He notes that this date corresponds to the Islamic AH 1260. Contains a variety of detailed charts.

Gundry, Robert H. Matthew: *A Commentary on His Literary and Theological Art*. Grand Rapids, Mich.: William B. Eerdman's Publishing Company, 1982.

Habershon, M. *A Dissertation on the Prophetic Scriptures*. London: James Nisbet, 1834. This book contains charts and discussions relating to both the 'Sabbath' rest and Daniel's prophecies.

Hales, Revd William. *A New Analysis of Chronology and Geography, History and Prophecy*, vol. II. London: C.J.G. & F. Rivington, 1830.

Hastings, James. *A Dictionary of the Bible*, vol. I. Edinburgh: T. & T. Clark, 1898.

Hendriksen, William. *New Testament Commentary*. Grand Rapids, Mich.: Baker Book House, 1973.

Henry, Matthew (1662-1714). *Matthew Henry's Commentary*, vols. I-VI. McLean, Virginia: McDonald Publishing Company, (no date). Matthew Henry was an evangelical Protestant Bible expositor. His commentaries have had a great influence on evangelical literature and are still widely used.

Hughes, David. *The Star of Bethlehem Mystery*. London: J.M. Dent and Sons Ltd, 1979.

Hunter, A.M. *The Gospel According to Saint Mark*. London: SCM Press Ltd, 1962.

Jenkins, Romilly. *Byzantium, The Imperial Centuries, AD 610-1071*. New York: Vintage Books, 1969.

Jonsson, Carl Olof, and Wolfgang Herbst. *The Sign of the Last Days - When?* Atlanta, Georgia: Commentary Press, 1987.

Kittel, Gerhard. *Theological Dictionary of the New Testament*, vol. I. Grand Rapids, Mich.: Wm. B. Eerdman's Publishing Company, 1977.

The Koran. Trans. N.J. Dawood. Harmondsworth, England: Penguin Books, 1974.

The Koran. Trans. Rodwell. London: Everyman's Library, 1971.

Kritzeck, James. *Peter the Venerable and Islam*. Princeton, New Jersey: Princeton University Press, 1964.

Küng, Hans. *Christianity and the World Religions*. Garden City, New York: Doubleday & Company, 1986.

Lachs, Samual Tobias. *A Rabbinic Commentary on the New Testament*. Hoboken, New Jersey: KTAV Publishing House, 1987.

La Cocque, André. *Daniel in His Time*. Columbia, South Carolina: University of South Carolina, 1988. Modern critical assessment of the Book of Daniel. Rejects the day/year theory and general Adventist approach to Daniel.

Land, Gary. *Adventism in America*. Grand Rapids, Mich.: Wm. B. Eerdman's Publishing Company, 1986.

Lange, John Peter (1802-84). *The Gospel According to Matthew*. New York: Charles Scribner's Sons, 12th edn., 1884. Highly respected German Protestant theologian and biblical scholar.

Lights of Guidance: A Bahá'í Reference File. Comp. Helen Hornby. New Delhi, India: Bahá'í Publishing Trust, 1983.

Lindsey, Hal. *The Late Great Planet Earth*. Grand Rapids, Mich.: Zondervan Publishing House, 1970.

McDowell, Josh. *Evidence that Demands a Verdict*. San Bernardino, Calif.: Here's Life Publishers, rev. edn., 1979.

Martin, Walter. *The Kingdom of the Cults*. Minneapolis, Minn., Bethany House Publishers, rev. edn.,1985.

Matthews, Charles D. *Palistine - Mohammedan Holy Land*. New Haven: Yale University Press, 1949. Contains two translations of early Islamic pilgrims' guides to Palestine.

Miller, William. *Evidence and Scripture and History of the Second Coming of Christ about the Year 1843*. Boston: Joshua V. Himes, 1842.

Momen, Moojan. *The Bábí and Bahá'í Religions, 1844-1944, Some Contemporary Western Accounts*. Oxford, England: George Ronald, 1981.

The Morning Watch; or Quarterly Journal of Prophecy and Theological Review, 7 vols. London: Dec. 1832.

Nabíl-i-A'zam (Muhammad-i-Zarandí). *The Dawn-Breakers, Nabíl's Narrative of the Early Days of the Bahá'í Revelation*. Wilmette, Ill.: Bahá'í Publishing Trust, 1974.

Nadwi, Abul Hasan 'Alí. *Saviours of Islamic Spirit*, vol. I. Trans. Mohiuddin Ahmad. Lucknow, India: Islamic Research and Publications, 2nd edn., 1976.

Naish, Reginald T. *The Midnight Hour and After*. London: Chas. J. Thynne and Jarvis, Ltd., 6th edn., 1926.

New Bible Dictionary. Wheaton, Ill.: Tyndale House Publishers Inc., 2nd edn., 1982.

Newton, Benjamin Wills (1807-1899). *Aids to Prophetic Enquiry*. London: The Sovereign Grace Advent Testimony, 3rd edn., 1881. B.W. Newton was an early Plymouth Brethren leader with strong Calvinist views.

---- *Thoughts on the Apocalypse*. London: The Sovereign Grace Advent Testimony, 2nd edn., 1853.

Newton, Sir Isaac. (See Withla, Sir William)

Newton, Thomas. *Dissertations on the Prophecies*. London: J.F. Dove, (no date).

Nichol, Francis D. *The Midnight Cry*. Washington, D.C.: Review and Herald Publishing Association, 1944, 2nd edn., 1945. (Seventh-Day Adventist.)

Olsen, V. Norskov. *Advent Hope in Scripture and History*. Washington, D.C.: Review and Herald, 1987.

'Origen de Principiis'. From *The Ante-Nicene Fathers*. Trans. The Revd Alexander Roberts and James Donaldson. Grand Rapids, Mich.: Wm. B. Eerdman's Publishing Company, 1979.

Parrinder, Geoffrey. *Jesus in the Qur'án*. New York: Oxford University Press, 1977.

Patte, Daniel. *The Gospel According to Matthew*. Philadelphia: Fortress Press, 1987.

Platt, Rutherford H. *The Forgotten Books of Eden*. New York: Bell Publishing Company, 1980.

Prophetic Studies of the International Prophetic Conference (Chicago, November, 1886). Chicago, Ill.: Fleming and Revell, 1886. Contains articles by many prominent clergymen of the time, including D.L. Moody, F. Godet, Franz Delitzsch, Wm. E. Blackstone and Nathaniel West. The secretary and organizer of the conference was the Revd George C. Needham.

The Holy Qur'án. Trans. & comp. A. Yusuf 'Alí. American Trust Publications for the Muslim Students' Association, 2nd edn., 1977.

Roberts, Revd Alexander, and James Donaldson, eds. *The Ante-Nicene Fathers*, vols. IV-V. Grand Rapids, Mich.: Wm. B. Eerdman's Publishing Company, 1979.

Rutherford H. Platt, Jr., ed. *The Forgotten Books of Eden*, New York: Bell Publishing Company, 1927, 1980.

Ryrie, Charles Caldwell (1816-1900). *The Ryrie Study Bible*. Chicago, Ill.: Moody Press, 1976.

Savory, R.M., ed. *Introduction to Islamic Civilization*. Cambridge, England: Cambridge University Press, 1976.

Schaff, Philip. *History of the Christian Church*, vol. V. Grand Rapids, Mich.: Wm. B. Eerdman's Publishing Company, 1907, 1988.

Scott, Thomas. *The Holy Bible Containing the Old and New Testaments with Original Notes*. New York: J. Seymour, 4th American edn., 1815.

Sears, William. *Thief in the Night*. London: George Ronald, 1961. Written by a noted Bahá'í. A book concerning prophecy, popular among Bahá'ís. Much of the book uses arguments and sources largely collected from Seventh-Day Adventist literature to support the divine claims of the Bahá'í Faith. The book is written in detective-story form.

Seiss, Joseph A. *The Last Times and the Great Consummation*. Philadelphia: Smith, English and Co., 1856, rev. edn., 1863. Includes a useful bibliography of books related to millenarian views.

Sheldon, Henry C. *History of the Christian Church*, vol. I. Peabody, Mass.: Hendrickson, 1895, 1988.

Shimeall, Revd Richard Cunningham. *Christ's Second Coming: Is It Pre-Millennial or Post-Millennial?* New York: John F. Trow, 1865.

---- *The Second Coming of Christ*. New York: Henry S, Goodspeed Co., Publishers,1873. This book was printed and bound into one volume together with a reprint of Shimeall's Reply to an Article on Eschatology which responds to Revd Prof. Shedd's article on eschatology published in his *History of Christian Doctrines*. Shedd's article was clearly an inadequate and inaccurate historical overview of Christian eschatology which prompted a number of Christian expositors to write responses. Shimeall's response is perhaps the most thorough and includes what he calls an 'Authentic History of Chiliasm' (ch. 3, 53-117).

Shoghi Effendi. *The Advent of Divine Justice*. Wilmette, Ill.: Bahá'í Publishing Trust, 1939, 1971.

---- *Citadel of Faith: Messages to America / 1947-1957*. Wilmette, Ill.: Bahá'í Publishing Trust, 1970.

---- *God Passes By*. Wilmette, Ill.: Bahá'í Publishing Trust, 1944, 1974.

---- *The Promised Day Is Come*. Wilmette, Ill.: Bahá'í Publishing Trust, rev. edn., 1980. In this book Shoghi Effendi surveys the turbulent events which transpired following the issuance of Bahá'u'lláh's message to the world, particularly His letters to various kings and leaders. These modern events are explored in relation to the prophesied Judgement Day.

---- *The World Order of Bahá'u'lláh*. Wilmette, Ill.: Bahá'í Publishing Trust, 1938, 2nd edn., 1974.

Smith, Ethan. *Key to the Revelation*. New York: J. & J. Harper, 1833.

Smith, Joseph. *Doctrines and Covenants*. Salt Lake City, Utah: The Church of Jesus Christ of Latter-day Saints, 1968.

Smith, Wilbur M. *A Treasury of Books for Bible Study*. Natick, Mass.: W.A. Wilde Co., 1960.

Snowden, James H. *The Coming of the Lord: Will It Be Premillennial?* New York: MacMillan Co., 1921.

Sours, Michael W. *Preparing for a Bahá'í/Christian Dialogue, Volume 2, Understanding Christian Beliefs*. Oxford, England: Oneworld Publications, 1991.

Speer, Robert E. *Missions and Modern History*, vol. I. New York: Fleming H. Revell, 1904.

Spicer, W.A. *Our Day in the Light of Prophecy*. Washington, D.C.: Review and Herald, 1918. (Seventh-Day Adventist.)

Stock, Eugene. *The History of the Church Missionary Society*, vol. III. London: Church Missionary Society, 1899.

Strong, James. *The Tabernacle of Israel*. Grand Rapids, Mich.: Kregel Publications, rev. edn., 1987.

Tacitus (c.55-117). *The Annals*. Trans. Alfred John Church and William Jackson Brodribb. Chicago, Ill: University of Chicago, Encyclopedia Britannica, (Great Books of the Western World, vol. 15), 1952.

Taherzadeh, Adib. *The Revelation of Bahá'u'lláh: Adrianople 1863-68* , vol. II. Oxford, England: George Ronald, 1977.

Tan, Paul Lee. *The Interpretation of Prophecy*. Winona Lake, Indiana: Assurance Publishers, 1974.

Taylor, Henry W. *The Times of Daniel, An Argument*. New York: Anson D.F. Randolph & Co., 1871.

Taylor, D.T. *The Great Consummation and the Signs That Herald its Approach*. Boston: Advent Christian Publication Society, 1906.

Thomas, John. *Elpis Israel*. Birmingham, England: C.C. Walker, 8th edn., 1903.

Townsend, Revd George (M.A., Prebendary of Durham and Vicar of Northallerton). *The Old Testament Arranged in Historical and Chronological Order* (On the Basis of Lightfoot's Chronicle). In Two Volumes. London: Rivington, 1826.

Trench, R.C. *Commentary on the Epistles to the Seven Churches of Asia*. London: Kegan Paul, Trench, & Co., 4th edn., 1886.

Vine, W.E. *Vine's Expository Dictionary of Biblical Words*. Nashville: Thomas Nelson, rev. edn., 1985.

Wale, Burlinton B. *The Closing Days of Christendom*. London: S.W. Partridge & Co., 2nd edn. 1883.

West, Nathaniel. *Premillennial Essays of the Prophetic Conference*. Chicago: F.H. Revell, 1879. Contains essays by many noted contributors and an article by West containing a detailed history of the Premillennial Doctrine.

White, E.G. *The Great Controversy*. Oakland, Calif.: Pacific Press, 1888. (Seventh-Day Adventist.)

Whitla, Sir William. *Sir Isaac Newton's Daniel and the Apocalypse ('With an Introductory Study of the Nature and Cause of Unbelief, of Miracles and Prophecy')*. London: John Murray, 1922. Sir Isaac Newton (1642-1717) is best known for his contributions to science, especially the theory of gravity. However, he was once regarded as an authority on biblical subjects and on the relationship between science and the Christian religion. Many Protestant expositors commonly cited Newton in defence of religion and their interpretations of prophecy, but few realized that Newton was inclined to many unorthodox views. Newton also wrote on biblical chronology and alchemy.

Wodrow, Robert. *The Past History and Future Destiny of Israel as Unfolded in the Eighth and succeeding Chapters of the Book of Daniel*. Glasgow: Blackie and Son, 1844.

GENERAL INDEX
(footnotes included in index)

BIBLICAL INDEX